2,50

PLANTERS AND SPECULATORS

PLANTERS
AND SPECULATORS

Chinese and European
Agricultural Enterprise in Malaya,
1786-1921

by

JAMES C. JACKSON
Leverhulme Fellow in Commonwealth Studies
University of Hull

KUALA LUMPUR
UNIVERSITY OF MALAYA PRESS
SINGAPORE
1968

Sole Distributors

Oxford University Press, Ely House, London W.1

GLASGOW NEW YORK TORONTO MELBOURNE WELLINGTON
CAPE TOWN SALISBURY IBADAN NAIROBI LUSAKA ADDIS ABABA
BOMBAY CALCUTTA MADRAS KARACHI LAHORE DACCA
KUALA LUMPUR HONG KONG TOKYO

Bangunan Loke Yew, Kuala Lumpur

● *University of Malaya Press 1968*

The University of Malaya Press is a joint enterprise of the
University of Malaya and the University of Singapore

PRINTED IN SINGAPORE BY CRAFTSMAN PRESS LTD.

TO

MY PARENTS

ACKNOWLEDGEMENTS

IN THE PREPARATION OF A WORK such as this assistance comes from innumerable people. For their courteous help in my search for information I should like to express my gratitude to the staff of the National Archives of Malaysia, the Singapore National Library, the Library of the Singapore Botanic Gardens and the University of Malaya Library. In the same connexion I am also indebted to the staff of the British Museum and the Public Records Office, London. To my former colleague, Dr. D.W. Fryer, go my heartfelt thanks for his constant encouragement and advice; indeed, without his inspiration this study would lack much of the value it may now possess. To Robert Ho, another former colleague, go my thanks for his guidance over many years and for his criticism of earlier drafts of the manuscript. Other people have helped, often unwittingly, to correct my ideas on particular subjects. From these I should like to single out Dr. D.K. Bassett and Dr. R.G. Cant for special mention.

In its original form this study was presented as a thesis for a Ph.D. degree in Geography to the University of Malaya, in 1965. Much of the material it contains was given in lecture-form and discussed in seminars and tutorials in the Department of Geography there between 1961 and 1966. This helped considerably to crystallize my ideas on various topics and it would be churlish not to acknowledge the debt I owe to the undergraduates concerned. Most married authors are indebted to their wives for their patience and forebearance, and in this I am no exception. To my Malaysian Chinese wife, Suk-Han, I extend thanks for listening critically to my ideas and for providing information on the Chinese community. Finally, I wish to acknowledge the work of Messrs. J. Ngai, V. Palani and K.H. Ching who drew the final copies of the maps and diagrams. The responsibility for any errors of fact or of judgement rests with me alone.

JAMES C. JACKSON

Department of Geography
University of Malaya
Kuala Lumpur
January 1966

CONTENTS

PART I

SHIFTING COMMERCIAL AGRICULTURE

PART II

SEDENTARY PLANTATION AGRICULTURE

PART III

THE RUBBER PLANTATION INDUSTRY

LIST OF FIGURES

between pages 268-9

LIST OF TABLES

CURRENCY AND WEIGHTS
AND MEASURES

Currency

THE NEED TO QUOTE PRICES in this work raises problems. During the nineteenth century the trade of the Malay Peninsula was conducted in silver dollars, including those coined in Hong Kong, Mexico, Peru, Bolivia and Spain. To these were added the American trade dollar from 1874 to 1895 and the Japanese yen from 1874 to 1898. The rupee was also legal tender in the Straits Settlements but, despite the attempts of the Supreme Government in India, it was never used for trade purposes. The exchange value of these silver dollars in terms of sterling and other gold currencies fluctuated with the price of silver. In the early nineteenth century the Spanish dollar was worth about 5s sterling and in the 1860's and 1870's the Mexican and Hong Kong dollars were worth a little over 4s sterling. The exchange value of the dollar in sterling from 1888 to 1905 is shown in Table A.

The use of these various silver dollars led to some confusion and in the second half of the nineteenth century there were several requests for the introduction of a British trade dollar. These were refused, and in 1890 the Mexican dollar was recognized as the standard coin. The decline in the price of silver at this time caused a reduction in the export of dollars from Mexico and therefore a shortage of currency in the East, and the minting of a British dollar began in Bombay in 1894. The depreciation of silver continued and trade with the non-silver world was growing, so in 1904 the Government began to demonetize the Hong Kong and Mexican dollars and to introduce a Straits dollar with a value fixed in terms of sterling. The change-over became fully effective in 1906: the Straits dollar was fixed at 2s. 4d sterling, at which it has since remained.

TABLE A

Exchange Value of the Dollar in Sterling, 1888-1905

YEAR	SHILLINGS	PENCE
1888	3	0
1889	3	0
1890	3	4
1891	3	2¼
1892	2	10
1893	2	6⅓
1894	2	1
1895	2	1½
1896	2	3/17
1897	1	11½
1898	1	11
1899	1	11⅓
1900	2	0
1901	1	11
1902	1	8½
1903	1	9
1904	1	10½
1905	2	0

Source: R. Emerson, *Malaysia: A Study in Direct and Indirect Rule*, New York, 1937, 522. See also G.C. Allen and A.G. Donnithorne, *Western Enterprise in Indonesia and Malaya*, London, 1957, 200-1; Chai Hon-Chan, *The Development of British Malaya, 1896-1909*, Kuala Lumpur, 1964, 84-96.

Weights and Measures

1 kati = 1.3 lbs.
1 pikul = 133.3 lbs.
1 orlong = 1⅓ acres.

INTRODUCTION

AT THE CLOSE of the eighteenth century the Malay Peninsula was a scantily-populated, jungle-covered wilderness politically divided into a series of small states of varying degrees of independence and isolation. Settlement was restricted to small, traditionally-organized and often temporary Malay coastal and riverine *kampongs*,[1] to a few diminutive mining centres in the foothills and to a shifting aboriginal population elsewhere. Internal communication was limited to the rivers and occasional jungle-tracks, and the peninsula produced little for export to the outside world save small quantities of tin, gold and jungle produce. It was a region almost totally devoid of export-orientated agriculture.

The nineteenth century witnessed sweeping changes in these patterns. A British Settlement was established on Penang Island in 1786 and a strip of the adjacent mainland, named Province Wellesley, was added in 1800. The Settlement of Singapore was founded in 1819 and five years later Malacca passed finally into British hands. With the addition of the Dindings, these separate British *points d'appui* were combined to form the Straits Settlements in 1826. They remained under the control of the Government of India until 1867 when, as a result of local pressures, they were constituted a separate Crown Colony. In the meantime, a policy of non-interference in the peninsular Malay States had emerged. This policy was reversed in 1874 when British protection was extended to the western Malay States of Perak, Selangor and Sungei Ujong. By 1889 Pahang and the remainder of Negri Sembilan had been added to the list of protected states, and in 1896 these were linked to form the Federated Malay States. The extension of British influence was completed in the period 1909-19 when the rulers of Johore and the former Siamese states of Trengganu, Kelantan, Kedah and Perlis agreed to accept British Advisers: these states then

---

[1] The Malay word *kampong* signifies a village or a cluster of buildings making up a large homestead or small hamlet together with the surrounding mixed gardens.

became known as the Unfederated Malay States (Fig. 1 inset).

The economic development of the peninsula proceeded rapidly, particularly in the second half of the nineteenth century, as pioneers carved land from the jungle for mining or agricultural purposes in order to export the produce. To a very great extent this pioneering was undertaken by immigrant aliens desirous of making a profit on the venture rather than of establishing permanent settlements. The economy of the peninsula quickly became tied to external trade, its development lay in the hands of immigrant pioneers most of whom intended, ultimately, to return to their homelands. Much of the published research on the history of the peninsula has centred on the political and administrative developments connected with the extension of British influence; the concurrent social and economic developments have received limited attention. The main purpose of the present study is to trace the development of export-orientated or 'plantation' agriculture in Malaya[2] during this period of rapid change.

Strictly speaking the term 'plantation' refers to any planting of export-orientated crops of whatever size. Plantation agriculture represents, therefore, a commercial venture producing for export. In the context of nineteenth-century Malaya the important distinction lies between export-orientated or plantation agriculture and domestic food-crop production or *kampong* agriculture. Size of unit was not a fundamental criterion in this distinction: it was the *object* of cultivation that marked the one from the other. The introduction of land regulations in the late nineteenth century which recognized a distinction between what are now termed 'smallholdings' and holdings comprising over 100 acres, termed 'estates', first established size of unit as a basic criterion. This new distinction was confirmed during the rapid expansion of rubber planting and of corporate ownership in export-orientated agriculture in the first two decades of the present century. Throughout this study the term 'plantation' is used in its literal sense and not as a synonym for the modern term 'estate'. Moreover, until the middle years of the first decade of the twentieth century when the official

---

[2] Throughout this study Malaya refers to the former Federation of Malaya together with the Island of Singapore.

statistics began to take 100 acres as the lower limit of 'estates' this latter term was also applied to holdings of a variety of sizes; it is similarly indiscriminately used for the earlier period in the pages that follow.

The development of plantation agriculture in Malaya in the nineteenth and early twentieth centuries was mainly the work of Chinese and European pioneers.[3] Entering a region largely devoid of commercial agriculture these pioneers responded in varying ways to the possibilities offered by the humid tropical environment. Much of what follows is, therefore, a study of a planters' frontier, of the reactions of pioneer agriculturalists to conditions that were new to them and to a situation in which the essentials for the development of plantation agriculture— credit facilities, labour and land with access to points of export —were severely limited. It is not, of course, a simple story. A number of different crops, with diverse requirements, producing different results and grown on varying systems attracted these pioneers at different dates. Moreover, the Chinese and the Europeans tended to respond in different ways and, in part, these reflected the social and cultural values of their respective origins. The Chinese agricultural pioneers looked for quick returns on a small capital investment. They were drawn to Malaya by the prospect of acquiring sufficient wealth to return to their homeland to a life of relative comfort, and the long-term development of land in an alien environment offered little attraction. To the nineteenth-century European settlers, on the other hand, long-term investment in land was considered the basis for the development of plantation agriculture, a concept which no doubt arose partly from the traditional European attitude towards 'landed estates' and partly from the experience of European planters with tropical crops in other parts of the British Empire.

The cardinal theme of this study is that for much of the nineteenth century the Chinese achieved greater success in their efforts to develop export-orientated agriculture than did their

[3] 'Chinese' is used throughout this study in its ethnic sense to include both immigrants from China and those whose forebears came from China. In terms of numbers the former were preponderant in nineteenth-century Malaya. As used locally 'European' also includes Americans.

European counterparts. In an attempt to indicate the factors involved in this success Part I focusses attention on the activities of Chinese planters using a system of cultivation reflecting their response to contemporary conditions. Towards the close of the century, however, the situation began to change noticeably and the European planters started to play an increasingly important role, culminating in the European domination of plantation agriculture in Malaya that accompanied the foundation of the rubber industry in the first two decades of the twentieth century. Part II is concerned with the earlier less successful attempts to develop plantation agriculture on the lines envisaged by the European settlers. It points to the emergence of factors more favourable to such development in the later years of the century. Undoubtedly most important in this respect were the inter-related effects of an expanding world economy and the spread of British control, for these gave planters in Malaya access to British capital, to the rapidly growing British market, and to cheap Indian labour at a time when plantation agriculture was generally regarded as the chief means of exploiting tropical colonies. The last section deals with the effects of the introduction and expansion of rubber planting in confirming this change. In examining this shift from Chinese to European domination considerable emphasis has been placed on the organization of the agricultural enterprises concerned, since in the last analysis it is this factor that determines their relative success under similar conditions.

Writing at the time of the rubber boom Willis remarked that 'enterprise of the kind now under consideration tends to run in grooves, the product that offers greatest attraction being alone taken up, as was lately the case with rubber'.[4] More recently, C.J. Robertson observed that the history of the plantation system, 'notably in both Ceylon and Malaya, shows the rise and fall of successive crops and on the whole a continuous successful adaptation'.[5] Plantation agriculture in Malaya in the nineteenth and early twentieth centuries was, in fact, highly

[4] J.C. Willis, *Agriculture in the Tropics*, Cambridge, 1914, 190.

[5] C.J. Robertson, 'The Integration of Plantation Agriculture in Economic Planning with special reference to Southeast Asia', *Pacific Viewpoint*, Vol. 4 No. 1, March 1963, 6.

speculative in nature; development followed a 'boom and bust' cycle tied closely to external economic conditions. Rising prices for particular agricultural products drove the pioneers to clear large areas of the Malayan jungle for planting purposes; falling prices resulted in declining interest, reduced acreages and frequently a change to some other relatively more profitable crop. Until rubber swept aside the nineteenth-century export crops there were noticeable regional concentrations on particular crops, and at any one time interest tended to centre on a single crop within each region. It is this fact that makes a treatment by individual crops desirable in the present context.

When a field is as uncharted as the economic history or historical geography of Malaya it is frequently necessary to establish the signposts of related disciplines before work can proceed satisfactorily on the task in hand. This the author has not hesitated to do whenever it appeared necessary. The result is a much broader survey than was originally intended, a survey which strays constantly beyond the bounds of what is more usually regarded as 'geography'. Nevertheless, as the work of a geographer, this book is more concerned with the effects of social and economic processes on the land than with the processes themselves.

Adjacent academic disciplines necessarily overlap, and many research topics lie in what might be regarded as the 'no man's land' in between, requiring as they do the application of a mixture of techniques and methods of analysis. In few fields of investigation is this so true as in the study of social and economic phenomena in the past, for here it is virtually impossible, nor does it seem desirable, to disentangle the traditionally-defined spheres of economics, geography and history. A central point of view can be adopted that is recognized as geographic, but only by probing beyond the limits of a single, traditionally-defined discipline can a satisfactory reconstruction of past social and economic phenomena be achieved.

Although it has become usual to regard geography as the study of the inter-relationships of the 'physical' and 'cultural' environments these are clearly part of a single entity which can only be divided artificially. If it is the task of the geographer to investigate Man's utilization of the earth and its resources, then all those factors which influence this utilization are pertinent to the investigation; conversely, those which are irrelevant should be ignored. Variations in relief, soil-type or climate may play important roles in determining agricultural patterns in temperate areas. In Malaya in the nineteenth and early twentieth centuries such factors were of minor importance and thus receive attention only when warranted by their influence. In contrast, what are generally termed 'historical' and 'economic' factors determined the very nature of plantation agriculture and the lines of development and expansion which it followed in this area and they deserve, therefore, pride of place in a study such as this.

In the past half decade there has been a growing clamour for the re-interpretation of Malayan history to provide what is termed an 'Asian-centred' perspective. In this study the author has attempted to trace the development of plantation agriculture in Malaya from the point of view of the people and the land involved, not from any particular 'perspective' nor as seen from the seats of officialdom in Malaya or in London. This subject, once termed 'one of the economic romances of the tropical belt',[6] has rarely received more than a few lines in published works on the history or geography of Malaya, yet plantation agriculture forms one of the twin pillars of the modern Malayan economy. Not even a general outline of this development has appeared in the past, and to some extent lack of published material has been taken to imply that such development was unimportant in the nineteenth century. Thus, in order to establish a sound factual background to support the interpretations suggested in this study it has been necessary to present a considerable amount of detail that has not previously appeared in print.

A brief comment on sources seems called for in this connexion, for very heavy reliance has been placed on English-language material. There is, in fact, no alternative, for the Chinese pioneers left little in the way of documents to mark their presence. This is not as serious a handicap as it might at first glance appear. For various reasons the Europeans showed

[6] F.C. Roles, 'Rubber Development in Malaya' in A. Wright and H.A. Cartwright, eds., *Twentieth Century Impressions of British Malaya*, London, 1908, 351.

considerable interest in the activities of the Chinese planters and the extant English language sources contain a great deal of information which, if carefully sifted, can help to fill the gap. Occasional works did appear by English-educated Chinese authors in the earlier years of this century and these have been used where appropriate. Nevertheless, much of the material upon which this book is based has been drawn from official reports and records. The European planting community, however, tended to be distinct from the body of Government officials and contemporary newspapers have proved a valuable source of information for the reverse side of the coin depicted in these official records. Although often fragmentary, the information which these various sources provide on the past agricultural economy is, in total, considerable; it is, however, rarely as complete as the author would have wished and gaps necessarily appear in the analysis that follows.

PART I

SHIFTING COMMERCIAL AGRICULTURE

1

THE BASES OF CHINESE AGRICULTURAL
PIONEERING

THERE IS A CLOSE RELATIONSHIP between the establishment of the British Settlements of Penang and Singapore and the beginnings of large-scale Chinese immigration to Malaya; indeed, the major focal point of Chinese settlement in the peninsula shifted from Malacca to Penang after 1786 and from Penang to Singapore after 1819. Although the southern Settlement attained the dominant role, throughout the nineteenth century all three British Settlements retained their positions as starting and controlling points for Chinese penetration into the relatively undeveloped and unknown Malay States which constituted their immediate hinterlands.

Chinese penetration into the Malay Peninsula was already in progress for both mining and agricultural purposes in the early years of the nineteenth century and in several regions had assumed significant proportions before the British first intervened directly in the Malay States in 1874. In fact, there is little doubt that the Chinese came to regard the Malay States as the natural economic hinterland of the Straits Settlements long before the British accepted this fact either politically or economically.

The close connexion in time between the extension of British control to the Malay States and a marked increase in their Chinese population has tended to create a belief that British intervention resulted in the establishment of 'real order and security' in these states and that this directly encouraged a tremendous influx of Chinese immigrants.[1] Undoubtedly there is a degree of truth in this belief, but Chinese pioneers were already at work, and in relatively large numbers, as either miners or agriculturalists, in several of the mainland states

[1] See for instance L.C.A. Knowles, *The Economic Development of the British Overseas Empire*, London, 1924, 54.

before the British intervened and in fact, their presence, and the problems which it created, were factors directly involved in producing the change in British policy.

The miners certainly extended their activities very considerably after 1874. Within a decade and a half however, the new British administration had evolved agricultural policies based on a conception of large-scale cultivation which was the antithesis of the cultivation system employed by the Chinese agricultural pioneers. Whilst the extension of British control to the western Malay States of Perak, Selangor and Negri Sembilan did much to foster a marked expansion of Chinese mining, it ultimately proved fatal to the early Chinese system of cultivation.

The importance of the establishment of British Settlements, and later the extension of British control in stimulating the rapid influx of Chinese to the Malay Peninsula in the nineteenth century rests mainly on its economic implications. The development of British free ports at Penang and Singapore provided the fundamental impetus for Chinese pioneers to move in increasing numbers into the hinterland of the Straits Settlements by opening to them the growing markets for raw materials in the industrially developing countries of Western Europe. As shipping facilities were improved the Chinese were quick to appreciate the economic possibilities that the Malay States offered, and they began to produce several items in increasing demand in the western world which could be sold profitably to European merchants, particularly in Singapore.

The spectacular effects that this had on the Malayan 'tin-rush' are generally recognized. It is less well-known that this new link with the markets of Europe also encouraged an extension of the activities of Chinese agricultural pioneers into several parts of the Malayan mainland. Apart from providing an *entrée* to the markets of Europe, the British Settlements, and in particular Singapore, developed into the headquarters of Chinese commercial activity in the western *Nan Yang* and provided the Chinese with a direct link with the markets and sources of labour and capital in the homeland.[2] To the Chinese

[2] See Wang Gungwu, *A Short History of the Nanyang Chinese*, Singapore, 1959, 19.

the British Settlements, with their commercial links with East and West, were the focal point of their activities, not only in the Malay Peninsula, but in a large part of South-East Asia.

One of the basic attractions of the Straits Settlements from the Chinese point of view was the *laissez-faire* attitude adopted by the British towards the immigrants. For much of the nineteenth century the Chinese were left almost entirely to themselves and were governed through headmen, or *Capitan China*, whom they themselves appointed. As a result the Chinese community developed its own internal organization distinct from, and almost completely lacking in integration with, the British administrative framework; in short, the Chinese established an *imperium in imperio* in the British Settlements. When they extended their operations into the mainland states they did so within their own organizational framework and it proved to be ideally suited to the frontier conditions that typified much of nineteenth-century Malaya.

All pioneer Chinese enterprises in nineteenth-century Malaya whether agricultural or mining were organized on the basis of what might be termed the *kongsi* system, a system showing variations in detail according to the type of enterprise involved. Strictly speaking, a *kongsi* was a Chinese association which existed for the economic benefit of its members by organizing their activities, but the secret societies and the *kongsis* were very closely related until the former were declared illegal in 1889.

Individual *kongsis* invariably consisted of members of a single dialect group, and usually of immigrants from the same small locality in south China. The system was ubiquitous in nineteenth-century Malaya because it provided a feeling of security and identity to widely different groups of Chinese immigrants in an alien environment. The *kongsi* system emerged as a replacement for the closely-knit village organization to which the immigrants were accustomed in south China. It developed because 'in Malaya, Chinese from different villages in China would be just as frightened of other Chinese not tied to them by social ties as they would be of Malays and others'.[3]

[3] W.H. Newell, *Treacherous River: A Study of Rural Chinese in North Malaya*, Kuala Lumpur, 1962, 19.

Pioneer ventures in the mainland states were financed by Chinese merchants and shopkeepers in the Straits Settlements. Clearly the arrangement was based on the existence of some degree of trust between the urban-based financiers and the pioneers, a situation favoured if they had clan association or other ties. It was also based on the fact that almost invariably the pioneers depended upon the financiers for the supply of provisions and for the ultimate disposal of their products. Usually the pioneer obtained his advances in return for a fixed proportion of his future products. Rates of interest on the advances were high because the risk of failure, and even of the pioneer absconding, were great. In some cases, at least, the Chinese financiers themselves borrowed money from European merchants to provide advances to these pioneers, but in general this system of promoting new ventures was divorced completely from the activities of the European residents.

The Chinese also evolved their own elaborate system of supplying the labour necessary for the extension of their agricultural and mining operations. Under this system, known as the 'Credit Ticket System', the passages of intending Chinese immigrants were arranged and paid by agencies who passed on the cost to the employers in Malaya. In return the new arrival, or *sinkheh*, was obliged to pay off, by his labour, the expenses incurred in bringing him to Malaya, and usually this involved working for at least a year at reduced wages. On arrival in Malaya the *sinkhehs* were dispatched to work for the headmen, or *towkays*, of mines or plantations in the interior and, in effect, came under the operation of a truck system whereby a large proportion of their wages took the form of food, clothes and opium. There is little doubt that the labourers, *towkays* and financiers of individual plantations or mines had the close connexions implied in the *kongsi* system or that usually they were, willy-nilly, members of the same secret society. The pioneer Chinese settlements in the interior were, therefore, the frontier outposts of a closely-knit organization controlled from the Straits Settlements.

The Chinese came to Malaya for strictly economic reasons. They were not drawn by the prospects of permanent settlement but by the hope of making a 'fortune' with which to return to their homeland. Coming only with a view to temporary residence they looked to economic activities that could give a quick return on a small capital investment. Thus, the Chinese agricultural pioneers spurned the subsistence farming of the indigenous Malays and abandoned the elaborate agricultural techniques and intensive use of land characteristic of China and turned instead to the cultivation of a small group of exportable crops suited to the conditions of a frontier economy in a humid tropical environment.

Outside the British Settlements the Malay Peninsula was very sparsely peopled in the early nineteenth century. Large tracts of virgin land were therefore available and the Chinese planters, recognizing that this land only had a value for them whilst it produced crops economically, employed a shifting system of cultivation which skimmed both profits and fertility from the soil and then left it to revert to *lalang* and *belukar*.[4] This tended to produce an expanding frontier of Chinese agricultural pioneering, for as old plantations were abandoned, fresh land was cleared either in regions of existing settlement or in completely new areas. They used this system, to their considerable gain, in many parts of southern Malaya during most of the nineteenth century. As the British extended their control and evolved an agricultural policy which looked to the long-term development of land, this shifting system, possible under frontier conditions and implying the complete lack of interest in anything but short-term results characteristic of the Chinese pioneers, was officially condemned. Moreover, later in the 1910's, the abolition of indentured labour and the government take-over of the opium monopoly undermined the whole basis of the early Chinese success—the control and exploitation of cheap labour.

By far the most important crops grown by the Chinese on this shifting system of cultivation in nineteenth-century Malaya were tapioca (*Manihot utilissima*), gambier (*Uncaria gambier*), and pepper (*Piper nigrum*). The first two, in particular, were ideally suited to the needs of the Chinese pioneers. They produced returns within a short time of planting, they would grow well in most localities, their cultivation was not labour-consum-

---

[4] *Lalang* is a coarse grass, *Imperata cylindrica; belukar* is the Malay term for secondary jungle.

ing nor did it require any particular skill, and the establishment of a plantation with the necessary processing equipment required a relatively small capital outlay. At the same time there was a growing demand for gambier as a dyeing and tanning agent in the leather industry of Europe and elsewhere and also for tapioca in the form of flake, flour or pearl. The pepper vine was slightly different, requiring greater care and taking longer to produce results, and its special position in the pioneer Chinese agricultural economy *vis-à-vis* gambier is discussed in Chapters 2 and 3. The production of these crops put the Chinese planters at the mercy of the economic situation in Europe. Prices fluctuated noticeably during the nineteenth century producing immediate responses among the Chinese planters, responses made possible by their attitude towards the land and by the short maturation period and life-cycle of the crops that they chose to cultivate.

The cultivation of these pioneer crops under Chinese management achieved a greater degree of success and embraced a larger area in Malaya than any other form of export-orientated agriculture prior to the advent of rubber. It is possible that, at one time or another during the nineteenth century, at least half a million acres of land may have been affected by the shifting cultivation of the Chinese agricultural pioneers, and at the turn of the century the produce exported annually from their tapioca and gambier and pepper plantations was valued at well over $8 million. In contrast, coffee never occupied more than about 20,000 acres in the western Malay States from which the total value of coffee exports never exceeded $1.2 million.

It is the purpose of this section to consider in some detail the various features of this important process of Chinese agricultural pioneering in the regions in which it had its most marked effects and in particular to emphasize the geographical effects of the shifting system of cultivation as the planters responded to fluctuating economic conditions.

2

CHINESE PLANTERS IN SINGAPORE
AND JOHORE*

THE EARLY EUROPEAN SETTLERS knew little of Singapore away
from the immediate environs of their new settlement but it is
clear that the island was not completely uninhabited and
uncultivated in 1819. There was already a small population of
Malays and Chinese, some of whom were engaged in agricultural activities, and by 1819 Chinese gambier plantations had
been established on the hills on the northern, western and
south-western periphery of the new town. Newbold, writing in
1839, estimated that the island had a population of approximately 150 in 1819, of whom about thirty were Chinese, and
in 1822 Colonel W. Farquhar indicated that some twenty
gambier plantations, belonging to both Malays and Chinese,
existed on Singapore when the British arrived.[1]
   The date of opening of these first plantations and the place
of origin of the Chinese settlers who worked them are unknown.
Purcell suggested that the first Chinese to settle in Singapore
on the establishment of the British Settlement came from
Malacca and Riau.[2] There were Chinese gambier planters in
Riau in the late eighteenth century and it is probable that some
of these moved to Singapore in the 1790's or early 1800's to
avoid the disturbances of that period. It seems likely that the
system of cultivation and financing associated with these pioneer

*This chapter is an amended version of an article by J.C. Jackson,
'Chinese Agricultural Pioneering in Singapore and Johore, 1800-1917',
JMBRAS, Vol. LXXXVIII, pt. 1, 1965, 77-105.

[1] T.J. Newbold, *Political and Statistical Account of the British Settlements in the Straits of Malacca*, London, 1839, Vol. 1, 279; letter from
Col. W. Farquhar to Lt. L.W. Hull dated 28 December 1822, quoted
by W. Bartley, 'Population of Singapore in 1819', *JMBRAS*, Vol. XI,
pt. 2, 1933, 177.

[2] V. Purcell, *The Chinese in Malaya*, London, 1948, 70.

plantations in Singapore, and subsequently with those in other
parts of the Malay Peninsula, came with these settlers from
Riau, although its origins may lie elsewhere in South-East Asia.[3]

In the first twenty-five years after the founding of Singapore
Chinese gambier and pepper planting expanded rapidly, particularly under the stimulus of high prices in the mid-1830's
(Table 1). By 1839 these plantations formed 'the only cultivation on the island which [had] yet assumed any degree of
commercial importance',[4] and the total area devoted to these
crops increased from 2,350 acres in 1836 to between five and six
thousand acres in 1841.[5] The planters had begun to push much
further into the interior of the island and some ten years later,
when there were estimated to be 24,220 acres under gambier
and 2,614 acres under pepper, it was noted that 'the whole of
the interior [was] occupied by Pepper and Gambier plantations
intermixed with primeval Forest'. Some plantations had also
been established in the northern and western parts of the
island.[6]

As a result the total quantity of gambier produced in Singapore increased markedly. In 1836 production was estimated to
total 22,000 pikuls. This rose to about 48,000 pikuls in 1839
and to 80,000 pikuls in 1848. In the latter year the Singapore
plantations also produced 30,923 pikuls of pepper, and these
two crops together occupied over three-quarters of the total
estimated cultivated area and accounted for nearly three-fifths
of the total value of agricultural produce on the island.[7]

---

[3] The Commissioner of Lands and Mines in Johore in 1914, writing of
this system, observed that 'It was certainly in existence very many
years ago, in some of the Dutch Islands.' Quoted in *New Atlas and
Commercial Gazetteer of the Straits Settlements and Federated Malay
States*, Shanghai, 1917, 71.

[4] *S.F.P.*, 28 March 1839 quoted by C.B. Buckley, *An Anecdotal History
of Old Times in Singapore*, Vol. 1, Singapore, 1902, 335.

[5] *S.F.P.*, 29 December 1836 quoted by P. Wheatley, 'Land Use in the
Vicinity of Singapore in the Eighteen-Thirties', *M.J.T.G.*, Vol. 2, 1954,
65; *S.F.P.*, Vol. 6 No. 46, 18 November 1841.

[6] J.T. Thomson, 'General Report on the Residency of Singapore, Drawn
up principally with a view of illustrating its Agricultural Statistics',
J.I.A., Vol. 4, 1850, 219; *Map of Singapore Island and Its Dependencies*,
1852, P.R.O., London, Straits Settlements No. 5.

Gambier was exported for use in both the silk and leather industries. Burkill maintains that the produce of the earliest Singapore plantations was exported to China, and it is probable that gambier was first shipped from Singapore to Europe in 1830.[8] Until the early 1830's gambier was subject to very heavy import duties on entry to Britain. These duties were then substantially reduced and already by 1834 gambier was regarded as being likely to become 'a staple article of export' from Singapore to Britain.[9] During the 1830's the amount dispatched to Britain increased steadily and it was to this destination that most of it was sent throughout the nineteenth century.

The System of Cultivation in Early Singapore

Pepper and gambier were not interplanted but allocated to separate parts of a plantation. Thus, Cameron observed in the mid-1860's that 'wherever there is a gambier plantation, pepper is sure also to be found growing in a small corner of a few acres near the homestead'.[10] The price of gambier was seldom high enough to justify its cultivation alone but the almost continuous collecting of the gambier foliage could be integrated with the highly seasonal cycle of pepper production thus ensuring regular employment throughout the year for the relatively large labour force required to care for the pepper vines.[11] Moreover, the refuse from gambier boiling provided virtually the only form of manure available for the pepper vines and the quicker-maturing gambier helped to provide an income

---

[7] Buckley, op. cit. Vol. 1, 241, 307 and 335; Thomson, op. cit. 219.

[8] I.H. Burkill, *A Dictionary of the Economic Products of the Malay Peninsula*, London, 1935, Vol. 2, 2202; H.N. Ridley, 'Gambir', *Agricultural Bulletin of the Malay Peninsula*, No. 2, February 1892, 20.

[9] *Singapore Chronicle*, N.S., Vol. 4 No. 18, 1 May 1834.

[10] J. Cameron, *Our Tropical Possessions in Malayan India*, London, 1865, 82.

[11] Once the gambier plant reached maturity the leaves and young branches could be cut about once every two months; otherwise the plant required little attention. Usually two crops of pepper were produced in a year, in December-January and in July-August, but the vines had to be carefully tended the whole year round.

until the pepper vines reached maturity.[12] As a general rule these crops were cultivated on a ratio of one acre of pepper to every ten acres of gambier.

The gambier and pepper planters used a shifting method of cultivation. Initially this was favoured by the Government, not least because it provided employment for the ever-increasing influx of Chinese immigrants. Within a short while, however, it became apparent that the practice was not altogether desirable for it resulted in the replacement of vast areas of virgin jungle by almost useless *lalang* and *belukar*.

Large-scale land clearance in connexion with gambier and pepper planting resulted from the operation of two separate factors. The Chinese cultivators wanted quick returns. Thus, when the soil began to show signs of exhaustion it was abandoned and they began again on virgin land. Once abandoned the land required a long fallow period before it would again be suitable for cultivation: on the one hand, gambier was an extremely exhaustive crop, and on the other, young vines would not thrive 'on old worn out pepper land'.[13] This process of frequent movement was facilitated by the fact that these Chinese planters were merely squatters with no legal title to the land.

In the second place, once collected, the gambier leaves had to be boiled as quickly as possible to extract the commercial product, for within twenty-four hours they became 'brown and worthless'. Therefore, each plantation had its own shed containing cauldrons for the boiling process. For this operation the planters required large reserves of firewood and it is estimated that a block of forest roughly equal in area to the cultivated holding was cleared to provide the necessary fuel.[14] These heavy fuel requirements helped to tie the gambier and pepper planters closely to the jungle fringe.

[12] S.W. Kirby, 'Johore in 1926', *Geographical Journal*, Vol. LXXI, 1928, 246. Returns could be obtained from gambier within fourteen months of planting; the pepper vines took about two and a half to three years to reach maturity.

[13] J. Low, *A Dissertation on the Soil and Agriculture of the British Settlement of Penang...*, Singapore, 1836, 43.

[14] *A.R.S.S., 1858-9*, 76; Ridley, 'Gambir', 31-35.

A gambier plantation became exhausted after about fifteen years, the pepper vines passed their peak of production in their fifteenth to twentieth years and the fuel supply was only expected to last at the most for some twenty-five years.[15] Consequently, by the mid-1830's many of the early plantations on Singapore were close to abandonment and as new plantations were opened larger and larger areas began to suffer both from soil exhaustion and deficiencies of firewood. Already by 1836 complaints were being made

... about the jungles being all cut down for firewood, and about plantations being deserted and allowed to run to lalang grass, while a fresh plantation was made in the nearest favourable site, and further devastation commenced.[16]

Only three-quarters of the existing plantations in Singapore were cultivated in 1850, and at that time it was felt that the cultivation was 'retrograding as the older plantations have all become exhausted'.[17]

The socio-economic background of the early Singapore plantations

Although the earliest Chinese planters on the island may have come from Riau, most of the plantations were opened by Chinese who had come direct from their homeland on the 'Credit Ticket System'. Generally speaking, after completing the one year's labour necessary to repay their passages many of these immigrants opened up small plantations of their own. They were financed by Chinese shopkeepers and merchants in Singapore town who usually claimed a proportion of future crops until the debt was discharged. This system of pledging the future plantation and its products was on conditions highly favourable to the capitalist. Thus, it was observed in 1841 that 'Almost the whole of the Pepper and Gambier plantations have been made, and are now it is believed up-held by borrowed

---

[15] *Singapore Chronicle*, N.S., Vol. 7 No. 36, 9 September 1837; Low, op. cit. 43; S.F.P., 28 March 1839 quoted by Buckley, op. cit. Vol. 1, 335.

[16] Buckley, op. cit. Vol. 1, 307.

[17] Thomson, op. cit. 137.

capital—so that the actual cultivators are nearly at the mercy of the Chinese merchants of the Town'.[18]

Many of these pioneer planters never cleared their original debt and remained under the control of Singapore financiers; indeed, it was believed that two-thirds of the plantations existing in 1839 were subject to encumbrances of this description. Moreover, according to the Chinese themselves 'the best of the plantations, when clear of all encumbrances yield the proprietor an annual profit of about $400, while the lowest barely pay their way'.[19]

An estimate of the Chinese population of Singapore in 1848 by a contemporary Chinese, himself involved in this agricultural enterprise, shows clearly that this form of cultivation was dominated by Tiechius. Indeed, over 90 per cent. of the Chinese gambier and pepper planters on the island at that date were members of this dialect group.[20]

Conditions on the pioneer plantations were extremely unpleasant. Housing was poor, the plantations were isolated, malaria, beri-beri and other diseases were rife. Speaking of the labourers in the late 1840's Siah U Chin observed that many 'get their legs and feet hurt with splinters [and] the broken skin being disregarded, large ulcers are formed'.[21] Not infrequently there are reports that labourers had been 'taken by tigers' and it has been suggested that because of this particular danger the employers on plantations in interior Singapore had to pay double wages to induce their labourers to remain.[22] Death and desertion resulted in a rapid turn-over of labour.

---

[18] S.F.P., Vol. 6 No. 46, 18 November 1841.

[19] S.F.P., 28 March 1839 quoted by Buckley, op. cit. Vol. 1, 335.

[20] Siah U Chin, 'The Chinese in Singapore', J.I.A., Vol. 2, 1848, 290. Although the accuracy of Siah's figures was questioned several years later on the basis of the Census taken in December 1849, there can be little doubt that they correctly indicate the relative dominance of this dialect group. See T. Braddell, 'Notes on the Chinese in the Straits', J.I.A., Vol. 9, 1855, 115-16; see also L.E. Williams, 'Chinese Leadership in Early British Singapore', Asian Studies, Vol. 2 No. 2, 1964, 177.

[21] Siah, op. cit. 287-8.

[22] S.F.P., Vol. 14 No. 21, 24 May 1849.

TABLE 1

SAMPLE PRICES QUOTED LOCALLY FOR GAMBIER AND BLACK PEPPER, 1831-61

(Spanish Dollars per Pikul)

Date	Gambier	Black Pepper
January 1831	1.30 to 1.75	5.00 to 5.25
January 1834	4.00 to 5.00	6.00 to 6.25
January 1837	3.00 to 3.25	6.75 to 7.00
January 1840	2.70 to 2.80	5.65 to 6.00
January 1844	1.50	4.20 to 4.30
January 1849	0.90 to 1.00	3.60
January 1855	3.15 to 3.20	6.50 to 6.75
January 1859	2.67 to 2.70	7.20
January 1861	2.85	6.75

Source: 'Prices Current' in the relevant issues of the *Singapore Chronicle*, S.F.P., *Penang Gazette* and *Straits Times*.

In the 1840's labourers' wages were not fixed, but varied according to the price of gambier. Significantly the price quoted locally for gambier fluctuated markedly, whereas pepper prices tended to be more stable (Table 1). By thus linking wages to market conditions the proprietors could minimize the effects of these changing prices. Nevertheless, the labourers were in a position to send money home to China annually and thereby partly fulfil the dream that had brought them to Malaya, although the ultimate aim of most was to return home with a 'fortune'. Few did so, and, as with so many Chinese enterprises in nineteenth-century Malaya, the bulk of the profits went directly or indirectly to Chinese financiers living in Singapore town. By providing capital to almost penniless immigrants this system of financing new gambier and pepper plantations took advantage of their 'get-rich-quick' desire. But without a system of financing of this type, extensive agricultural colonization could never have occurred in early nineteenth-century Singapore.

Expansion into Johore

There seems little doubt that the declining area available for new plantations in Singapore, and increasing Chinese immigra-

tion into the island, stimulated Chinese planters to expand into
nearby Johore. It is possible that some Chinese were already
cultivating gambier and pepper in Johore at the beginning of
the nineteenth century.[23] After 1819 the proximity of Singapore
facilitated imports of provisions, exports of products and contacts with financiers. These attractions were enhanced by
'accounts of the richness of the soil in the river valleys' of
Johore, and since the state was so large and the population small
there were vast areas of virgin land available. The Chinese
believed that the Malay ruler of Johore—the Temenggong—
would grant them the same measure of protection that he himself enjoyed under the Colonial Government as a resident of
Singapore. The Temenggong's attitude towards the Chinese
planters in fact did much to encourage the expansion of
gambier and pepper planting in Johore.[24]

This movement into Johore may have begun in the late
1820's. Once started it rapidly gained momentum and by the
1840's and 1850's numerous Chinese planters were pioneering
on the mainland. An observer in June 1845 reported that within
the previous six months fifty-two new plantations had been
commenced by Chinese from Singapore; of these twenty were
on the Skudai river, twelve on the Sungei Melayu, fifteen on
the Sungei Danga and five on the Sungei Tebrau. There were
about five hundred people in all engaged in these plantations
and it was thought that 'the immigration will increase as the
gambier and pepper plantations on this island [i.e. Singapore]
wear out, which, from their age, many of them are fast doing'.[25]
Clearly at this date the new gambier and pepper plantations
on the mainland concentrated along the rivers flowing into the

[23] See A. Hamilton, *A New Account of the East Indies* edited by Sir
William Foster, London, 1930, Vol. 2, 51. Burkill notes that in 1758
the gambier plant was taken to Malacca from 'Puntain' (Pontian?),
in Johore. Burkill, op. cit. Vol. 2, 2202.

[24] C.M. Turnbull, 'The Johore Gambier and Pepper Trade in the mid-
nineteenth Century', *J.S.S.S.*, Vol. XV, pt. 1, 1959, 44; *S.F.P.*, Vol. 11
No. 1, 1 January 1846; D.F.A. Hervey, 'A Trip to Gunong Blumut',
JSBRAS, No. 3, 1879, 90; H. Lake, 'Johore', *Geographical Journal*,
Vol. 3, 1894, 295.

[25] Article in *S.F.P.*, June 1845 quoted by Buckley, op. cit. Vol. 2, 431.

Johore Strait. These provided the most convenient means of entry for settlers moving from Singapore.

The movement of Chinese across the Johore Strait during the 1840's and 1850's may have been augmented by a migration from the exhausted plantations of Riau. By the early 1860's there were about 1,200 gambier and pepper plantations in Johore, employing a labour force of some 15,000. Although the majority were still concentrated on the rivers flowing into the Johore Strait some had appeared 'further North on the rivers flowing into the open sea'.[26]

This movement into Johore was basically an extension of Chinese gambier and pepper planting in Singapore. Thus it was dominated by the Tiechius, although other dialect groups were involved in the establishment of individual settlements.[27]

The Kangchu System

There were no roads in mid-nineteenth century Johore and rivers served as highways of immigration and later as arteries of commerce. Based on these all-important river valleys a system of settlement, cultivation and landholding emerged in connexion with gambier and pepper planting. It is a system which appears also to have been used in Singapore and which had a counterpart in the Chinese gambier and pepper plantations that appeared in southern Selangor and coastal Negri Sembilan later in the century (see next chapter). Described by a later Chinese observer as being 'an entirely unique and perhaps efficacious system of land-tenure and co-operative cultivation'[28] it was a means whereby pioneer Chinese agricultural colonies were established in previously sparsely populated areas.

In these valleys small villages or river depots were established, each of which was known as a *kangkar* (literally 'foot of the river' in the Tiechiu dialect), and from which cultivation

---

[26] Turnbull, op. cit. 46.

[27] Tan Tek Soon, 'Chinese Local Trade', *The Straits Chinese Magazine*, Vol. VI No. 23, September 1902, 91; F. Lees, 'Chinese Settlement in the Kulai Sub-District of Johore, Malaysia', in R.W. Steel and R.M. Prothero, *Geographers and the Tropics: Liverpool Essays*, London, 1964, 282.

[28] Tan Tek Soon, op. cit. 91.

extended 'only from the river bank to the nearest watershed'.[29] The Chinese settlers were expected not to interfere with any property, land or village already occupied by Malays within the area granted, nor were they to engage in trade with them.[30] In most cases however, the *kangkars* were established in areas containing a very small existing population. Some were established in areas where the sole inhabitants were groups of transient aborigines, others in unpopulated areas.

Each *kangkar* and its section of the valley was governed by a semi-feudal Chinese headman known as a *kangchu* ('lord of the river'), who held the land under a title known as a *surat sungei* ('river document') granted to him by the Malay ruler. The earliest recorded *surat sungei*, issued for part of the Skudai river, is dated 1833.[31] In the mid-nineteenth century specific powers were delegated to the *kangchu* in the form of a *tauliah* ('letter of authority'). This gave him a legal position both as head of his community and as representative of the Sultan's authority.[32]

This system, usually termed the *kangchu* system, was well-suited to conditions in nineteenth-century Johore. The state was sparsely populated and almost entirely covered with virgin jungle. The absence of roads made administration difficult. Accordingly, each *kangchu* was officially recognized by the Malay authorities as the *penghulu* or headman, of the Chinese in his *kangkar* and was given virtually a free hand to administer the settlement and its lands.

The *kangchu* paid rents or taxes for the whole area and in fact took the responsibility of the territory worked from his *kangkar* off the shoulders of the government. He was obliged to construct and maintain the paths leading to the various plantations within the *kangkar,* and to provide for 'the upkeep of the river communications'.[33] In addition to his administrative

---

[29] Loc. cit. Coope states that the *Kangchu* was granted 'a vague area limited only by the watersheds of the next two rivers'. A.E. Coope, 'The Kangchu System in Johore', *JMBRAS*, Vol. XIV, pt. 3, 1936, 247.

[30] Coope, op. cit. 248.

[31] Ibid. 247.

[32] Lees, op. cit. 280.

[33] Tan Tek Soon, op. cit. 91.

powers, within his *kangkar* he held the opium and gambling 'farms', together with exclusive rights of pawnbroking, selling liquor, slaughtering pigs and selling pork—all lucrative sources of income in pioneer Chinese settlements in Malaya, whether mining or agricultural.

The organization of the *kangchu system* was in accord with the clan structure of Chinese society and, as Cowgill notes, 'had much to commend it as a method of controlling Chinese peasant folk'.[34] From the point of view of the Malay authorities its basic advantage was that local administration lay in the hands of a person of the same race, and usually dialect group, as the settlers and this person was their leader in the development and expansion of the settlement.[35] Agricultural colonization and development by immigrant aliens could proceed within the organizational framework introduced by the immigrants, superficially integrated into the Malay administration in that the Temenggong was recognized as its titular head, but in practice standing almost entirely outside the jurisdiction of the existing local authorities.

As on Singapore Island the financing of the gambier and pepper plantations in Johore was controlled by residents of Singapore town. Thus, an observer in 1846 noted that 'The plantations in Johore being owned by Chinese Merchants in Singapore the whole produce is of course brought to this market, and the supplies required by the cultivators furnished from this place'.[36] In 1864 the Chinese merchants of Singapore claimed that they had advanced over one million dollars to develop these plantations, although in fact most of this money had been borrowed originally by them from European merchants. At this date there were 100 gambier shops and over 200 provision stores in Singapore which relied almost entirely on the Johore trade.[37]

Most of the *kangchus* had borrowed money from Chinese merchants in Singapore to develop their *kangkars* and were

[34] J.V. Cowgill, 'Chinese Place Names in Johore', *JMBRAS*, Vol. 11, pt. 3, 1924, 221.
[35] Lees, op. cit. 281.
[36] *S.F.P.*, Vol. 11 No. 1, 1 January 1846.
[37] Turnbull, op. cit. 46.

subject to the same obligations as their counterparts on the island. Usually they also had to buy their provisions from their creditors. In some cases however, *kangchus* themselves owned the boats which brought the provisions up-river to the settlements; some also owned shops in Singapore from which the provisions were bought. In addition to their monopolies of opium, pawnbroking, and liquor and pork selling, they also held a monopoly of all other provisions moving into their settlements and controlled the transportation of all exports. In this connexion Tan Tek Soon notes that

... the several traders interested in a river or its vicinity and the Kangchu would furnish the necessary capital between them to build a gambier tongkang of sufficient capacity to carry off the produce in fortnightly trips... The freight of produce is placed at as low a rate as possible, chargeable to the planters... Owing to its importance and the vested interests which have in time grown around this traffic, no competition is ever permitted.[38]

Many *kangchus* became very wealthy, some of the richer commanding an annual income of several thousand dollars, and by the late 1870's many of the more prosperous had retired to Singapore and delegated their authority to representatives in Johore. In such cases a *kangchu* was often the owner of more than one *kangkar*.

The *kangchu* system continued to be used in Johore, and if place-name evidence is to be trusted, in Singapore also, throughout the whole of the nineteenth century. In 1873 a special *Law of the Kangchus* was passed in Johore.[39] This laid out in detail the privileges, duties and responsibilities of the *kangchus* in the eyes of the Malay authorities, and provides much information on the workings of the system later in the century. It appears doubtful however, whether the *kangchus* generally fulfilled their obligations meticulously. The system was finally abolished by *The Kangchu Rights (Abolition) Enactment* of 1917 under which all remaining *kangchus* were compensated financially for the loss of their former rights. By this time rubber had come to claim the main interest of Chinese planters

[38] Tan Tek Soon, op. cit. 92.
[39] Coope, op. cit. 252-61.

in Johore. That the system had survived almost intact for so long is due to the suitability and closeness of its organization and to the fact that it was a recognized institution among the Chinese.

Plantations, Kangkars and Bangsals

There has been much confusion over the use of the terms 'plantation', *'kangkar'* and *'bangsal'* in contemporary documents. It is evident however, that the term 'plantation' was somewhat loosely applied to any patch of land upon which, or area within which, gambier and pepper were planted. On the other hand, the terms *'kangkar'* and *'bangsal'* clearly had specific and different meanings.

The term *kangkar* was used to signify both the riverine village headquarters of the *kangchu* and the whole 'area' of land worked from the headquarters. In the latter case it is synonymous with the Malay term *kawasan* (area), sometimes used in contemporary sources. It refers to the area recognized by the Malay authorities as having been granted to the *kangchu* in his *surat sungei*, an area which contained, besides the village, both cultivated land and virgin jungle. *Kangkars* or *kawasans* varied widely in size; some of the smaller ones contained less than 2,500 acres, many of the larger ones comprised more than 20,000 acres of land (Fig. 7B).

On the other hand, *bangsal* was a term strictly reserved for the small patches of land actually planted with gambier and pepper in which there would be a gambier cauldron and furnaces for boiling purposes. Each *kangkar* or *kawasan* would therefore contain many *bangsals* (Figs. 2 and 6). Although the *bangsals* varied in size they probably averaged between ten and fifty acres, producing annually some 100-200 pikuls of gambier and 50-150 pikuls of pepper each.[40]

It appears that although the *kangchu* had control over the whole area worked from his settlement, each *bangsal* was worked by a different group of planters. Both in Singapore and Johore each *bangsal* employed about nine or ten men. Initially

[40] *S.F.P.*, 28 March 1839 quoted by Buckley, op. cit. Vol. 1, 335; Thomson says that the average size of a 'plantation' in Singapore was thirty acres. Thomson, op. cit. 137.

they were financed by the *kangchu* and obtained provisions and sold the produce through him. Although all the planters within a *kangkar* were in one way or another under the control of the *kangchu* he did not, by custom at any rate, own all the land. Anyone within his area who planted land with his permission was treated as having a freehold. By virtue of the system of cultivation however, it was not the land as such that had the greatest value but the commercial products that it yielded.

After a period of fifteen to twenty-five years, when the initial *bangsals* began to show signs of soil exhaustion and depletion of firewood, the planters moved elsewhere within the *kangkar* to open new *bangsals* and the old ones reverted to *lalang* and *belukar*. Although it is impossible to be certain, the existence of occasional cases of two *kangkars* close together on the same small river with the suffixes *lama* (old), and *bahru* (new), e.g. Kangkar Temon Lama and Kangkar Temon Bahru may indicate that when the areas under cultivation within the *kangkar* boundaries had spread sufficiently far from the initial village headquarters it became necessary to establish a new river depot further inland (Fig. 3). A schematic plan of the author's interpretation of the relationship of *bangsals* to *kangkars* has been shown in Figure 2.[41]

There is considerable evidence to support the suggestion that *bangsal* refers only to the cultivated blocks within a *kangkar* or *kawasan*. The word *bangsal* usually indicates a shed or lean-to shelter in Malay, in which case it could refer to either the gambier boiling shed or the shed housing the workers or both, within a cultivated clearing. It was defined by Hervey in 1879 as meaning 'cooly shed' and it was observed in 1893 that the 'plantations' were 'commonly termed bangsals'.[42] Moreover the ratio of *bangsals* to *kangkars* in Singapore in 1885 (Fig. 4) can best be explained in terms of a system such as that suggested. Contemporary map evidence for north-western Johore

---

[41] Given the fact that the terms *bangsal* and *kangkar* had these specific meanings, it is obvious that in many documentary references 'plantation' has been applied indiscriminately to both terms; it is similarly used in this chapter when it is impossible to make the distinction.

[42] Hervey, 'Trip to Gunong Blumut', 92; *S.F.P.*, 28 March 1839, quoted by Buckley, op. cit. Vol. 1, 335.

provides additional support (Fig. 6). That the term was in use in Johore is shown by the existence of the element *bangsal* in several place-names on modern topographic maps of the state.

A relationship of this type is also suggested by several early references to Johore. Tan Tek Soon for instance, noted that the *kangchu* was responsible for the construction and maintenance of 'the paths leading to *the several plantations under his control*'.[43] H. Lake, who was engaged in surveying in Johore in the early 1890's, gives a clearer picture of the system and the village headquarters.

> *Each group of plantations possesses what is known as a 'kangka',* or village. Here resides the 'kangchu', or Chinese headman, also the representatives of the various syndicates, or 'Kongsees' of Chinese speculators. The gambling-house, with the opium store, is also here. Around the central buildings, which are often of a substantial character, are grouped the shops and stores, the eating-houses and innumerable pig-pens,—everything built on the ground, of bamboo and round poles thatched with palm leaf.[44]

This system whereby small clearings of gambier and pepper were cultivated by separate groups of planters under the jurisdiction of the *kangchu* owed its origins to the methods of financing new ventures current amongst the Chinese immigrants. After securing the backing of a number of gambier and pepper traders in Singapore the prospective *kangchu* proceeded to an unoccupied district in Johore and selected an area of jungle-land on the banks of some river or stream. He then arranged with a number of semi-dependent planters to open up the jungle and plant gambier and pepper; a sufficient acreage was allocated to each of these planters for present cultivation and future expansion. They were induced to undertake the enterprise by an arrangement under which for the first eighteen months the *kangchu* supplied them with all the necessities of life, implements, seeds and cuttings, the cost of which he debited to their account. When the first crop was harvested a settlement was made and the *kangchu* distributed the planters'

---

[43] Tan Tek Soon, op. cit. 91. The italics have been inserted.
[44] Lake, op. cit. 290. The italics have been inserted.

debts and their plantations to his own creditors. Thereafter
each planter was financed by his own town trader who supplied
him with provisions and additional advances and received his
produce in exchange at prices regulated after 1867 by the
Gambier and Pepper Society. These prices were generally about
30 per cent. below the actual market value.[45] The planters rarely,
if ever, became financially independent of the merchant-
financiers in Singapore town.

In essence this was a truck system based on a hierarchy
headed by the urban-based merchants of Singapore. Next in
line came the *kangchus,* and in turn the planters in charge of
individual *bangsals,* each employing about ten wage-earning
labourers. Thus the *kangchu* system was much more complex
and closely knit than has been recognized previously. Its
organization, similar in form to so many types of Chinese enterprise in nineteenth-century Malaya, was ideally suited to the
financial requirements of impecunious immigrant pioneers
establishing agricultural colonies in a virgin area. Moreover, it
is more than likely that all those involved were members of the
same secret society within which the same hierarchy existed.

Gambier and Pepper Planting in Singapore, c.1850-1913

The extension of this form of agricultural enterprise to Johore
did not signify its disappearance in Singapore. By the 1850's
plantations had been established in the heart of the island and
in its northern and western parts, which thus represented a
considerable outward expansion from the original areas of
concentration. Although the shifting method of cultivation and
an increase in the number of planters were important causes
of this expansion, the growth of Singapore town and mounting
interest in the agricultural possibilities of the island on the part
of its European settlers also played their parts. Davidson noted
that even before the mid-1840's some of the gambier and pepper
clearings were 'being purchased by Europeans .... This drives

---

[45] Tan Tek Soon, op. cit. 91. The Gambier and Pepper Society (or *Kong-
kek*) was established in Singapore in 1867 for the mutual protection
of financiers and planters and for the protection of the trade between
Johore and Singapore.

back the squatter, who, like his brethren all over the world, is ever willing to sell and move further inland'.[46]

Gambier and pepper planting showed signs of decline in Singapore in the late 1850's and 1860's. In 1855 there were 543 gambier and pepper 'clearings' on the island but the majority of these were nearing the end of their productive lives for approximately two-thirds of all the gambier plants and pepper vines which they contained were classed as 'old' or 'decaying'; little more than 1 per cent. of all the plants were classed as 'young'.[47] Clearly the reduced prices of the late 1840's and early 1850's acted as a strong deterrent to new planting (Table 1). Prices improved in the mid-1850's, but at that time all 'squatters' on the island were called upon to take out titles to their land and to pay rents.[48] By the very nature of their system of cultivation most planters were reluctant to do this and they were also wary of new planting. Moreover, secret society disturbances resulting in a wave of rioting on the gambier and pepper plantations in the early 1850's may have induced some planters to leave for Johore. Thus, although there was very little virgin jungle left in Singapore, by 1860 there were only six to seven thousand acres planted with these crops, yielding approximately 20,000 pikuls of gambier and 10,000 pikuls of pepper.[49]

By the late 1860's the situation had improved 'because more labour was imported, and the demand from Europe became stronger'.[50] In 1870 Singapore exported approximately 580,600 pikuls of gambier, about half of which had been grown on the island, and the amount exported had risen to 782,129 pikuls by 1880. By the mid-1880's gambier and pepper plantations were widespread in the northern and western parts of the island (Fig. 4).

[46] G.F. Davidson, *Trade and Travel in the Far East*, London, 1846, 43-44. Although the process is clear from this quotation, it is difficult to see how a 'squatter' could sell his land, unless he was paid some form of compensation by the new 'owner' for abandoning it.

[47] *S.F.P.*, Vol. 22 No. 20, 17 May 1855.

[48] *A.R.S.S.*, *1855-6*, 13.

[49] *A.R.S.S.*, *1857-8*, 76. *A.R.S.S.*, *1860-1*, Appendix VII.

[50] W. Makepeace, G.E. Brooke and R.St.J. Braddell, *One Hundred Years of Singapore*, Vol. 2, London, 1921, 80.

In 1890 there were still about 11,000 acres devoted to these crops in Singapore. The following year however, this had declined to 6,100 acres, and between 1891 and 1907 the area planted with gambier and pepper on the island tended to fluctuate around a total of 6,000 acres (Fig. 5). After about 1905 these crops quickly lost favour among the Chinese planters whose interests were turning to other forms of cultivation. The total area under gambier and pepper fell to 600 acres in 1912 and to 75 acres the following year.

Gambier and Pepper Planting in Johore, c.1850-1917

A similar outward expansion from the initial areas of concentration occurred in Johore. By the early 1870's there were twenty-nine Johore rivers with Chinese plantations on their banks; ten years later double that number of rivers had been opened.[51] For some time extension into new areas in Johore was limited to the west coast where navigable rivers facilitated penetration into the interior. Yet even here it is probable that gambier and pepper plantations were restricted to the Batu Pahat area and a few of the rivers further south until the 1880's. Indeed, it is unlikely that expansion into the old kingdom of Muar occurred until after the Maharaja of Johore was elected its ruler in 1877, and expansion here was a phenomenon of the last twenty years of the century (Fig. 6).

Expansion into the areas drained by rivers flowing into the South China Sea dates almost entirely from the early 1880's. The Johore correspondent of the *Singapore Free Press* provides a clear date for this movement by noting in November 1884 that 'The last two or three years have witnessed a number of Chinese gambier and pepper planters rushing into the Sedeli districts and locating themselves principally on the banks of the Sedeli Besar River . . . . Some of the plantations have already commenced manufacturing gambier'.[52]

The 1880's and 1890's were, in fact, a period of rapidly increasing demand for gambier in the British and North Ameri-

---

[51] R.O. Winstedt, 'A History of Johore (1365-1895 A.D.)', *JMBRAS*, Vol. X, pt. 3, 1932, 117.

[52] *S.F.P.*, N.S., Vol. 1 No. 9, 29 November 1884.

can markets, the main destinations of the Singapore exports. The price of gambier rose from about $5 per pikul in 1884 to over $8 for a time in 1889 whilst that of black pepper rose from about $12 per pikul in 1880 to over $20 in 1889. As a result production in Johore increased markedly. In 1880 the State exported to Singapore 316,063 pikuls of gambier and 56,203 pikuls of pepper. Three years later there were estimated to be some four thousand gambier factories in Johore, and by 1889 output had risen to 400,544 pikuls of gambier and 117,024 pikuls of pepper. In 1894 Dato Abdul Rahman, Secretary to the Sultan of Johore, was moved to say 'seven or eight years ago we produced most of the gambier used all over the world'.[53] Under the stimulus of increased prices gambier and pepper planting achieved greater significance and spread into many new areas in Johore in the last two decades of the century. Already by the early 1890's, when there were estimated to be about 210,000 Chinese in the state 'who were chiefly gambier and pepper planters', *kangkars* occupied the whole of the lower valleys of the rivers flowing to the Johore Strait; they were also to be found along the Sungei Sanglang and the Sungei Benut and the Batu Pahat and Muar river systems on the west coast. On the east coast they had been established on the Sungei Sedili Kechil and along the Sungei Sedili Besar system, but not, apparently, on the Sungei Endau[54] (Fig. 7).

By the 1890's the opening up of gambier and pepper plantations in other parts of Malaya had tended to reduce the relative importance of Johore as a producing State (see next chapter). But although the cultivation of other crops, notably Liberian coffee and rubber, had begun, gambier and pepper remained

---

[53] Lake, op. cit. 298. Dato Abdul Rahman was speaking in the discussion following the reading of Lake's paper.

[54] Ibid. 290-6. The figure of 210,000 Chinese in Johore in the early 1890's is probably an over-estimate for there were only 63,410 at the time of the 1911 Census. It is possible, however, that there was a decline in the Chinese population of Johore after the turn of the century for another source maintains that there were 150,000 Chinese in the state in the early 1890's. *Précis of Information Concerning the Straits Settlements and the Native States of the Malay Peninsula*, prepared in the Intelligence Division, War Office, London, 1891-2, 155.

the most important items of cultivation in Johore until the
end of the first decade of the twentieth century. Exports of
gambier fell by over 40 per cent. between 1890 and 1910. In
1913 the General Adviser noted that much gambier had been
interplanted with rubber and much had been eradicated to
make room for rubber. 'The falling prices of gambier, the
difficulties, in the face of competition from rubber estates, of
obtaining labour on the old terms, and the greater profits hoped
for from rubber planting', he said, 'all had their effects in reducing the output of gambier and the associated product, pepper'.[55]
Between 1912 and 1917 exports of both gambier and pepper
declined by 60 per cent., each year showing a substantial fall.
The death knell of gambier and pepper planting was sounded
in 1917 with the abolition of the *kangchu* system.

The Distribution of Kangkars in Johore

The distribution of *kangkars* on Singapore Island at various
dates in the nineteenth century is indicated by cartographic
evidence (Fig. 4). Similar evidence for Johore is limited to three
maps dating from the later years of the *kangchu* system: those
produced by Dato Bintara Luar in 1887 and 1904 and that by
H. Lake in 1893. Documentary material in English is also
scanty.

Place-names form the most important source of evidence for
the extent of Chinese agricultural colonization in Johore during
the nineteenth century, the elements of significance being
kangkar and *kangchu* or *chu kang*.[56] Although in many parts
of Malaya existing place-names, as recorded on modern maps
and in official use, are in Malay and therefore contain no
indication of the history of settlement in predominantly Chinese
areas, the Chinese names for the same places, in the appropriate
dialect, can often be extremely valuable. A list of ninety-eight

---

[55] *A.R. Johore, 1913,* 4.

[56] Both in Singapore and Johore it is not infrequently the case that the
village headquarters carry a family name in combination with the
element *kangchu* or *chu kang*, rather than the element *kangkar*.
Kangkar was usually used in combination with the name of the river
upon which the settlement stood; where this was not, or could not be
the case, a name combining the term *kangchu* or *chu kang* with the
family name of the headman appears to have been in vogue.

kangkar names (apparently romanized in the Tiechiu dialect)
with the Malay equivalents was produced in 1887.[57] This provides the earliest information on distributional patterns for the
state as a whole (Fig. 7A). J.V. Cowgill produced a similar list
in 1924 which contains the names of eighty *kangkars,* many of
which do not appear in the earlier list.[58] These lists add considerably to the number of *kangkars* for which the correct
location is known. They have also preserved the names of many
for which the present-day Malay name gives no indication of
their former state; Ayer Hitam, for example, appears in
Cowgill's list as *Chai Sing Kang* (*kar*). Similarly the lists record
several place-names which, although they have retained their
Chinese form, with the passage of time have lost the all-
important element: thus Yong Peng appears as *Yung Peng
Kang* (*kar*). In addition to the names contained in these lists
there are many place-names on the modern topographic maps
of Johore which contain the prefix *kangkar.*[59]

There must also have been other settlements for which
evidence is no longer extant; settlements which were founded
and for various reasons disappeared during the course of the
nineteenth century as the tide of gambier and pepper planting
flowed on. The total number of *kangkars* existing in nineteenth-
century Johore and the precise limits of those parts of the state
affected by this form of colonization will probably never be
known.

The distribution of all known *kangkars* is shown in Figure
8 which attempts a synthesis of the various types of evidence.
Although it indicates the parts of Johore affected by this form
of Chinese agricultural colonization, it is merely a composite
picture showing the location on one map of a whole series of

---

[57] *Singapore and Straits Directory, 1887,* 249-50. All except four of the
names contained in this list have been located on Fig. 7A; three of
those for which the location cannot be ascertained were on the Batu
Pahat river system.

[58] Cowgill, op. cit. 224-47.

[59] Because of the re-grouping of a large part of the Johore population,
particularly Chinese, into 'New Villages' during the 'Emergency'
(1948-60), pre-1948 maps are more useful in this connexion than more
recent editions.

settlements which may well have existed at different dates as centres of gambier and pepper cultivation. Moreover, it would be unwise to assume that blank areas necessarily indicate an absence of past Chinese agricultural settlements.

Clearly the greatest concentration of *kangkars* was always in southern Johore, particularly along the rivers flowing into the Johore Strait. On the east coast the settlers entered the state mainly along the Sungei Sedili Besar and to a much more limited extent along the Sungei Sedili Kechil and the Sungei Endau. In the west the mangrove-fronted, swamp-backed coast between Kukup and Batu Pahat, to which no major river flows, inhibited penetration into the interior, and the main concentrations were along the Muar and Batu Pahat river systems.

The planters appear to have preferred relatively low, flat or undulating areas and avoided the steeper hillsides and altitudes above two or three hundred feet. The major topographic limitation to their extension into interior areas was their complete dependence on the rivers as a means of communication with Singapore. It is for this reason that many *kangkars* were sited at or near the limit of tidal influence on the rivers upon which they were of necessity located, and also that the gambier and pepper planters never penetrated more than a few miles from their *kangchu's* headquarters.

The Changing Frontier of Gambier and Pepper Planting

A significant feature of Chinese agricultural colonization both in Singapore and Johore was the fluctuating nature of the pioneer fringe. Virgin land was constantly required to accommodate new immigrants and to facilitate the shifting method of cultivation. The nineteenth century was characterized, therefore, by a more or less continuous outward expansion from the initial areas of concentration within which large stretches of *lalang* and *belukar* were the chief relict features in the landscape. By 1843 the Tanglin district of Singapore consisted of 'barren looking hills covered with short brushwood and lalang. This was the result of the deserted gambier plantations . . .'; in Johore the former 'plantations' between Ulu Tiram and the

Sungei Plentong had been deserted by 1896 and 'immense lalang plains now reign in their stead'.[60]

Nevertheless, the outward expansion of the frontier of colonization in Johore did not signify abandonment and de-population of areas 'back of the frontier' in the way that it did, for instance, in the coffee-growing areas of Sao Paulo in Brazil.[61] Nor was it the result of 'some disaster or deterioration in the already settled areas' as it was in early New South Wales.[62] The factors causing the frontier to expand also resulted in further land clearance in the older zones of settlement. Thus, in 1896 in the Kota Tinggi area of Johore 'new gambier and pepper gardens [were] being extensively opened up, and there [was] a steady influx of Chinese into the country', although the initial colonization of this area had taken place several decades earlier.[63] Within the older zones of settlement land appears to have been colonized, abandoned and then reoccupied at a later date. Whilst the over-all frontier of colonization extended out-wards to the ultimate limits suggested by Figure 8 the distri-bution of cultivated land within the occupied areas fluctuated continually.

The situation in Singapore was slightly different. By the mid-1880's gambier and pepper plantations concentrated in the northern and western parts of the island (Fig. 4). This could suggest that the frontier of cultivation had gradually advanced northwards and westwards across the island, and that by 1885 the planters were in the process of exhausting these the last strongholds of the *kangchu* system in Singapore. But there is also the possibility that communication with the *kangkars* of northern and western Singapore was around the coast by boat and that penetration into the interior was effected by means of the rivers as it was in western and eastern Johore; certainly the produce from the plantations in northern Singapore was carried around the island by boat in the 1840's.[64] Whether this

[60] Makepeace, and others, op. cit. Vol. 2, 82. *S.F.P.*, 3rd Series, No. 452, 24 March 1896.
[61] Preston E. James, *Latin America*, London, 1941, 499-500.
[62] T.M. Perry, *Australia's First Frontier: The Spread of Settlement in New South Wales, 1788-1829*, Melbourne, 1963, 122.
[63] *S.F.P.*, 3rd Series, No. 457, 28 April 1896.
[64] *S.F.P.*, Vol. 11 No. 1, 1 January 1846.

ultimate expansion was by land or by sea and river, the general thesis of a frontier advancing across the island is in accord with all the known facts. In the case of Singapore however, this frontier advance was accompanied by the engulfment of the older plantations by the expanding margins of the town.

Chinese gambier and pepper planting was the dominant form of agricultural pioneering in Singapore and Johore throughout the nineteenth century. Using a system of organization particularly well-suited to the conditions of a sparsely peopled and undeveloped area the Chinese had pushed the frontiers of commercial agriculture a considerable distance inland before rubber appeared on the scene.

3

GAMBIER AND PEPPER PLANTERS IN
WESTERN MALAYA

THE TYPE OF AGRICULTURAL PIONEERING reviewed in the previous
chapter appeared later and in a less spectacular way, in other
parts of western Malaya. During the last four decades of the
nineteenth century Chinese gambier and pepper planters opened
plantations in the British Settlement of Malacca and in the
Malay States of Negri Sembilan and Selangor. Despite the
differences between the administrations of each of these areas,
and between those of these states and Johore, a similar organizational framework—the *kangchu* system—formed the basis of
Chinese gambier and pepper planting wherever it appeared.
However, several other avenues of enterprise were also open to
Chinese immigrants to these west coast states, which already
contained unevenly distributed but sizeable Malay populations,
and gambier and pepper planting was of considerably less
importance in expanding the frontier of colonization.

Introduction and Expansion in Malacca

Both pepper and gambier were cultivated in Malacca in the
early nineteenth century, but they were not grown jointly by
Chinese planters for export. Pepper was grown on a fairly
extensive scale by Chinese planters in the 1820's, but then
declined rapidly in importance and had virtually disappeared
twenty years later (see Chapter 6). Malay smallholders probably
began to plant gambier in the second half of the eighteenth
century, but they only produced 'chewing' gambier for local
consumption. Commercial production of gambier for export,
in association with pepper cultivation, was first begun by Chinese
planters in Malacca in the mid-nineteenth century.

This form of agricultural enterprise did not rise to real
importance in Malacca until the 1870's and 1880's. The initial
interest occurred at a time when gambier prices were rising as

a result of increasing demands from local tanners and dyers and from Singapore merchants for export to Europe.[1] Until this time the interests of the Malacca Chinese had centred on tapioca planting. By the early 1880's however, tapioca prices were very low, the industry was declining and the Government was taking a less favourable view of the Chinese tapioca planters (see next chapter).

Apparently at this time the administration did not regard gambier and pepper planting as an undesirable alternative form of agriculture. Indeed, in 1882 the Resident Councillor, Hervey, remarked on the advantages of gambier and pepper. They were, he said, 'cultivations which last for thirty years, three times the period of tapioca under the present system of cultivation, nor does their cultivation require anything like the area used for tapioca'.[2] From the mid-1880's this form of agriculture was encouraged by the granting of twenty- to thirty-year leases for the cultivation of gambier and pepper, a period ideally suited to the Chinese system of cultivation.

Planting expanded rapidly during the 1870's. Between 1871 and 1879 exports of gambier from Malacca almost trebled and exports of pepper increased by more than three times. As in the case of Johore, these exports were destined, in the first place, for Singapore. In 1877 there were twenty-one gambier factories in Malacca and cultivation was restricted to the two areas which were to remain henceforth the nuclei of the industry—the mukims of Ayer Molek and nearby Serkam to the east of Malacca town, and the Sungei Baru area in the extreme west of the state. By 1880 Malacca contained 148 gambier factories, three-quarters of which lay in mukim Sungei Baru Ilir; two years later this number had increased to 171, more than four-fifths of which were in this mukim[3] (Fig. 9A).

Gambier and pepper planting appears to have declined temporarily in importance in Malacca in the early 1880's for total exports of gambier fell by almost 25 per cent. between 1882

---

[1] Kernial Singh Sandhu, 'Chinese Colonization of Malacca', *J.T.G.*, Vol. 15, 1961, 14.

[2] *Accounts and Papers*, 1884, Vol. LIV, C-4015, No. 16, *A.R. Malacca, 1882*.

[3] *S.S.B.B.*, 1871, 1877, 1879, 1880 and 1882.

and 1886. If a recession did occur during this period it was not the result of reduced gambier prices (see Chapter 2). It may have been caused by the steady improvement in tapioca prices between mid-1885 and 1888, or by the difficulty of procuring labour consequent upon the current heavy demand for Chinese workers in the tin mines of the Malay States.[4] Alternatively it may reflect the abandonment of exhausted land on the initial *plantations* followed by a short period of reduced production while new clearings were planted. Certainly land was abandoned in the Sungei Baru and Ayer Molek areas in the early 1880's[5] and the period 1882 to 1887 is characterized by an outward expansion from the earlier centres of concentration (Fig. 9).

New land was taken up for gambier and pepper planting in the late 1880's and by 1888 almost 3,800 acres were devoted to these crops. Exports increased rapidly and in 1889 stood at 11,509 pikuls of gambier and 1,855 pikuls of pepper.[6] Nevertheless, gambier and pepper planting was still of limited importance in Malacca and a contributor to the *Malacca Weekly Chronicle* in December 1889 commented 'It is clear enough that in Malacca there are all the conditions favourable for the production of gambier, and it is somewhat hard to understand why planters have not engaged more actively in the cultivation'.[7] Unbeknown to this observer the Malacca planters were already taking advantage of the favourable conditions and between 1888 and 1890 the acreage devoted to gambier and pepper in Malacca almost doubled (Fig. 10).

Generally the 1890's were a period of expansion and prosperity for this form of agriculture in Malacca. By mid-decade a total of 7,325 acres were in the hands of gambier and pepper planters and 264 gambier factories were in operation in the state. Although the Sungei Baru area remained the major centre of concentration, mukim Ayer Molek had again appeared as an important secondary centre and planting activities on a smaller scale had extended into mukims Ayer Panas and Bukit Katil

[4] *N.S.S.F., Sel. 507/94; Malacca Weekly Chronicle*, Vol. 1 No. 41, 13 October 1888.

[5] *A.R. Malacca, 1883, S.S.G.G.*, 1884, No. 248, 658.

[6] *A.R. Malacca, 1888*, 58; *S.S.B.B.*, 1889.

[7] *Malacca Weekly Chronicle*, Vol. 11 No. 103, 21 December 1889.

adjacent to Ayer Molek, into mukim Bukit Rambai on the coast to the west of the town and into mukim Chabau in the extreme north-eastern corner of the state (Fig. 11A).

This expansion was not strictly a frontier advance. Rather it represented small-scale expansion over-stepping land already occupied for other purposes into the few areas within which virgin land was still available. By the mid-1890's the extension of gambier and pepper planting in Malacca was limited by the widespread existence of Malay *kampongs* and rice-fields, large tapioca concessions and Government Forest Reserves (Fig. 11B). In Johore gambier and pepper planting was the chief form of agricultural pioneering; in Malacca it was but one of several types. Nevertheless, within these limits some expansion occurred, and by 1897 the total area devoted to gambier and pepper in Malacca had reached a record peak of 11,511 acres for the nineteenth century (Fig. 10).

Negri Sembilan and Selangor, c.1850-1900

Chinese were planting gambier and pepper in what later became the Coast District of Negri Sembilan before British intervention for in 1874 J.W.W. Birch noted of Sungei Raya that 'about 200 Chinese plant gambier close by on which they pay a rent to the Raja'.[8] Eight years later Paul stated that at Sungei Raya there were 'large pepper gardens *with vines of 30 years old* still in bearing, the manure consisting of refuse gambier leaves. These gardens [were] cultivated solely by Chinese . . .'.[9]

The implication is that this activity started as early as the 1850's and in fact, there seems little reason why this should not have been the case. This was the period during which expansion from Singapore to the mainland was gaining strength and given the encouragement, some of the planters presumably would have been prepared to move into this coastal area. In the 1850's a large Chinese population was mining at near-by Lukut

[8] 'A Glance at Selangor in '74', *Selangor Journal*, Vol. 1 No. 1, 23 September 1892, 10.

[9] *Accounts and Papers*, 1884, Vol. LV, C-4192, Encl. 3 in No. 13, *A.R. Sungei Ujong, 1882*. The italics have been inserted.

and shipping facilities for export to Singapore must have existed. Moreover, the enlightened and enterprising Raja Juma'at, who had done much to encourage the mining industry, would hardly have opposed the settlement of Chinese planters within his territory.

Nevertheless, large-scale expansion of Chinese gambier and pepper planting in these states did not occur until after British intervention. In September 1876 the Sultan of Selangor, on the advice of the British Resident, granted a twenty-year concession for gambier and pepper planting to Toh Eng Siew for an area of land not exceeding 20,000 acres at Sengkang in the Sungei Raya district (Fig. 12). The land was to be held rent-free and no duty was to be levied on the gambier and pepper exports.[10] For the next ten years Chinese gambier and pepper planting in Negri Sembilan was almost entirely concentrated in this coastal area adjacent to Malacca where the Sungei Linggi provided a means of communication. Thus, of the 2,728 pikuls of gambier and 401 pikuls of pepper exported from Sungei Ujong in 1881 all the pepper and all except nineteen pikuls of the gambier came from the Sungei Raya area. As late as 1886, when gambier and pepper planting had begun in other areas, the Sungei Raya district remained the major centre of production. By this date there were 7,000 acres under these crops on Toh Eng Siew's concession and in addition there were about 2,000 acres of cultivated land in the nearby Lukut district, principally planted with gambier and pepper.[11]

A marked expansion of gambier and pepper planting occurred in the late 1880's as a direct result of the simultaneous introduction in 1884 of special regulations designed to encourage this form of agriculture in Sungei Ujong, Selangor and Perak. These regulations, which were to remain in force for a period of seven years, stipulated that no premium was to be charged on land taken up for gambier and pepper planting,

---

[10] N.S.S.F., P.D. 1435/95. This concession is dated 30 September 1876; it was replaced by rent-paying titles for about 5,000 acres in 1896, A.R. Negri Sembilan, 1896, 3.

[11] Accounts and Papers, 1882, Vol. XLVI, C-3428, Encl. 3 in No. 5, A.R. Sungei Ujong, 1881 and Accounts and Papers, 1888, Vol. LXXIII, C-5566, Encl. 3 in No. 1, A.R. Sungei Ujong, 1886.

that the land was to be surveyed at the end of three years and
the customary survey fees charged, after which a lease would
be granted bearing a quit-rent of ten cents an acre per year,
and that an export duty of thirty cents per pikul of pepper and
fifteen cents per pikul of gambier would be levied at the port
of export.[12]

These terms proved attractive to the Chinese planters, not
least because they were well-adapted to their shifting system of
cultivation. The response in Selangor was immediate and a
block of over 10,000 acres was taken up by Chinese at Sepang
in Kuala Langat District, while smaller plantations were begun
in the Districts of Kuala Lumpur and Ulu Langat.[13]

In Sungei Ujong the introduction of the special regulations
immediately induced 'many people to come forward'. During
1885 alone applications were submitted for 1,800 acres in the
Pasir Panjang area and 6,000 acres at Lukut, and by 1887
gambier and pepper planting was beginning to supersede tapioca
planting as the chief form of agricultural enterprise in Sungei
Ujong. Up to that date 1,466 acres had been taken up for
gambier and pepper planting in the state under the special
regulations and considerable extensions were being made to
existing plantations. By 1887 there were almost 1,500 Chinese
in the coastal district of Sungei Ujong, 1,000 of whom were
employed on the Sengkang concession and another 300 in the
Pasir Panjang area.

One of the difficulties of attracting more Chinese gambier
and pepper planters to Sungei Ujong at this date was the
existence of a monopoly of the preparation and sale of opium.
The sale of opium to their labourers was a remunerative source
of income for the leaders of all pioneer Chinese communities
in nineteenth-century Malaya. In particular, it was an important
right held by the *kangchus* in Singapore and Johore for it was
one of the foundations of the truck system that they operated.
It was probably also an excellent means of ensuring that the
labour force did not abscond since it brought with it addiction

[12] *A.R. Sungei Ujong, 1884*, *S.S.G.G.*, 1885, No. 171, 392; *S.S.G.G.*, 1885,
No. 569, 1648; *A.R. Selangor, 1884*, *S.S.G.G.*, 1885, No. 333, 1001.

[13] *A.R. Selangor, 1884*, *S.S.G.G.*, 1885, No. 333, 1001; *A.R. Selangor,
1892*, 10.

and indebtedness. But, in the Malay States under British administration exclusive rights to import, prepare and sell opium in specified areas were 'farmed' out to individual Chinese who paid the Government for the privilege. The British Resident, Paul, believed that so long as this monopoly existed in Sungei Ujong:

...none will settle in the country as the difference between the cost of prepared opium bought from the farmers, and that of opium imported and cooked by the importer, may just turn the scale, and, in a plantation, make a considerable difference in or even swallow up the profits.[14]

He maintained that 'nothing will throw the country open but the abolition of the Chandu [opium] farm,' and in the late 1880's several large blocks of land were granted to Chinese gambier and pepper planters on leases carrying special exemption from the opium monopoly. In particular, a 5,000-acre concession was granted to a Chinese in Lukut in 1887 and in July 1888, 6,145 acres at Tanah Merah, adjacent to the Sepang concession in Selangor, were leased for thirty-six years to Loh Cheng Keng and Loh Tee Seng. In January 1889 a further 9,371 acres in this area were leased to the same people for a thirty-six year period, and hereafter this block of over 15,000 acres is referred to as the Tanah Merah concession (Fig. 12). All three leases carried special provisions regarding opium.[15]

Several other smaller blocks were leased to Chinese gambier and pepper planters in Sungei Ujong in the late 1880's. At the same time these crops aroused interest in the states of the old Negri Sembilan. Thus, Tan Kim Guan and Tan Yu Pek applied for about 2,000 acres for gambier and pepper planting in Gemencheh in 1888 and before 1890 these crops had also been planted on a relatively large scale by the Chinese tapioca planters of Rembau and Tampin. In addition, gambier was grown by

[14] *Accounts and Papers*, 1888, Vol. LXXIII, C-5566, Encl. 3 in No. 5, *A.R. Sungei Ujong, 1887*. In this context the term 'farmer' refers to the holder of the opium monopoly.
[15] *N.S.S.F., Chinese 3801/1900*. Under the Gambier and Pepper Regulations introduced in Selangor in August 1884 planters had the right to prepare opium, free of charge, for the use of persons employed on their plantations.

small-scale Chinese planters around Lubok China in Rembau who cultivated 'patches of gambier sufficient to employ one or two men each'.[16] But although Rembau, Tampin, Gemencheh and Johol exported over 1,000 pikuls of gambier in 1888, further expansion here was limited because of competition with tapioca. Moreover, in the late 1880's the Chinese here did not receive the official encouragement to plant gambier and pepper given to their counterparts in Sungei Ujong.[17]

It has already become apparent, and further evidence is provided later, that the different forms of Chinese agricultural enterprise in nineteenth-century Malaya were controlled by urban-based financiers located in one or other of the Straits Settlements; that in fact Malacca town was the focal point for the Chinese tapioca industry and that Singapore served the same function for the gambier and pepper planters. Although special gambier and pepper regulations were introduced in Perak in 1884 Chinese gambier and pepper planting was never of any significance there. Generally speaking Perak lay within the sphere of influence of the Penang Chinese and this fact, coupled with its distance from Singapore, probably explains the failure of the new regulations. In fact, from the late 1880's onwards Chinese gambier and pepper planting in the western Malay States was concentrated mainly in the block of 25-30,000 acres of land held by Loh Cheng Keng and his associates lying astride the Negri Sembilan-Selangor boundary (Fig. 12).

This remained the predominant form of export-orientated agriculture in coastal Negri Sembilan and southern Selangor throughout the 1890's. Up to 1890 approximately 22,000 acres had been leased for these crops in Sungei Ujong of which some 10,000 acres were estimated to be cultivated. In Lukut and Sungei Raya in particular a large proportion of the land alienated for this purpose was already planted and more was being

---

[16] N.S.S.F., K.P. 371/88; Report on the District Consisting of the States of Rembau, Tampin with Keru and Gemencheh, 1888 in N.S.S.F., K.P. 243/88; Accounts and Papers, 1887, Vol. LVIII, C-4958, Encl. 3 in No. 11, A.R. Sungei Ujong, 1885.

[17] See Accounts and Papers, 1889, Vol. LVI, C-5884, Encl. in No. 2, A.R. Negri Sembilan, 1888 where Lister wrote 'I consider it very important to discourage, as far as possible, the growing of gambier'.

cleared. Development proceeded rapidly on the Tanah Merah concession and by 1890 it gave employment to 'upwards of 1,000 coolies'. It contained 'a rising town with substantial shops' and a cart-road eight miles long was under construction between Sepang and Tanah Merah by which the produce of the Selangor concession was to be brought to Tanah Merah for shipment.[18] In 1891 this concession exported about 6,000 pikuls of gambier, and from that date onwards was the leading producer in Sungei Ujong, a position formerly held by the Sengkang concession at Sungei Raya.[19]

Nevertheless, the development of this type of agriculture in Negri Sembilan and Selangor in the early 1890's was not limited to the Tanah Merah area. Apart from the opening of a number of small plantations along the coast several larger blocks were also taken up in the same area. These included 500 acres granted to See Koh Lye at Lukut in 1890, and a pepper estate belonging to J. Waddell Boyd and V.R. Wickwar by the side of the railway near Port Dickson which was bought by Chan Kong Piau in 1893. Chan was granted a further 150 acres adjoining this estate in 1895 bringing his total holding to over 1,000 acres. Moreover, in 1890 Maxwell remarked that 'operations on a large scale [were] being carried on at the Chinese gambier and pepper plantation at Sepang' in Selangor. In 1890 this latter concession employed about 1,000 Chinese and produced 11,740 pikuls of gambier, more than either the Tanah Merah or Sengkang concessions in the adjacent state, and greater in value than any other export from Selangor with the exception of tin.[20]

By the mid-1890's tapioca prices had fallen to a level at which it did 'not pay to sell' (see Chapter 4). Douglas, Collector and Magistrate of the Coast District, estimated that an independent gambier plantation of 150 acres (including fifty acres of forest for firewood) at the high prices prevailing in 1894 would suffer a loss of $1,915 on the first year's working, but would produce

---

[18] *Accounts and Papers*, 1892, Vol. LVI, C-6576, Encl. 3 in No. 1, *A.R. Sungei Ujong*, 1890.

[19] *Accounts and Papers*, 1893–4, Vol. LXI, C-6858, Encl. 3 in No. 1, *A.R. Sungei Ujong and Jelebu*, 1891. In 1891 the Sengkang concession exported 4,227 pikuls of gambier.

[20] *N.S.S.F.*, *Land 876/90 P.D. 1023/93*, and *P.D. 1452/95*; *A.R. Selangor*, 1890, 21.

TABLE 2

GAMBIER AND PEPPER PLANTATIONS, COAST DISTRICT,
NEGRI SEMBILAN, 1901

Locality	Registered Owners	Acreage
Tanah Merah-Jimah	Loh Tee Seng & Loh Kong Yu	6,145
,,	Loh Cheng Keng & Loh Tee Seng	9,371
,,	Li Hui	743
,,	Others	144
Total for Tanah Merah-Jimah		16,403
Sengkang	Toh Choon Yong	7,709
Pasir Panjang	Koh Chap Siam & Chua Wi Kiat	1,778
,,	Tan Hong Soon	904
,,	Sim Toh Nio & Chua Meng Peng	113
,,	Others	59
Total for Pasir Panjang		2,854
Port Dickson	Chan Kong Piau	1,199
,,	Toh Boon Kiat	79
Total for Port Dickson		1,278
Si-Rusa	Toh Poan Him	348
,,	Toh Miow	115
,,	We Che Ann & We Tuan Sang	108
,,	Others	124
Total for Si-Rusa		695
Linggi	Tiew Loon	181
,,	Koh Tiew	86
,,	Tan Seh	25
Total for Linggi		292
TOTAL		29,231

Source: *N.S.S.F., P.D. 2472/1902.* These figures include 'all the principal estates' in the Coast District, but some small areas of under fifty acres were omitted from the returns.

net profits of $1,240 and $2,834 respectively in the second and third years. Thus, at this time an unencumbered planter could expect to make a *net* profit of over $28 an acre within three years of opening a gambier plantation.[21] As a result the tapioca planters of Negri Sembilan showed an increasing desire either to combine gambier and tapioca planting or to plant gambier on partly recuperated tapioca land. The total acreage devoted to gambier and pepper in the state increased sharply and as these new plantings matured in the later years of the decade, exports trended upwards (Fig. 13).

By 1901 almost 30,000 acres were in the hands of gambier and pepper planters in the Coast District of Negri Sembilan, representing roughly half the total area alienated for agricultural purposes. The most important concentration, as it had been for the previous decade, was the Tanah Merah region (Fig. 12 and Table 2). At the same date the Sepang concession in Selangor comprised a total of 13,500 acres and it is possible that some gambier and pepper had been planted on Loke Yew's huge agricultural concession in Ulu Selangor.[22] At the turn of the century Chinese gambier and pepper planters held between forty and fifty thousand acres of land in Negri Sembilan and Selangor.

The socio-economic framework

In Malacca, Negri Sembilan and Selangor these crops were cultivated on a shifting system very similar to that employed by the Chinese in Singapore and Johore. In these western states however, there would appear to have been two different types of *plantation*. On the one hand, there were several large concessions comprising anything up to 20,000 acres. These included

---

[21] *Accounts and Papers*, 1895, Vol. LXX, C-7877, *A.R. Sungei Ujong and Jelebu, 1894.*

[22] Loke Yew originally applied for this land in Ulu Selangor for padi planting in 1897. He was granted a 20,000-acre concession on which nothing was done for several years, and on which padi was never planted. By 1905 gambier and pepper, interplanted with rubber and coconuts, were cultivated on the concession. *M.R., Ulu Selangor,* November 1897, *S.G.G.,* 1898, No. 31, 13; *A.R. Selangor, 1905,* 2. Both the Changkat Asa and Kalumpang Estates in Ulu Selangor were originally part of this concession.

the Sepang concession in Selangor and the Tanah Merah and
Sengkang concessions in Negri Sembilan. In Malacca by the
early 1890's there were 'two or three large plantations carefully
cultivated by the Chinese on one of which 800 acres had been
planted with gambier'.[23] In size at least, these large *plantations*
are reminiscent of the *kangkars* or *kawasans* of Johore. In
marked contrast in coastal Negri Sembilan and western Malacca
there were a number of small *plantations*, registered in the
names of individual Chinese most of which averaged between
twenty and seventy acres in size (Fig. 11B); these resemble the
individual *bangsals* or planted clearings in Singapore and
Johore.

In total there is considerable evidence to indicate that gambier
and pepper planting by Chinese in these states was organized
on a system very similar to the *kangchu* system of Johore and
Singapore.[24] The same terms were used with reference to the
larger concessions in Negri Sembilan and Selangor and clearly
had more or less equivalent meanings. It was noted in 1894 for
instance, that ' "Kangchu" is the racial appellation for Towkay
Loh Cheng Keng', the managing proprietor of the Sepang and
Tanah Merah concessions.[25] Similarly the term *kangkar* was
used by the Chinese planters to refer to the village headquarters
or river depot from which the *kangchu* operated and at which
the products were collected for export.[26] The term *bangsal* was
used on these concessions but generally it seems to have been
reserved specifically for the sheds housing the labourers and
the gambier cauldron and the term *ladang* was applied to the
cleared blocks of land.

In these states, as in Johore, groups of labourers, under their
headmen, cultivated and processed the products of patches of

[23] Ridley, 'Gambir', 24 and 38.
[24] In fact, in 1891 the District Officer of Kuala Langat stated that the
plantations at Sepang were 'worked by Chinese, much in the same
way as similar plantations in Singapore and Johore'. *A.R. Selangor,
1891*, 16.
[25] *Selangor Journal*, Vol. 2 No. 10, 26 January 1894, 152.
[26] For example, the old police station at Sungei Tanah Merah was 'known
to the Chinese as "kangkah" ' in the mid-1890's, at which time the
Chinese also referred to the village of Sepang as *kangkar*, *N.S.S.F.,
Pol. 2608/95; Selangor Journal*, Vol. 2 No. 10, 26 January 1894, 152.

gambier and pepper (i.e. *ladangs* or *bangsals*), scattered throughout the large concessions (i.e. *kangars* or *kawasans*), granted by
the Government to Chinese proprietors known colloquially as
kangchus.[27]

There is little evidence of the relationship between the headmen and the *kangchus,* or of the methods of financing the
plantations, in these western states. In 1910 however, the Protector of Chinese remarked that the method of working the
Bute Estate, formerly part of the Sepang concession, was to
distribute fifty-acre lots to every ten men in a *kongsi* to plant
gambier, pepper and rubber. When ready for shipment the
gambier and pepper were taken to the estate office where they
were weighed and shipped to Singapore and sold according to
market rates. Various charges, including 20 per cent. tribute,
cash advances, customs duty, freight and broker's commission
were deducted from the proceeds of the sale and the remainder
was distributed among the labourers.[28] This was late in the
history of gambier and pepper planting in these states and the
expansion of rubber planting and European estate ownership
were beginning to have effects. Nevertheless the system in force
contains many elements reminiscent of that used by the planters
in Singapore and Johore at an earlier date. In short, it is likely
that the headmen of the individual clearings within the large
concessions owed financial and other allegiance to the proprietors or *Kangchus,* that they received credit facilities and
provisions from the proprietors and were obliged to sell their
products to them.

The position with regard to the smaller plantations in coastal
Negri Sembilan and western Malacca is more problematic. On

[27] In writing of the *ladangs* or *bangsals* on the Sepang concession an
observer in 1894 noted that these clearings 'include both pepper and
gambier plantations and are scattered broadcast over the whole of
the large concession in the midst of which Sepang is built, the ladang
paths raying out in every direction'. *Selangor Journal*, Vol. 2 No. 10,
26 January 1894, 152. There was an average labour force of about 15,
including the headman, at each clearing on the Tanah Merah concession in 1895; this figure is closely in accord with similar averages
for Singapore and Johore. *N.S.S.F., Pol.* 2487/95.

[28] Report on the Bute Estate by the Protector of Chinese, Selangor and
Negri Sembilan, 20 August 1910. *N.S.S.F., Misc.* 2437/1910.

the face of it these appear to be independent smallholdings registered in the names of individual Chinese; in fact until the 1890's the cultivation of gambier and pepper by Chinese in Malacca was largely confined to plantations of this type.[29] Lack of evidence prohibits definite conclusions regarding the organization of gambier and pepper cultivation on these smaller plantations. They may reflect however, the adjustment of the *kangchu* system to suit conditions in British administered territories in the late nineteenth century.

Large concessions of land granted on special terms to Chinese gambier and pepper planters were an unusual feature in these western states. An established local administration already existed. Population, although unevenly distributed, was denser than in early nineteenth-century Johore and land regulations requiring the payment of rents and premiums were already in force. Except in the special case of the large concessions these circumstances inhibited the full development of the *kangchu* system in the form in which it appeared in Johore. Other prospective gambier and pepper planters in these western states would only apply for as much land as they required immediately, so that the small plantations probably represented planted clearings together with the necessary reserves for firewood. Although superficially this would create differences in the system, particularly the fact that individual planters held their own land direct from the Government and paid rent for it, there is no reason to suppose that this necessarily implies that the same type of commercial organization did not still apply.

Conditions in Malacca, Negri Sembilan and Selangor made it unnecessary to encourage large-scale Chinese agricultural colonization. New settlements created by the planters as centres for their operations were rare. Nevertheless the organizational framework that typified this form of agricultural pioneering in Singapore and Johore also seems to have existed with some modifications in the western states.

The Chinese gambier and pepper planters in Malacca, Negri Sembilan and Selangor had close ties with Singapore town. In speaking of these crops in his report on Selangor for 1886 Rodger noted that 'some Chinese *from the Straits Settlements* are

[29] *S.F.P.*, 3rd Series, No. 451, 17 March 1896.

rapidly developing an extensive plantation at Sepang' and three years later the importance of the trade that had sprung up there had induced the Chinese to run a small steamer from Singapore to take out the produce.[30] By 1897 the Sengkang concession was in the hands of a Singapore Chinese firm, Chop Guan Ho Seng, who employed a resident manager at Sungei Raya and owned their own *tongkang* for import and export purposes.[31] Throughout the period under review most of the gambier and pepper produced in Malacca, Negri Sembilan and Selangor was shipped to Singapore and some, at least, of the provisions required on the plantations came from this southern Settlement. In these states connexions between the plantations and Chinese merchants in Singapore town must have resembled those already described in the case of Johore. Fundamentally Chinese gambier and pepper planting in Malacca, Negri Sembilan and Selangor merely represented a late nineteenth-century extension of operations already in progress in Singapore and Johore.

Most of the gambier and pepper planters in Singapore and Johore were Tiechiu. This was also the case on the Sepang concession in the early 1890's.[32] By 1904 however, the labour force at Sepang also included Hainanese, Cantonese and Hokkiens. In 1910 the majority of the labour at Tanah Merah consisted of Hainanese; at the same date the Chinese labour force on the Bute Estate comprised three-fifths Hainanese, one-fifth Tiechiu and one-fifth Liu Chiu.[33] Many of the names contained in grants of land for gambier and pepper planting in the Coast District are Hainanese family names; several dialect groups are represented by the names of land-holders in Malacca. The Chinese labour force on the plantations in these states appears

[30] *Accounts and Papers*, 1888, Vol. LXXIII, C-5566, Encl. 2 in No. 1, *A.R. Selangor, 1886;* the italics have been inserted. *A.R. Selangor, 1889*, 18.

[31] *N.S.S.F., Misc. 1302/97.*

[32] J.C. Jackson, 'Population Changes in Selangor State, 1850-1891', *J.T.G.*, Vol. 19, 1964, 61.

[33] Report on the Jimah Estate by the Protector of Chinese, Selangor and Negri Sembilan, 19 August 1910 and Report on the Bute Estate by the Protector of Chinese, Selangor and Negri Sembilan, 20 August 1910. *N.S.S.F., Misc. 2437/1910.*

to have been more varied than was the case in Singapore and Johore.

An Expanding Frontier of Chinese Agricultural Colonization?

In these western states Chinese gambier and pepper planting did not serve as a major agent of colonization in the way that it did in Singapore and Johore. In general, this form of agriculture appeared later in Malacca, Negri Sembilan and Selangor and it developed within an administrative framework governed by British officials and on land terms granted by these officials. It appeared in areas which generally contained an existing Malay population and in conjunction with the parallel development of other types of export-orientated agriculture associated with different crops. Here it was but one form of agricultural pioneering and development in the late nineteenth century.

It was, nevertheless, an important form of agricultural pioneering in these states for about thirty years. However, although the planters employed a shifting system of cultivation requiring the abandonment of the original clearings after about fifteen to twenty years, gambier and pepper planting did not exist long enough here for an advancing frontier of colonization to appear. Certainly there were fluctuations in the numbers of cultivated clearings within each concession as exhausted *ladangs* were abandoned and fresh land was cleared and planted. Thus, the Sepang concession included forty-four *bangsals* or *ladangs* in 1886; during 1903, seventeen new *ladangs* were opened and by 1904 the enlarged concession contained sixty-seven cultivated clearings.[34] But the need to acquire fresh land which drove the planters in Singapore and Johore into new areas was not felt by the majority of planters in Malacca, Negri Sembilan and Selangor until the end of the nineteenth century. By this time Government agricultural policy was unfavourable to shifting types of cultivation and severely restricted the future possibilities of gambier and pepper planting.

[34] *Accounts and Papers*, 1888, Vol. LXXIII, C-5566, Encl. 2 in No. 1, *A.R. Selangor, 1886; A.R. Kuala Langat, 1903*, 2; *A.R. Kuala Langat, 1904*, 2.

Some evidence exists to show that when possible the planters did expand their operations in the way that their counterparts were wont to do in southern Malaya. A clear example of this occurred in the case of the Sepang concession. In 1897 it was reported that the plantations here were 'not being looked after well' and for the three subsequent years exports of both gambier and pepper showed a marked decline[35] (Fig. 14). Towards the end of 1898 the Chinese of Sepang submitted applications for about 500 acres of land lying between Labu and Chinchang, and the following January 214 Chinese applied for blocks of twenty-five acres or less for gambier and pepper planting between the boundaries of the Sepang concession and the Sungei Labu. In February 1899, as a result of these applications, over 190 blocks of about twenty acres each, aggregating between three and four thousand acres, were granted to Chinese for these crops in mukim Labu.[36] The *towkay* upon whom these planters depended died in December 1900. Because nobody took his place many of these blocks were abandoned and others showed only slow progress. The land reverted to the state but was re-alienated for gambier and pepper in 1901. Since the area of the Sepang concession was 13,500 acres in 1904, this newly alienated land must have been included within the area worked by the *kongsis* on that concession.[37] In 1901 the Tanah Merah concession comprised 15,516 acres; three years later it occupied 18,205 acres.[38] The shifting system of cultivation, resulting in soil exhaustion and depletion of firewood reserves, appears to have also stimulated an outward expansion in the case of this concession. However, gambier and pepper planting was a declining form of agriculture before this outward expansion on the part of established planters could become a widespread feature.

[35] *A.R. Lands, Mines and Surveys, F.M.S., 1897*, 20. The decline in exports in 1899 was partly caused by the difficulty in procuring and keeping labour owing to the much higher wages paid to construction workers on the Labu Valley Railway. *A.R. Kuala Langat, 1899*, 3.

[36] *A.R. Kuala Langat, 1898*, 2; *A.R. Kuala Langat, 1899*, 3; *M.R. Kuala Langat*, February 1899, *S.G.G.*, 1899, No. 148, 87.

[37] *A.R. Kuala Langat, 1900*, 2; *A.R. Kuala Langat, 1901*, 3; *A.R. Kuala Langat, 1904*, 2.

[38] *N.S.S.F., N.S. 576/1904*.

The Causes of Decline

A policy of only granting land to Chinese who agreed to combine the planting of gambier and pepper with some 'permanent' crop such as rubber or coconuts was introduced by the Negri Sembilan Government in 1900.[39] A similar attitude was also current in Malacca and Selangor. Fundamentally, the new policy was designed to make gambier little more than a catch-crop which would disappear when the 'permanent' crop approached maturity. The introduction of this policy coupled with the growing profitability of rubber cultivation made the decline of gambier and pepper planting in these west coast states inevitable.

Gambier prices rose markedly in the first two years of the twentieth century and many applications for land for gambier and pepper cultivation were submitted by Chinese planters. Very little new land was actually granted however, 'owing to the reluctance of the Chinese to agree to combine a permanent cultivation—such as rubber or coconuts—with tapioca and gambier'.[40]

By 1903 the Chinese planters appear to have been willing to agree to the regulations having realized that this was the only way to acquire new land. In 1903 forty acres were granted to Eu Fong at Linggi for rubber and gambier and he fully realized that 'the gambier [would] probably be killed out by the rubber in five years' and in 1904 200 acres were granted to Sin Ah Kok in mukim Labu for gambier, pepper and coconuts.[41] In many cases these grants stipulated that rubber must be planted first, often at a rate of not less than seventy-five trees per acre and that gambier could only be planted when the rubber trees were several months old. Most planters complied conscientiously with the regulations. There are, however, instances in the early years of the century in which rubber was clearly only planted to satisfy the authorities so that the planters could grow gambier on their new land. There are also a few cases in which the planters agreed to the terms of the grants but made no attempt to plant a 'permanent' crop.

[39] N.S.S.F., Tampin 3864/1900.
[40] A.R. Negri Sembilan, 1902, 3.
[41] N.S.S.F., P.D. 5044/1903 and Land 5942/1904.

The price of gambier fell sharply in 1903 and pepper prices dropped from an average of $33.75 per pikul in 1903 to $28.46 in 1904.[42] In addition in 1904 the pepper vines on several plantations were attacked by the caterpillars of the nettle moth.[43] This combination of unfavourable circumstances was reflected in decreasing acreages and declining production (Fig. 13). In fact, gambier and pepper planting was already declining in relation to other forms of agriculture and by the end of 1905 there were 20,497 acres in the hands of gambier and pepper planters in the Coast District of Negri Sembilan. This represented about two-thirds of the estimated 1901 acreage and about 30 per cent. of the total area alienated for agricultural purposes.[44]

There was a further fall in gambier prices in 1905 and 1906, and as a result the Chinese planters began to take an increasing interest in rubber. Many small gambier plantations were abandoned, in several instances the land reverting to the state, and the number of applications from Chinese for land solely for rubber cultivation increased noticeably.[45]

Stimulated by the success of Tan Chay Yan and his colleagues, the Malacca Chinese turned quickly to the new crop (see Chapter 10). By 1905 the planters on the Sepang concession in Selangor were seeking 'to substitute rubber for their present crops', and a similar process was occurring on Loke Yew's concession in Ulu Selangor and on the concession at Tanah Merah in Negri Sembilan.[46] The initial move towards rubber planting on these plantations took the form of interplanting, for gambier in particular was well-suited to act as a catch-crop during the maturation period of the rubber. Thus, although the Chinese planters were now turning to rubber, the gambier acreage showed no sign of decline. In fact, in the case of Malacca there was a noticeable expansion of the area devoted to gambier

[42] *A.R. Negri Sembilan, 1903*, 4; *A.R. Negri Sembilan, 1904*, 5.

[43] *A.R. Lands and Mines Department, Coast District, 1904*, 4. N.S.S.F., P.D. 839/1905. It was reported in 1904 that 'On one estate alone several hundred vines are said to have been destroyed in this manner.'

[44] *A.R. Coast, 1905*, 2.

[45] *A.R. Coast, 1906*, 2. The price of gambier fell from an average of $10.47 in 1905 to $9.18 in 1906.

[46] *A.R. Selangor, 1905*, 6.

between 1909 and 1913 (Fig. 10). But as the rubber trees approached maturity the gambier was cut out, and the total gambier acreage in Negri Sembilan and Selangor declined rapidly after 1909. By 1912 the Sepang and Tanah Merah concessions, both still Chinese-owned, were largely planted with rubber. In the Coast District of Negri Sembilan the area estimated to be under gambier declined from 12,451 acres in 1910 to about 900 acres in 1917. In Malacca the area planted with this crop fell from 12,550 acres in 1912 to 5,875 acres in 1914. After 1915 the total area planted with gambier in Malacca never again exceeded 1,000 acres (Fig. 10).

One other factor played a part in the extinction of Chinese gambier and pepper planting in these western states. The rapid rise of rubber prices caused a tremendous upsurge in the demand for land from European planters and particularly from European-owned planting companies. In many instances these were prepared to pay very high prices for land already planted with rubber for this reduced the period that they had to wait for the initial profits and thereby could help to attract investors. The Chinese planters were not slow to take advantage of this new method of acquiring wealth quickly. Already by 1907 many were interplanting rubber with their gambier 'with an eye to the European purchaser'.[47] A year later it was obvious that gambier and pepper planting in the Coast District was doomed for 'on only one estate [was] new land being opened up for the cultivation of gambier'; several of the older estates had already passed into European hands, and it appeared 'likely that others [would] follow'.[48]

In 1909 part of the old Sengkang concession was sold to a European syndicate, the United Sua Betong Rubber Estate Limited. The following year Loh Kong Yew sold 810 acres of the Tanah Merah concession to a European syndicate for a total of $150,000 which he received half in cash and half in shares in the newly formed Jimah Rubber Estate Limited. This sale provides a clear example of the rapid disappearance of all trace of the gambier and pepper plantations that usually accompanied such a transference to a European company. At the time

[47] *A.R. Coast, 1907,* 1.
[48] *A.R. Coast, 1908,* 2.

the land concerned contained about 400 acres planted with gambier, pepper and rubber and provided employment for almost 400 Chinese; within a year the gambier and pepper were being 'cleared out', the total labour force had been greatly reduced and a large proportion of the Chinese labourers had been replaced by Tamils and Malays.[49]

By the beginning of the First World War Chinese gambier and pepper planting had ceased to be the most important form of export-orientated agriculture in southern Selangor and coastal Negri Sembilan and the crops were rapidly disappearing from Malacca. The pioneer Chinese plantations had given way to rubber estates, many of which were European-owned; within a short while the landscape was transformed and new agricultural patterns emerged which contained very few features to indicate the nature of their predecessors.

[49] Report on the Jimah Estate by the Protector of Chinese, Selangor and Negri Sembilan, 19 August 1910. N.S.S.F., Misc. 2433/1910; N.S.S.F., Misc. 2675/1911.

4

THE CHINESE TAPIOCA INDUSTRY

APART FROM GAMBIER AND PEPPER, the Chinese agricultural pioneers also produced large quantities of tapioca for export. Tapioca may have been introduced to Malaya at least as early as the eighteenth century, but large-scale commercial cultivation did not begun until the middle of the following century.

Tapioca will grow almost anywhere in Malaya and requires very little attention once planted. A small labour force can therefore plant and maintain large areas. The most labour-consuming part of the operation consists of harvesting the roots and conveying them to the processing factory. Transport costs were, in fact, the largest item of expenditure for the nineteenth-century Chinese planters. The first returns could be expected within two years of planting on virgin land, and at times during the period of high prices culminating in the 1880's gross yields of over fifty dollars per acre were achieved from a single crop. The processing operation required only simple equipment and, apart from the steam engines which were widely introduced after the 1870's, factories could be established to deal with the root produced on large plantations for a relatively small capital outlay.

The tapioca flour, flake and pearl which were exported were produced from the roots of the plant. Harvesting involved cutting off the stem and pulling up the roots by hand. The large and bulky roots were taken to a factory, soaked in water for twenty-four hours and then peeled either by hand or by machine. The roots were then crushed, the pulp strained and the mixture of water and tapioca directed into settling tanks. Here the tapioca settled to the consistency of cheese; it was then removed to a drying shed, broken into small pieces and dried to form tapioca flake. Tapioca pearl was produced by swinging the small pieces in a cradle until they were reduced to pellets which were then dried. To produce tapioca flour the small pieces were passed through a series of sieves prior to drying. Processing was, therefore, a simple operation and the typical factory employed about twenty workers. On average one acre produced seventy pikuls of tapioca root; usually ten pikuls of root yielded one and a half to two pikuls of exportable tapioca.[1]

Thus, tapioca is a crop peculiarly adapted to the conditions of a frontier economy; it was well-suited to the needs of nine-teenth-century Chinese immigrants desirous of quick returns on a small investment. Pioneered by Chinese planters the tapioca industry grew to large proportions in Malacca and the old Negri Sembilan[2] in the second half of the nineteenth century. It was the cornerstone of Chinese commercial agricul-ture, and indeed of almost all forms of Chinese enterprise, in these states for over fifty years. It ultimately occupied over 160,000 acres at the turn of the century and probably affected in total a much larger area. A flourishing export trade develop-ed, supplying mainly the British market; for a considerable period this trade was valued at over $2 million annually.[3]

The Chinese System of Tapioca Cultivation

As in the case of gambier and pepper, the Chinese grew tapioca on a system of shifting cultivation. Although it would grow in almost any reasonably well-drained locality, it soon caused soil exhaustion. This, coupled with the fact that large supplies of firewood were necessary to keep the factories in production, meant that vast tracts of virgin jungle were cleared,

[1] This account of processing is based on descriptions in *N.S.S.F.*, *P.D. 5548/1904*, Cameron, op. cit. 384-5 and R.N. Jackson, *Immigrant Labour and the Development of Malaya, 1786-1920*, Kuala Lumpur, 1961, 27-28.

[2] Throughout this chapter the term 'Negri Sembilan' refers to the modern state of the same name. The term 'old Negri Sembilan' refers to the old group of small states to the north of Malacca which included Johol, Gemencheh, Rembau, Tampin, Sri Menanti and Jempol; these small states have been amalgamated to form the modern districts of Rembau, Tampin and Kuala Pilah (Fig. 1).

[3] A few Europeans also planted tapioca but achieved little success. See J.C. Jackson, 'Tapioca: a Plantation Crop which Preceded Rubber in Malaya', *Malaysia in History*, Vol. 10 No. 2, 1967, 13-24.

cultivated and abandoned by the Chinese planters. Indeed, all contemporary European observers agreed that 'the method of tapioca cultivation . . . [was] wasteful and devastating'.[4]

Generally a planter proposing to open a tapioca plantation acquired a concession of between 1,500 and 5,000 acres, preferably located near an existing road. A factory was built within the concession as close as possible to a source of clear water for washing purposes because the quality of the tapioca produced depended largely on an adequate supply of water. The first factories in Malacca were driven by water power; by the early 1870's, however, most were powered by steam engines. A continuous supply of both tapioca roots and firewood was necessary to keep these factories in operation.

Initially part of the concession was cleared and planted. The District Officer, Tampin, in 1904 claimed that no fixed proportion of the total area was planted each season, the acreage varying according to the amount of capital available and other circumstances. At the same time, however, his colleague in the Coast District maintained that about one tenth of the total area was opened at a time. He continued 'one factory can work from 100 to 200 acres of tapioca, but a few of the very large estates here and in Malacca have planted up as much as 1,000 acres at one time'.[5] Clearly, the amount of tapioca planted on a concession at any time would depend upon a variety of circumstances including, among others, labour supply, prices, size of factory and available capital. As a rule, a well-run steam-powered tapioca factory required an area of about 5,000 acres to keep it supplied with tapioca roots and firewood under the system of cultivation employed.

Newly cleared land was cultivated for three to five years and then abandoned. During this period two or three crops were obtained, the successive crops being valued at $60, $45 and $30 per acre respectively in 1881. Abandoned land took as much as fifteen to twenty-five years, and often longer, to recuperate sufficiently to allow further cultivation and even then could

[4] A.B. Rathborne, *Camping and Tramping in Malaya*, London, 1898, 37.
[5] *N.S.S.F., N.S. 3557/1905.*

provide hardly enough firewood to supply the factory.[6] Under this system of shifting cultivation a concession was likely to suffer from soil exhaustion and fuel deficiency within a matter of twenty to twenty-five years from the date of first opening. Although under favourable conditions the sections of a concession which had been cultivated and abandoned first could eventually be re-planted, it was more usual for the planters to abandon a once-used concession completely and to acquire new land elsewhere. In this way their system of cultivation, designed to obtain maximum profits from the land with no intention of permanent occupation, produced a situation in which activity tended to concentrate along an expanding frontier behind which abandoned land was the sole witness to the former extensive tapioca plantings (Fig. 16B).

The Chinese always combined large-scale tapioca planting with pig-rearing. Pigs could be fed on factory waste and there was an evergrowing demand for pork among the Chinese in the mining areas. Moreover, the sale of pigs provided an important additional source of income that was not dependent upon tapioca prices. As early as 1871 Malacca exported 839 pigs; by 1881 this number had more than doubled, and in 1889 3,467 pigs were exported from Malacca mainly to Selangor.[7] A similar development occurred in Negri Sembilan. Thus, in 1896 the tapioca planters of Tampin exported over 4,000 pigs, and two years later this total had risen to 6,400 which 'were probably taken to Kinta in Perak'.[8]

Tapioca Planting in Malacca, c.1850-96

Until the mid-nineteenth century the interests of the Chinese in Malacca centred on trade and commerce in the town itself and on tin-mining in the Durian Tunggal, Ayer Panas and Kesang areas. By mid-century, however, Malacca had been eclipsed as a trading centre by the more recent Settlements of

[6] N.S.S.F., P.D. 5548/1904; Accounts and Papers, 1883, Vol. XLV, C-3642, No. 14, A.R. Malacca, 1881.

[7] Kernial Singh Sandhu, 'Chinese Colonization of Malacca', 13; S.S.B.B., 1889.

[8] A.R. Negri Sembilan, 1896, 4; A.R. Negri Sembilan, 1898, 3.

Penang and Singapore. Moreover, the rich stanniferous areas of the Malay states were proving more attractive to mining capital and labour and tin-mining based on meagre deposits was a short-lived enterprise in Malacca. In their search for a profitable alternative the Chinese of Malacca turned to the cultivation of export crops and tapioca was the first to attract their attention in the early 1850's.[9]

In 1860 there were estimated to be about 1,000 acres under tapioca in Malacca producing some 2,000 pikuls and located within a ten-mile radius of the town. Two years later the crop was extensively planted, and by the late 1860's occupied about 10,000 acres in a roughly shaped crescent in the centre of the state (Fig. 15A). Before the end of the decade tapioca had become a 'very paying crop' and the industry was 'fast increasing'; large tracts of land were already either owned or rented on twenty-year leases by the Chinese planters.[10]

The industry expanded rapidly during the 1870's and early 1880's. Between 1872 and 1880 total exports from Malacca, which included a small amount originating in the Malay States, showed a five-fold increase. The area held by tapioca planters in the state rose from 19,900 acres in 1871 to over 58,000 acres in 1880 and by 1882 reached a peak of almost 93,000 acres (Fig. 17).

This period of rapid growth was marked by the expansion of tapioca planting outwards from the original centres of concentration, an expansion aided by the road-building operations of the Malacca government. By the early 1880's the frontier of cultivation had reached the Negri Sembilan boundary in the north-west and had extended into the coastal mukims of the south-east (Figs. 15B and 16A). At the same time the earliest zone of cultivation was beginning to decline in importance as factories were closed and exhausted land was abandoned.

The tapioca planters watched the state of the market very

[9] R.N. Jackson, op. cit. 91; I.H. Burkill, 'Pepper, Nutmegs and Rubber, Part 11', *British Malaya*, November 1953, 649.

[10] *A.R.S.S.*, *1860-1*, Appendix VII; Cameron, op. cit. 385; *A.R.S.S.*, *1865-6*, 45; *Accounts and Papers*, 1868-9, Vol. XLIII, *A.R. Malacca, 1867*, 50 and 53.

closely and responded quickly to price changes (Figs. 17 and 18). This initial era of prosperity and rapid expansion came to an abrupt end in the early 1880's when prices fell disastrously and a new Government policy towards the industry emerged.

As early as 1882 the Resident Councillor observed 'the failing of some planters consequent on the fall in price of tapioca'.[11] Conditions deteriorated and by 1884 Chinese were leaving the state; indeed, it was estimated that 6,000 left Malacca within twelve months. By October 1884 one-third of the tapioca plantations had been abandoned and another third had stopped manufacturing. The remainder were only producing about half their usual output. The situation was so bad that one abandoned plantation of 2,100 acres, on which the rent had not been paid, was put up for auction by the Government and the highest bid was eleven dollars.[12] In November 1884 the Malacca correspondent of the *Singapore Free Press* estimated that 'the combined tapioca planters [had] sustained here, through the low price of the produce, losses to the large sum of $956,000'.[13]

In consequence, tapioca virtually disappeared from the earliest centres of cultivation where many plantations were already partially or completely exhausted and were therefore yielding diminished returns; several blocks of abandoned tapioca land reverted to the Government. The remaining plantations were restricted mainly to a semi-circular frontier zone of recently planted land some twelve to seventeen miles from the town (Fig. 16A).

By 1885 prices had risen slightly but they were not high enough to induce planters to increase output and plantations were kept open only so that crops already planted could be harvested. Most manufacturers were holding on to their stocks in the hope that prices would reach a more satisfactory level.[14]

A concurrent change in Government policy towards the tapioca industry tended to exacerbate the effects of this drastic

---

[11] *Accounts and Papers*, 1884, Vol. LIV, C-4015, No. 16, *A.R. Malacca, 1882.*

[12] *S.F.P.*, N.S., Vol. 1 No. 4, 25 October 1884.

[13] *S.F.P.*, N.S., Vol. 1 No. 8, 22 November 1884.

[14] *S.F.P.*, N.S., Vol. 2 No. 3, 17 January 1885.

fall in prices. As in the case of gambier what had been regarded at first as a useful means of providing employment for Chinese immigrants and of stimulating land clearance was soon looked upon as an evil causing the 'devastation' of large tracts of valuable forest.

As early as 1881 the Malacca Government restricted the issue of new tapioca leases to cases where the applications were of long standing, and the following year it was stated officially that 'tapioca cultivation on leased land has been put a stop to as far as possible'.[15] By 1885 Government policy was clearly designed to suppress the industry for it was remarked that

... the Government are bound, and have recognised the obligation to provide the present manufacturers with such additional land from time to time as may be required to give employment to their machinery, while no land will be given to persons desiring to start fresh enterprises in tapioca.[16]

But during the depression many plantations were abandoned and between 1881 and 1885 more than a fifth of the factories were closed. It was believed that under these circumstances the existing factories would eventually close down and the industry would disappear.

TABLE 3

TEN-YEAR AGRICULTURAL LEASES ISSUED IN MALACCA, 1879-85

Year	Number	Acres
1879	35	17,602
1880	103	28,966
1881	20	13,576
1882	5	4,534
1883	4	572
1884	Nil	Nil
1885	10	11,872

Source: A.R. Malacca, 1881, 1882 and 1885.

[15] Accounts and Papers, 1883, Vol. XLV, C-3642, A.R. Malacca, 1881; Accounts and Papers, 1884, Vol. LIV, C-4015, No. 16, A.R. Malacca, 1882.

[16] Accounts and Papers, 1886, Vol. XLV, C-4904, A.R. Malacca, 1885.

The combined effects of the fall in prices and the change in Government policy were immediately apparent. The number of ten-year agricultural leases issued, which were almost entirely used for tapioca, had fallen to nil by 1884 (Table 3). The area held by tapioca planters declined from 92,900 acres in 1882 to 13,200 acres in 1886 (Fig. 17), and total exports of tapioca from Malacca decreased from 241,755 pikuls in 1882 to 178,820 pikuls in 1886. The tapioca industry was the mainstay of the Malacca economy and all aspects of Malacca's trade suffered during this depression.[17]

The situation began to improve in the later years of the decade. Not all Government officials were convinced that the disappearance of the tapioca industry was to Malacca's advantage. In 1885 Hervey expressed concern about the decrease in revenue that would result from such an occurrence for approximately four-fifths of Government receipts under the head of 'rents' came from the tapioca planters. Isemonger, acting Resident Councillor the following year, maintained that although the industry had certain disadvantages these should be set against the important advantages it possessed from the point of view of the Government. Huge areas of forest had been cleared, but the resulting plantations produced a large revenue for the Government from premiums and rents. The industry also resulted in the introduction of a large tax-paying population which materially affected the main source of revenue—the opium and spirit 'farms'. In view of these considerations the official attitude towards the industry began to relax and new land was granted for tapioca planting[18] (Table 3 and Fig. 17).

Nevertheless, rising prices were mainly responsible for the increased activity of the late 1880's and early 1890's (Fig. 18). By 1887 tapioca was again yielding large profits, and it was generally felt that prices were unlikely to fall 'owing mainly to the alleged increase and growing consumption of the manu-

---

[17] Between 1882 and 1884 the total value of all exports from Malacca fell by almost 25 per cent. and imports fell by 27 per cent. *A.R. Malacca, 1884, S.S.G.G.*, 1885, No. 321, 950.

[18] *Accounts and Papers*, 1886, Vol. XLV, C-4904, *A.R. Malacca, 1885; Accounts and Papers*, 1887, Vol. LVII, C-5071, No. 12, *A.R. Malacca, 1886.*

factured article in China',[19] which thus broadened the potential market. The planters responded immediately. The acreage devoted to tapioca in Malacca more than doubled between 1887 and 1890 (Fig. 17). Despite the improved conditions the planters continued to avoid the earliest zone of tapioca cultivation and concentrated instead in the northern and eastern parts of the state (Figs. 16A and 16B).

At this time several of the Malacca planters extended their operations into the adjacent parts of Muar in Johore, an area favoured by easy communication with Malacca town. But this activity never became widespread because the Chinese planters in Johore were chiefly involved in gambier and pepper cultivation. Nevertheless, tapioca planting by Chinese continued in Johore well into the second decade of the twentieth century concentrating particularly in the Muar and Segamat Districts close to the Malacca boundary.[20]

The planters had lost much of their labour during the depression of the mid-1880's and the high demand for Chinese labour in the rapidly expanding tin mines of the Malay States made it difficult to obtain *sinkhehs* for work on the Malacca tapioca plantations in the later years of the decade. This frustrated the attempts of many planters to extend their acreage and persuaded some to experiment with Indian immigrant labour. The experiment failed and for the expansion of the late 1880's and early 1890's the planters relied, as always, upon a predominantly Chinese labour force.[21]

[19] *Accounts and Papers*, 1889, Vol. LIV, C-5620-3, *A.R. Malacca, 1888.*
[20] *M.R. Tampin*, April 1896, *N.S.G.G.* Vol. 1, 1896, No. 96, 138; *New Atlas and Commercial Gazetteer of the Straits Settlements and Federated Malay States*, 70.
[21] The first batch of eighty-six Indian immigrants was introduced by Lee Keng Liat and Koh Seck Chuan in early November 1888, mainly for work on plantations at Gading and Nyalas. The following April the immigrants complained that they had not been provided with suitable accommodation. After an inquiry the Indian Immigration Agent ruled that the immigration would be stopped unless the Government appointed a special officer to look after the interests of Indian labourers on the tapioca plantations. This was not done and no further attempts were made to introduce Indian immigrant labour. *Malacca Weekly Chronicle*, Vol. 1 No. 44, 3 November 1888 and Vol. 2 No. 67, 13 April 1889.

This resurgence of the industry was short-lived. In 1888 it was estimated that a price of four dollars per pikul would cover the expenses of tapioca planters working with borrowed capital and that three dollars per pikul would cover the expenses of those using their own money;[22] a large proportion of the planters were in the first category. Towards the end of 1889 prices began to decline; by the mid-1890's they had fallen below four dollars per pikul,[23] (Fig. 18). By June 1896 the situation was such that at current prices it did not pay to sell and nearly every planter had thousands of bags stored up waiting for the price to rise. One planter offered to give the use of his land and factory to his labourers free, letting them make what they could out of the tapioca they could make and sell; they declined the offer, 'knowing full well that at the present price of tapioca they would not get as much for it as they now receive in wages'.[24]

As always the change in market conditions was reflected immediately in a declining crop area (Fig. 17). This time, however, there was the beginning of a change in policy on the part of the planters. Having lost much of their confidence in tapioca many began to turn their attention to other crops. Tan Hun Guan tried both coffee and tea at Durian Tunggal and others, notably Tan Chay Yan, began to experiment with different types of rubber (see Chapter 10).

Expansion into Negri Sembilan, c.1875-1901

The Chinese tapioca planters of Malacca began to extend their operations into the adjacent parts of Negri Sembilan in the 1870's; in the following decade the process was greatly accelerated. By the 1880's soil exhaustion characterized the earlier zones of tapioca cultivation in Malacca and large tracts of land were already held by tapioca planters towards the state boundaries. In addition, increasing Government antagonism towards the industry, coupled with the demarcation of special

---

[22] *Accounts and Papers*, 1889, Vol. LIV, C-5620-3, *A.R. Malacca, 1888.*
[23] *Malacca Weekly Chronicle*, Vol. 2 No. 102, 14 December 1889; *S.F.P.*, 3rd Series, No. 446, 11 February 1896. The average prices in February 1896 were tapioca pearl $3.65 to $3.70 per pikul and tapioca flake $3.75 to $3.90 per pikul.
[24] *S.F.P.*, 3rd Series, No. 463, 9 June 1896.

Forest Reserves, restricted further extension in Malacca. In the old Negri Sembilan large areas of unoccupied land were available and there were none of the difficulties of obtaining firewood already besetting the planters in Malacca.

Until the early 1890's land in the old Negri Sembilan was granted on considerably more attractive terms than those offered to the tapioca planters in Malacca. For a concession in Rembau, for instance, a planter paid a premium of 50 cents per acre and was exempt from paying rent, being charged a duty of 25 cents per pikul on exports. In Malacca a planter paid a premium of $5 per acre and an annual rent of 75 cents per acre for the whole concession until the scale of premiums was reduced in 1892.[25] This contrast in land terms played a major part in shifting the zone of planting activity across the Malacca state boundary in the late 1880's and early 1890's. The attractions of land over the state boundary were enhanced by the existence of a road system linking the new plantations with the commercial centre of the industry in Malacca town. Although the location of these new plantations beyond the Malacca boundary necessitated increased transport costs these were offset by the more favourable terms upon which land was granted.

Expansion into Negri Sembilan first occurred during the period of high prices in the later 1870's, a period when development in Malacca was most rapid. The first plantations were opened in south-eastern Sungei Ujong soon after British intervention when several short-term leases were granted by the new Government.[26] By the early 1880's the crop was 'largely cultivated' on the lower ground of Sungei Ujong and in 1881 a total

---

[25] A.R. Malacca, 1893, 6-7.

[26] In 1879 Murray, the British Resident in Sungei Ujong, reported that 'Several Tapioca plantations are in progress'; a year later, when the road from Seremban to Linggi was completed, 'tapioca and other plantations [were] being opened from the Linggi terminus and [were] gradually spreading inland'. Accounts and Papers, 1881, Vol. LXV, C-3095, Encl. 3 in No. 1, A.R. Sungei Ujong, 1879 and No. 6, Weld to Kimberley, 31 May 1881, The Progress of the Protected Native States, 1880.

of 14,370 pikuls of tapioca was exported, almost entirely from Linggi.[27]

In the old Negri Sembilan, and particularly in Rembau, concessions were granted to Chinese tapioca planters by the Malay authorities before the extension of British protection to these states. Indeed, expansion into this area clearly pre-dates the price-fall of the early 1880's. Tapioca planting extended into the Malacca mukims of Taboh Naning and Pulau Sebang in the late 1870's; from these the planters moved across the boundary into the adjacent states of Rembau and Tampin. In 1879 a twenty-five year lease for 5,000 acres was granted by the Malay authorities to Baba E See Kiat, Baba Song Gee Gwan and Syed Alui Alkadree at Tiang Merbau, Batang Malaka; five years late Skinner noted of Rembau that 'in recent years, tapioca has been cultivated by the Chinese, which has material-ly increased the prosperity of its people'.[28] Lister stated that of the area held by tapioca planters in the old Negri Sembilan 'the principal portion was granted by the Chiefs before British proctection', and that this was almost entirely the case in Rembau.[29] The planters quickly extended their operations into Gemencheh, and also acquired large blocks of land along the Tampin-Kuala Pilah road.

As in Malacca, the low price of tapioca in the early 1880's caused a temporary recession in Negri Sembilan. Very little new land was brought into cultivation on the recently acquired con-cessions in the old Negri Sembilan; in Sungei Ujong by 1883 nearly all the plantation owners were abandoning tapioca and some had accepted favourable terms from the Government and were 'entering into the experiments of cultivating other pro-ducts on the tapioca grounds, on a large scale'.[30] The industry was revived by rising prices in 1886. This revival, however, did

[27] A.M. Skinner, *A Geography of the Malay Peninsula and Surround-ing Countries*, Part 1, Singapore, 1884, 43; *Accounts and Papers*, 1882, Vol. XLVI, C-3428, Encl. 3 in No. 5, *A.R. Sungei Ujong, 1881*.

[28] *N.S.S.F., K.P. 470/88*; Skinner, op. cit. 48.

[29] *Accounts and Papers*, 1893-4, Vol. LXI, C-6858, Encl. 4 in No. 1, *A.R. Negri Sembilan, 1891*.

[30] *Accounts and Papers*, 1884, Vol. LV, C-4192, Encl. 3 in No. 21, *A.R. Sungei Ujong, 1883*.

not apply to Sungei Ujong where tapioca planting was of relatively little significance by 1890. Henceforth, the major zone of activity lay in Rembau, Tampin, Gemencheh and Johol.

This change in the relative importance of the two areas concerned during the first decade and a half of the industry's history in Negri Sembilan can be attributed to a combination of circumstances. By the late 1880's the interests of the Chinese planters in what later became the Coast District were firmly fixed on gambier and pepper cultivation and rising tapioca prices were not sufficient to divert these interests. Moreover, by virtue of its close connexions with Malacca, the tapioca industry in Negri Sembilan was tied closely to the road network that provided the most convenient links with Malacca town. This particularly favoured the areas along Malacca's northern boundary which were already served by roads and which were some ten miles nearer than the plantations in Sungei Ujong.

The leases granted by the Malay authorities in the old Negri Sembilan prior to British intervention were on more favourable terms than those issued by the Government of Sungei Ujong in the 1870's. Most of the early Malay leases in the former area were for a period of twenty to twenty-five years; those granted in Sungei Ujong were only of five to seven years' duration. By 1882 many of the latter were drawing to a close and in 1890, when little tapioca remained in Sungei Ujong, it was observed that 'when the present leases have expired, there will in all probability be still less'.[31] In contrast, in the late 1880's officials in the old Negri Sembilan still favoured tapioca planting as a means of stimulating land clearance and immigration 'in order to lay the foundations of the Revenue'.[32] Even when the old Malay leases in this area were replaced by titles issued by the new Government the planters were not required to pay rent for the land but instead paid export duties on the produce. Such a system of payment was well-suited to the shifting form of cultivation for the planters would hardly have agreed to pay rent on land lying fallow and unproductive for long periods. The change-over from Malay to British authority did not

[31] *Accounts and Papers*, 1892, Vol. LVI, C-6576, *A.R. Sungei Ujong*, *1890*.
[32] *N.S.S.F., K.P. 280/88.*

diminish the attractions of the land across Malacca's northern boundary.

Lister, Superintendent of the old Negri Sembilan, estimated that by 1887 a total of 75,000 acres had been taken up in Tampin, Gemencheh and Johol for tapioca and in Rembau for tapioca and gambier and pepper, of which 8,000-10,000 acres were already under tapioca. A year later, he remarked that 36,000 acres had been granted for this purpose in Johol 'to big firms in Malacca' and he estimated that in Rembau 'the estates when surveyed will show an acreage of twenty-five to thirty thousand. In Tampin from fifteen to twenty thousand. All these acreages are in process of development and tapioca is being exported and Chinese coolies are more and more required as the estates develop'.[33]

It is possible that by 1888 the tapioca planters held as much as 90,000 acres in the old Negri Sembilan, made up of large concessions averaging over 1,500 acres each (Table 4). Such figures, however, must be merely estimates for the old Malay leases were not based upon a survey and contained a very imprecise description of boundaries. Although soon after intervention the new Government began to replace the Malay leases by titles based on a survey, at the end of 1888 most of the land in Rembau in particular was still held on the old leases. Moreover, land had been planted outside the concessions and 'the natives allow[ed] tapioca planters to plant tapioca on the secondary growth behind their house and garden for a consideration'.[34]

The available evidence is fragmentary, but in total it indicates a very marked expansion of tapioca planting to the north of the Malacca boundary in the late 1880's. Thus, the number of factories required to process tapioca produced in this area rose from six in 1887 to eighteen in December 1888 and to twenty-five twelve months later. Simultaneously Chinese agricultural labourers were imported to work the tapioca concessions. A census of the Chinese population of the old Negri Sembilan

[33] *Memorandum on the Negri Sembilan with a Railway Scheme, 1888,* (*N.S.S.F., K.P. 234/88*).

[34] *Accounts and Papers,* 1888, Vol. LXXIII, C-5566, Encl. in No. 6, *A.R. Negri Sembilan, 1887.*

TABLE 4

LAND HELD BY TAPIOCA PLANTERS IN THE OLD
NEGRI SEMBILAN, 1888

Locality	Surveyed (acres)	Unsurveyed (estimates) (acres)	Total (acres)
Rembau	8,171	22,470	30,641
Tampin and Keru	—	15,000	15,000
Gemencheh	3,459	17,000	20,459
Johol	—	20,300	20,300
Inas	—	3,600	3,600
Total	11,630	78,370	90,000

Source: *Accounts and Papers*, 1889, Vol. LVI, C-5884, Encl. in No. 2, *A.R. Negri Sembilan*, *1888*.

The replacement of Malay leases by titles based on surveys probably explains the discrepancy between the following figures and those quoted above. Although the difference in the totals is of small magnitude, the variations in certain individual figures reveal the difficulty of acquiring reliable statistics concerning this industry in its early stages.

TAPIOCA CONCESSIONS IN THE OLD NEGRI SEMBILAN, 1888

Locality	Number of concessions	Acres
Rembau	31	31,591
Tampin	5	8,700
Gemencheh	7	22,459
Johol	9	22,400
Total	52	85,150

Source: *N.S.S.F., K.P. 622/88*.

taken in September 1887 gave a total of 1,200 with the number of Chinese 'daily increasing'. According to censuses taken by the police this total increased to 2,107 in 1888 and 3,885 in 1890.[35]

In the late 1880's tapioca planting progressed farthest in Rembau; much of the land held by the planters in Tampin,

[35] *N.S.S.F.*, *K.P. 257/88, K.P. 291/90* and *B.R. 3324/1902; Accounts and Papers*, 1888, Vol. LXXIII, C-5566, Encl. in No. 6, *A.R. Negri Sembilan*, *1887*.

Gemencheh and Johol remained unused. By 1888 the thirty-one concessions in Rembau occupied about 31,000 acres and produced over half of the 54,793 pikuls of tapioca exported from the old Negri Sembilan; in fact, about 20,000 pikuls were produced on the plantations lying in the western corner of Rembau.[36] At this date this small state contained over two-fifths of all the Chinese in the old Negri Sembilan, together with three-fifths of the factories already in production (Tables 5 and 6).

TABLE 5

TAPIOCA FACTORIES IN THE OLD NEGRI SEMBILAN, 1888

Factories	Rembau	Tampin and Keru	Gemencheh	Johol	Total
Steam-powered factories	4	1	2	2	9
Steam-powered factories in the course of construction	2	2	1	—	5
Steam-powered factories planned for 1889	1	—	3	2	6
Steam-powered factories outside the state	2	2	—	—	4
Water-powered factories	5	—	—	—	5
Total	14	5	6	4	29

Source: Accounts and Papers, 1889, Vol. LVI, C-5884, Encl. in No. 2, A.R. Negri Sembilan, 1888.

There was little increase in the total planted acreage in the old Negri Sembilan during the 1890's. By mid-decade tapioca prices were very low and it was Government policy to grant fresh land for tapioca only in exceptional circumstances. There was, however, a noteworthy change in the distribution of the planted area. By the early 1890's much of the land planted in Rembau during the initial wave of expansion was exhausted

[36] Accounts and Papers, 1889, Vol. LVI, C-5884, Encl. in No. 2, A.R. Negri Sembilan, 1888.

and firewood was becoming scarce;[37] this small state had been 'completely denuded of forest, and [was] now for the most part a lalang plain'.[38] Rembau therefore declined in importance in relation to the neighbouring states of Tampin, Gemencheh and Johol. In particular, large areas were planted with tapioca along the Tampin-Kuala Pilah road.

At the same time there was a revival of tapioca planting in Sungei Ujong, especially in what is now the Coast District. New land was granted by the Government and by 1893 there were seventeen tapioca plantations in Sungei Ujong occupying in total about 26,000 acres. By the turn of the century tapioca planters held over 100,000 acres of land in Negri Sembilan; half lay in Tampin District (the former states of Tampin and Gemencheh), a quarter in Kuala Pilah District, and about a fifth in the Coast District.[39]

Tapioca Planting in Other Parts of Western Malaya

Chinese tapioca planting was heavily concentrated in Malacca and the adjacent parts of Negri Sembilan and Johore. Elsewhere the industry developed intermittently and on a smaller scale, as it did, for instance, in Kedah, Perak and Selangor. There are several reasons for this marked regional concentration.

The tapioca industry in nineteenth-century Malaya was largely controlled by its originators, the Malacca Chinese; it evoked little interest among other Chinese planters and merchants. They had started the industry when few alternative forms of enterprise were available to them. During the 1860's and 1870's it had proved a remunerative and reliable investment, especially in comparison with the troubled mining industry of the Malay States. Malacca town took on a new significance as the commercial centre of the tapioca industry. The close connexions between the industry and Malacca particularly favoured areas accessible by road from the town. Once established on an im-

---

[37] In 1891, for instance, one planter, Yeow Chiah, applied for additional land in Rembau 'to enable [him] together [sic] firewood for [his] factory'. *N.S.S.F., Land 179/91.*

[38] *Accounts and Papers*, 1892, Vol. LVI, C-6576, *A.R. Negri Sembilan, 1890.*

[39] *N.S.S.F., K.P. 2470/1902.*

portant scale in Malacca and Negri Sembilan the strong hold of the Malacca merchants on credit and trade facilities tended to inhibit its appearance elsewhere. Moreover, the Chinese in other parts of Malaya were already involved in tin-mining or the commercial production of different crops and there was rarely sufficient incentive to induce them to turn to large-scale tapioca planting.

The development of the tapioca industry in the Malacca hinterland was favoured by the terms upon which land was granted to the early planters in the areas concerned, and in particular by the terms offered in the old Negri Sembilan. British protection was extended to Perak and Selangor over a decade before the territories on Malacca's northern boundary. In both these states land regulations were already under consideration before the tapioca planters extended their operations outside Malacca. Basically these regulations were designed to encourage the opening of *permanent* estates by granting land on long-term, rent-paying leases. Land terms of this type held little interest for the tapioca planters.

The governments of Perak and Selangor received a large revenue from tin-mining; moreover, these states had begun to attract the attention of European planters by the 1880's. Thus, it was deemed unnecessary to turn to Chinese tapioca planters as agricultural pioneers or as revenue producers. Finally, the development of export-orientated agriculture in other parts of Malaya was associated with crops other than tapioca, and usually with crops officially considered more desirable. In some cases other dialect groups had initiated this development;[40] in others, Chinese planters became involved in agricultural enterprises introduced by Europeans which differed markedly from tapioca planting.

Nevertheless, tapioca planting did claim the attention of Chinese in a few areas outside the Malacca hinterland in the late nineteenth century. In Selangor the industry had appeared in the neighbourhood of the Kuala Lumpur mines before the British intervened in 1874. The *Capitan China*, Yap Ah Loy, certainly owned a tapioca plantation in the late 1870's and

[40] Tapioca planting in the Malacca hinterland was mainly in the hands of the Hainanese; this point is discussed later.

early 1880's; this plantation formed part of the 12,000 acres
of jungle land that he held on the old Damansara-Kuala
Lumpur road. When tapioca prices fell in the early 1880's it
was completely abandoned.[41]

Interest in tapioca planting in Selangor was revived when
prices rose later in the decade. But the industry never gained a
firm foothold and was confined to the 3,000-acre Jeang Eng Hin
Estate, located about two miles from Batu Tiga on the old
Damansara road, and opened up in 1887. This lone concession
in Selangor was rapidly cleared and planted and production
increased from 3,829 pikuls in 1890 to 5,386 pikuls in 1892.[42]
The planters, however, found difficulty in obtaining sufficient
Chinese labour; moreover, by 1894 about half the concession
had been used for shifting tapioca cultivation and the remainder
was expected to be exhausted within another six or seven years.
At the turn of the century there was little or no tapioca left and
exports ceased. A little later the concession passed into the
hands of a European rubber planting company.[43]

In Perak the tapioca industry developed in two different
ways. It developed in a small way during the 1890's as a pioneer

[41] In 1879 Swettenham observed that the *Capitan China* had planted
'a tapioca estate larger than any in the Colony [i.e. Straits Settlements],
the flour being obtained by machinery put up at Kwala Lumpor, and
now under the superintendance of an English engineer'. *Accounts
and Papers*, 1881, Vol. LXV, C-3095, Encl. 1 in No. 2, *Special Audit
Report on the Selangor Accounts, 1879*. The location of this tapioca
factory is probably commemorated in the local Cantonese name for
Petaling Street, colloquially known today as *Shu Chong Kai*, or
'Tapioca Factory Street'. See also *Selangor State Council Minutes*,
33rd Meeting, Kuala Lumpur, 31 October 1882 and J.M. Gullick,
'Kuala Lumpur, 1880-1895', *JMBRAS*, Vol. XXVIII, pt. 4, 1955, 58-59.

[42] This particular concession was held on a rent-paying lease but 'with
no conditions as to the mode in which the cultivation of tapioca is to
be carried out or the number of crops to be taken off the land'.
Selangor Journal, Vol. 2 No. 25, 24 August 1894, 415. See also *A.R.
Klang, 1890*, S.G.G., 1891, No. 323, 461 and *A.R. Selangor, 1892*, 10.

[43] By 1890 they had begun to employ indentured Indian labour and by
1896 almost 46 per cent. of the total labour force consisted of non-
Chinese, *M.R. Klang*, December 1890, *S.G.G.*, 1891, 43; *Selangor
Journal*, Vol. 5 No. 12, 19 February 1897, 196. See also *Selangor
Journal*, Vol. 2 No. 25, 24 August 1894, 415.

planting enterprise near the coast in Matang District. Here, at Temerloh, Goh Hooi Chew obtained a small concession in 1893. Although evidence is limited there were clearly other tapioca plantations in this area in the early 1890's. But this burst of activity was short-lived. By the end of the decade little tapioca remained. Goh's plantation was interplanted throughout with coconuts and durians and his attention had been diverted to sugar planting on another concession he had recently acquired.[44]

Chinese tapioca planting also became temporarily significant in Perak and Province Wellesley in the first decade of the twentieth century as a form of catch-cropping, mainly in connexion with the conversion of sugar estates to rubber or coconuts, but also occasionally as a temporary stand-by among rubber on new estates. By 1904 tapioca had been widely planted for this purpose on the Chinese sugar estates in Krian and several tapioca factories were opened in the District.[45] This was, however, merely a temporary phase, intended to tide the planters over the maturation period of their permanent crops.

Tapioca was probably the first crop to be grown on a plantation basis in Kedah. Planting was begun by Chinese in the 1890's in the mining districts of the southern half of the state where large concessions were granted for the purpose. The crop increased in popularity with the turn of the century and was frequently used as a catch-crop for rubber. By 1906 over 50,000 acres had been alienated for tapioca alone or for tapioca with rubber or coconuts. This was restricted to the Districts of Kuala Muda, Kulim and Bandar Bharu and most, but not all, lay in Chinese hands. The planted area increased steadily from 10,000 acres in 1911 to almost 30,000 acres in 1915. The ill-effects of shifting tapioca cultivation had already been recognized, however, and measures were introduced to minimize them. Rubber planting followed closely on the heels of tapioca in Kedah and the two crops were usually interplanted. As the

---

[44] A.R. Matang, 1893, P.G.G., Vol. 7, 1894, No. 328, 238 and A.R. Matang, 1900, 1. Rubber was first planted on Goh Hooi Chew's concession in 1907. In 1910 it became the property of Temerloh Coconut and Rubber Estate Limited.

[45] A.R. Larut and Krian, 1904, 5. The amount of tapioca exported from Perak rose from 3,923 pikuls in 1906 to 95,187 pikuls in 1909.

rubber matured, interplanting ceased. By 1919 there were 18,000 acres under tapioca and thereafter the decline continued.[46]

During the nineteenth century the Chinese tapioca industry never developed on a large scale outside the Malacca hinterland. Where it did appear it was either the result of the efforts of individual Chinese planters in search of a new investment or of the fact that tapioca was ideally suited to serve as a catch-crop for more permanent products.

Socio-economic Features of the Chinese Tapioca Industry

Malacca town was the commercial centre, the focal point, for the tapioca industry of western Malaya. Indeed, a circle with a radius of thirty or thirty-five miles drawn with Malacca town as its centre would include most of the tapioca plantations in nineteenth-century Malaya. Communication facilities and transport costs were of fundamental importance to the Chinese planters and strictly limited the outward expansion of the industry.

The tapioca industry in Negri Sembilan represented little more than an extension of that in Malacca. Many planters, such as Lee Keng Liat, Yeoh Sioh, Tio Koh, Tan Hun Guan and Chan Seh Peng, with headquarters in Malacca town, owned plantations in both states. Tapioca roots produced on several plantations in the old Negri Sembilan were transported by bullock cart to factories in Malacca for processing.[47] This movement was sometimes a two-way process for in the first decade of the present century certain planters took tapioca root produced on plantations in Malacca to be processed at their factories in Negri Sembilan and then re-exported the produce. At various times it is possible to discern a similar two-way

[46] See Zaharah Haji Mahmud, *Change in a Malay Sultanate: An Historical Geography of Kedah up to 1939*. Unpublished M.A. Thesis, University of Malaya, April 1966, 231-60.

[47] As late as 1905 Low Kay Seng of Malacca carted tapioca from his plantation at Kundor in Rembau to his factory at Sungei Baru in Malacca for which, in his own words, 'I have to employ 30 carts daily for each of which I am forced to pay $3.75 per trip'. *N.S.S.F., Chinese 998/1905*.

movement of firewood.[48] These were bulky materials and the Chinese planters built networks of cartroads within their concessions upon which large numbers of carts moved constantly between the factories, the cultivated land and the sources of firewood. In 1888, Hale, the Magistrate at Tampin, noted that the 'Chinese are not disinclined to make roads for the convenience of working their estates', in fact in many cases they received 'grants-in-aid' from the Government for the purpose.[49]

Some of the tapioca produced in Negri Sembilan was taken to the Sungei Linggi whence it was exported to Singapore by steamer. Most, however, was transported to Malacca town by bullock cart for shipment to the southern Settlement. The bulk of the provisions consumed on the tapioca plantations and the majority of the Chinese immigrants who formed the labour force were imported from Malacca town by this same means. Consequently, transport costs, which rose from twenty-five cents per bag of tapioca in the early days to forty cents a bag in 1897, formed a significant proportion of the planters' expenditure.[50] This carrying trade was in the hands of Malacca Chinese. Although many of the tapioca planters probably owned their own carts, or had interests in the business, the high costs incurred were undoubtedly a major cause of the outburst of indignation among the Malacca Chinese in 1888 regarding the route of the proposed Sungei Ujong railway, a route which lay so far away from the plantations that it would in no way help to reduce these costs.[51] Similarly complaints about the state of the roads leading from various parts of the old Negri Sembilan to Malacca town were common during the 1890's.

A small group of Chinese, with their headquarters in Malacca town, controlled the tapioca industry and its ancillary activities and were its chief beneficiaries. Thus, as with most Chinese enterprises in nineteenth-century Malaya, the lion's share of the profits derived from this industry went to make the fortunes

[48] E.g. *N.S.S.F.*, *Tampin 1352/1909* and *Tampin 1626/1909*.

[49] *N.S.S.F.*, *K.P. 243/88*.

[50] *N.S.S.F.*, *Tampin 2186/97*.

[51] *Malacca Weekly Chronicle*, Vol. 1 No. 6, 11 February 1888 and No. 8, 25 February 1888.

of a small group of urban-based financiers in the Straits Settlements, in this case in Malacca town.

Tapioca cultivation is not labour intensive. Nevertheless, the
marked expansion of planting activities that occurred between
the 1860's and the early 1890's necessitated a greatly increased
labour force. The tapioca planters relied on both Malay and
Chinese labour. Malays were employed in smaller numbers and
probably were engaged mainly in clearing jungle and in felling
and collecting firewood. On the other hand, the cultivation and
processing of tapioca were carried out almost entirely by Chinese
labour. Large numbers of new immigrants, or *sinkhehs*, were
brought to Malacca by junk under the Credit Ticket system and
shipped to the interior to work on the tapioca plantations. Thus,
the Chinese population of Malacca almost doubled between 1860
and 1881, and the number of Chinese in the old Negri Sembilan
more than trebled between 1887 and 1890.[52] Most of the
sinkhehs were youths who lived and worked under trying conditions. As usual they had to work for a year for very low wages
to repay their passages from China and most of the wages that
they did receive were swallowed by the inflated prices of provisions, including opium, charged on the plantations.

The importation as well as the employment of these immigrants was controlled by Chinese based in Malacca town.
Strictly speaking, some of these were *Baba* or 'Straits' Chinese,
but most had Hainanese family names. The *sinkhehs* too, were
mostly members of this dialect group. Table 6 reveals that
almost half the Chinese employed in the old Negri Sembilan
in 1890 were Hainanese, although several other groups, notably
the Hokkiens, were also represented in the labour force.

Little evidence exists to indicate how the tapioca industry
was financed. However, analogy and deduction, coupled with
the available evidence, suggests the existence of a hierarchy
based on some form of contract system resembling the *kangchu*
system. Here again the organization of Chinese agricultural
pioneering was based on the need for credit facilities, a need
satisfied by wealthy Chinese residents of Malacca town in

---

[52] Kernial Singh Sandhu, 'Chinese Colonization of Malacca', 8; *Accounts
and Papers*, 1888, Vol. LXXIII, C-5566, Encl. in No. 6, *A.R. Negri
Sembilan, 1887; N.S.S.F., B.R. 3324/1902.*

TABLE 6

CHINESE POPULATION OF THE OLD NEGRI SEMBILAN, 1890

State	Hainanese	Hokkien	Tiechiu	Hakka	Others	Total
Rembau	882	373	36	35	348	1,674
Tampin	484	107	170	38	417	1,216
Gemencheh	432	186	3	124	242	995
Total	1,798	666	209	197	1,007	3,885

Source: Draft A.R. Tampin, 1890. N.S.S.F., B.R. 3324/1902.

search of a remunerative investment. As individuals, or as groups forming kongsis, the Malacca Chinese owned the tapioca concessions of both Malacca and Negri Sembilan. They also owned the factories which processed the tapioca produced on those concessions. Planting was undertaken by contractors using sinkheh labour. The contractors received advances in kind and cash from the proprietors and were obliged to sell their produce to them at fixed rates. Until it was prohibited in the early 1880's this system was also extended to include Malay planters in Malacca.[53]

Underlying these socio-economic features of the tapioca industry was a closely-knit organization that provided both the credit facilities and the agricultural labour necessary for the establishment of plantations in areas where neither were available. It was a system of organization made possible by the presence of a wealthy Chinese class in Malacca town who financed and controlled the industry, and by the widespread desire of the poverty-stricken south Chinese to seek material improvement in the Nan Yang. The existence of this organizational framework in the form of the kongsi system can alone explain the success of Chinese tapioca planting in the pioneer conditions of both Malacca and Negri Sembilan at a time when

[53] In 1881 it was stated that 'the Chinese manufacturers supplied the Malays with funds, and the Malays began, without authority, to clear the forests in all directions, and to plant tapioca, which they afterwards sold to the manufacturers on the manufacturers' terms'. Accounts and Papers, 1883, Vol. XLV, C-3642, No. 14, A.R. Malacca, 1881.

European planters were only beginning to take an interest in this same area.

Chinese Tapioca Planting: an Ephemeral Form of Pioneering

In the early 1870's tapioca planters held about 20,000 acres of land in the Malacca hinterland almost entirely confined to the British Settlement. By the turn of the century they held over 160,000 acres, less than a third of which lay within the Malacca state boundary. Clearly, very marked changes characterized the industry in the last quarter of the nineteenth century; the most obvious changes were an increase in the planted area and a movement of the major zone of activity further from Malacca town. But did Chinese agricultural colonization occur in the Malacca hinterland in the way that it did in nineteenth-century Johore?

When the Chinese planters first entered Johore the state was very sparsely peopled. Gambier and pepper planting was relatively labour intensive and as this industry expanded increasing numbers of Chinese immigrants poured into the almost empty areas of Johore. Here they established village headquarters many of which have survived to form the nuclei of permanent settlements. Gambier and pepper were cultivated on a shifting basis but only small blocks of land were planted at any one time; shifting tended to occur within the confines of the territory attached to the village headquarters. If more land was required then new river depots were established either further inland on the same river system or in new areas. Chinese agricultural settlement in nineteenth-century Johore had many features characteristic of colonization in a frontier environment.

In contrast, in the Malacca hinterland tapioca planting expanded into an area that already contained a sizeable Malay population.[54] It was an area characterized by numerous small valleys in each of which Malay *kampongs* with their padi-fields

[54] Malacca had an average population density of about 100 per square mile when tapioca planting began in the early 1850's, and those parts of Negri Sembilan into which the industry expanded later had densities of 25-30 per square mile at the time of this expansion.

and fruit trees had already been established but which were separated by jungle-clad interfluves as yet unoccupied. It was also an area with an existing local administrative framework. In most respects the tapioca industry was completely divorced both from the economy and the administrative framework of these Malay settlements. The Chinese planters used land for agricultural purposes which had been avoided by the Malays, except as a source of jungle produce. The Chinese were present only temporarily, they were organized on their own *kongsi* system with ultimate control in the hands of the Malacca Chinese, their agricultural enterprise in no way competed with the subsistence farming of the Malay villagers, and their needs were supplied by imports. The expansion of tapioca planting occurred as a wave of activity passing quickly across the landscape, making use of the unoccupied hillslopes between the Malay valley settlements, and leaving nothing in its wake but abandoned land.

The industry began in Malacca in a semi-circular zone several miles inland, thus avoiding the *kampongs* and padi-fields that already ringed the town. As land in this initial zone became exhausted and the industry grew in popularity the wave of planting activity flowed outwards almost in concentric circles.[55] New land was obtained in two ways. Either the Chinese planters were granted new concessions by the Government, or they made unauthorized encroachments beyond the limits of their original leases. Thus, the area held by the tapioca planters was frequently in excess of official estimates.[56]

During the 1870's and 1880's this wave of activity passed beyond the boundaries of the British Settlement and here again land was planted and abandoned in quick succession as the Chinese planters skimmed their profits from the soil and

---

[55] By 1876 Malacca already contained about 12,000 acres of abandoned tapioca land. *Accounts and Papers*, 1877, Vol. LIX, *A.R. Malacca, 1876*.

[56] It is probable, for instance, that in Malacca the planters held between 55,000 and 58,000 acres in 1877 as compared with the official figure for that year of 32,000 acres. *Accounts and Papers*, 1878-9, Vol. 1, C-2273, *A.R. Malacca, 1877* and *S.S.B.B.*, 1877.

moved on.[57] Clearly, the expansion of the tapioca industry did
not signify Chinese colonization of sparsely populated areas.

An important cause of this fundamental difference between
Chinese agricultural pioneering in Johore and in the Malacca
hinterland lies in the difference between tapioca and gambier
and pepper planting. Large areas of tapioca could be cultivated
by a relatively small labour force and it is unlikely that the
total number of Chinese involved in tapioca planting in the
Malacca hinterland ever exceeded 10,000. Moreover, land
planted with tapioca was abandoned within five years and a
concession was completely exhausted within about twenty-five
years. In contrast, an individual gambier and pepper *bangsal*
was cultivated for fifteen to twenty-five years. The tapioca
industry was characterized by larger planted areas and by very
much more frequent shifting than gambier and pepper planting. Village headquarters were never established by the tapioca
planters for their stay in one place was short and their numbers
small; permanent settlements of the *kangkar* type never
emerged in connexion with this form of Chinese agricultural
pioneering.

Tapioca planting was undertaken in an area and in a manner
which focussed attention on the outer edge of an expanding
wave of activity behind which the abandoned interfluves were
only rarely re-occupied for tapioca planting. The void remaining when the wave passed on was almost invariably left unfilled
until rubber planting permitted permanent agricultural utilization at a later date.

The Decline of Chinese Tapioca Planting

The devastating effects of this shifting system of cultivation
were already apparent in Malacca in the 1880's and a Govern-

---

[57] It is for this reason that Rembau was 'for the most part a lalang
plain' in 1890, that Gemencheh had been 'denuded of forest by
tapioca planters' by 1899, and that by the turn of the century there
were immense stretches of *lalang* 'extending for miles in the
neighbourhood of Linggi' in the Coast District; a similar situation
existed in Tampin and Johol. *Accounts and Papers*, 1892, Vol. LVI,
C-6576, *A.R. Negri Sembilan, 1890; A.R. Negri Sembilan, 1899, 4;
A.R. Coast, 1905, 2.*

ment policy emerged which was designed to suppress the industry. This move was quickly followed by Government officials in the neighbouring areas.[58] By the mid-1890's Lister was refusing all applications for tapioca land in the old Negri Sembilan 'except where it seems necessary to keep an existing factory going'.[59] Simultaneously a corresponding policy emerged in Sungei Ujong.[60]

Official concern regarding the effects of shifting tapioca cultivation in Negri Sembilan led to the passing of a special Order in Council in May 1892. This stipulated that henceforth no more than two crops of tapioca could be taken in succession from the same piece of land, defaulting planters being subject to a $200 fine.

The new regulation was not designed to kill the tapioca industry, but rather to produce a situation which would allow the forest to regenerate on abandoned land and so permit the planters to practise continuous shifting cultivation within the concessions already granted to them. It was thus intended to contain the industry within existing boundaries whilst allowing it to continue otherwise unchanged.[61] In practice, however, the new regulation merely increased the shifting nature of the industry. Moreover, from experience the planters knew that land took longer to recuperate than this regulation allowed if it was to yield reasonable returns and they continued to prefer virgin jungle for new clearings. But there was also a growing prejudice in Government circles against granting fresh land for tapioca.

Although the tide of official opinion turned against the tapioca

[58] As early as 1888 Lister announced that in the old Negri Sembilan 'except under exceptional circumstances such as an entirely new district or special products there is no necessity for even entertaining demands for Tapioca land'. *N.S.S.F., K.P. 538/88.*

[59] *N.S.S.F., C.S. 2472/95.*

[60] In 1879 the British Resident of Sungei Ujong announced that 'this Government positively refuses to grant any more forest land for that purpose [i.e. tapioca planting] except a sufficiency to supply firewood and wood for building purposes'. *Accounts and Papers, 1881, Vol. LXV, C-3095, Encl. 3 in No. 1 A.R. Sungei Ujong, 1879.*

[61] *Accounts and Papers, 1893-4, Vol. LXI, C-6858, Encl. 4 in No. 1 A.R. Negri Sembilan, 1891.*

planters in the last decade of the nineteenth century, the
industry was still regarded as one of the most important agents
of agricultural pioneering in previously unopened areas. In
1897 Bathurst, District Officer in Jelebu, proposed a scheme to
encourage tapioca planters to enter his hitherto neglected
District. The British Resident supported the proposal and the
Chinese planters of Kuala Pilah and Tampin were informed
of the decision.[62] The offer was ignored, however. Presumably
it did not attract the Chinese because the inaccessibility of this
area in relation to Malacca town would have made transport
costs excessive; it is also probable that the planters no longer
had confidence in the Government's attitude towards them.

The titles or 'permits' introduced by Lister in the old Negri
Sembilan in the late 1880's to replace the Malay leases contained
a clause to the effect that 'the land when abandoned will revert
to the state unless special application is made to the contrary'.
In this context it was held that 'abandoned' meant 'the cessation
from the cultivation of successive crops'.[63] By the turn of the
century large areas formerly planted with tapioca in both the
Coast District and the old Negri Sembilan had become *lalang*-
covered wastes as the wave of activity passed on. The existence
of these large tracts of apparently 'abandoned' land raised the
problem of how the titles issued by Lister should be interpreted
now that rubber cultivation was expanding and the Government was receiving an increasing number of applications for
land on which rents could be charged.

Belfield, the acting British Resident, was of the opinion that
'these permits must be held to have lapsed, and the land there-
under to have reverted to the state' under the terms and
conditions printed on them. In May 1906, however, the legal
adviser to the Federated Malay States Government proclaimed
that the permits should be interpretated to mean that the
holder must continuously cultivate tapioca in such a manner
that eventually three crops would have been planted on every
part of the concession. The land should not revert to the state,
he said, 'until entire cessation, over the whole area, of the
cultivation of successive crops of tapioca, continual succession

of a crop on one part of the land to a crop on another part thereof being sufficient to avoid "abandonment" '.[64]

Exports of tapioca from Negri Sembilan fell by about 60 per cent. between 1902 and 1906. By this time vast areas of former tapioca land had been 'abandoned', even under the interpretation of the permits decided upon by the legal adviser. In August 1906 notices of impending reversion of large tracts of tapioca land were published in the *Negri Sembilan Government Gazette*. After allowing the owners three months in which to protest, most of the abandoned tapioca concessions in Negri Sembilan reverted to the state in January 1907. In consequence the area held by tapioca planters in this state declined from over 100,000 acres in 1901 to about 8,750 acres in 1909.[65] Similarly the acreage devoted to this crop in Malacca fell by 84 per cent. between 1904 and 1911.

In both states the decline was accompanied by a change in the interests of the Chinese planters. In the late 1890's they began to experiment with various crops including tea, coffee, gambier and rubber, as possible substitutes for tapioca. Coffee and tea never proved sufficiently successful to oust tapioca completely, but rubber cultivation was soon a remunerative occupation, either for its own sake or so that the land could be sold for large sums to European companies. Tapioca was ideally suited to serve as a catch-crop with newly-planted rubber, and probably initially also served as a useful 'face-saver' for the early Chinese rubber planters. In effect the interplanting of rubber and tapioca prolonged the life of the tapioca industry by several years.

As in the case of gambier planting, an important cause of this change in interest in Negri Sembilan was the introduction of a special cultivation clause into the titles of all new land granted for tapioca after 1900. This clause stipulated that the land 'shall be planted with permanent cultivation simultaneously with Tapioca' at a fixed number of trees per acre. The permanent crops which must also be planted to satisfy the new

[64] *N.S.S.F.*, *N.S. 3557/1905*.
[65] *N.S.G.G.*, Vol. 11, 1906, No. 341; *N.S.S.F.*, *Tampin 99/1907* and *R.G. 1178/1910*.

regulations included *geta rambong*, para rubber, coconuts, arecanuts and betel nuts.[66]

This new cultivation clause was intended to eliminate the wasteful system of shifting cultivation. Nevertheless it did not deter Chinese planters from taking up new land with an apparent willingness to comply with the requirements. In fact many took up new land for tapioca and merely planted a 'permanent' crop, such as rubber, to keep the authorities at bay.[67]

Consequently, Government became suspicious of any Chinese applicant who requested permission to plant tapioca, even as a catch-crop, and little new land was granted. Moreover, the Negri Sembilan Government was exerting every effort to foster rubber planting alone, particularly by European planters (see Chapter 10). In the case of land held by those planters who complied conscientiously with the cultivation clause rubber gradually replaced tapioca. By the later years of the first decade of the twentieth century many of the Chinese planters had begun to accept the change, precipitated by Government policy and made desirable by rising rubber prices, and were applying for land for rubber alone.

In 1904 the Negri Sembilan Government introduced special *lalang* terms to encourage planters to take up abandoned tapioca land for rubber or coconuts.[68] European planters and companies immediately took advantage of the offer of land on favourable terms. Although by the later years of the decade their example was followed by several Chinese planters, a large area of land which was formerly held by Chinese tapioca planters and had reverted to the state passed into the hands of European companies.[69]

---

[66] A similar regulation was introduced in Kedah in 1906 by which time tapioca was widely planted in the southern half of the state.

[67] The District Officer of Kuala Pilah remarked in 1903 that 'the grantee in such cases simply plants tapioca and rubber and then neglects the rubber and the State is no better off than it was before'. *N.S.S.F.*, *K.P. 1539/1904.*

[68] *N.S.G.G.*, Vol. 9, 4 January 1904, No. 20.

[69] Perhaps the best example of this process is the acquisition of five to six thousand acres of *lalang* land near Batang Malaka by the Dunlop Rubber Company in 1916. *A.R. Negri Sembilan, 1916, 11.*

The decline of tapioca planting resulting from these various official measures was stimulated in the early 1900's by falling prices. Between 1894 and 1904 the cost of cultivation is estimated to have risen by about one-third;[70] in 1903 and 1904 tapioca prices were extremely low (Fig. 18). In Tampin District the year 1903 was described as 'a most disastrous one for tapioca planting owing to the low prices which ruled in the Singapore market'. A large estate in mukim Keru went bankrupt; another in mukim Gemencheh was sold on foreclosure of mortgage; and others tided over the crisis with great difficulty.[71] The plantations in Rembau and the Coast District also suffered severely. Tapioca prices rose again in 1905 but this short depression had coincided with the introduction of several new Government regulations and rapid replacement by rubber was already in progress. For a short period Government action aimed at eliminating the tapioca industry had been reinforced by strong economic forces acting in the same direction. In combination these had permanent effects and the pioneer character of Chinese agricultural enterprise in the Malacca hinterland speedily disappeared.

There was a slight resurgence of the tapioca industry in 1913 when rubber prices fell and tapioca prices rose, and also in the period 1917-20 when rubber prices again declined and the Director of Food Production in the Federated Malay States ordered an increase in food production because of war-time shortage. Rubber, however, had replaced tapioca as the major crop in the Malacca hinterland before 1910 and new agricultural patterns had already begun to emerge (see Chapters 10 and 11).

[70] *N.S.S.F., P.D. 5548/1904.*
[71] *A.R. Tampin, 1903,* 1.

PART II

SEDENTARY PLANTATION AGRICULTURE

5

EXPERIMENT AND TRANSITION

PART I WAS CONCERNED WITH the attempts of Chinese pioneers to develop export-orientated agriculture in the scantily-populated, largely jungle-covered Malay Peninsula during the nineteenth century. But the desire to exploit the agricultural potentialities of this region was not restricted to the Chinese. Concurrently, other forms of export crop production developed, forms differing noticeably from those adopted by the pioneer Chinese and approximating much more closely to the forms of commercial agriculture that ultimately evolved in early twentieth-century Malaya. To a large extent these forms represent a European reaction to conditions in nineteenth-century Malaya, a reaction that was at once experimental and transitional.

The European settlers in early nineteenth-century Malaya had little knowledge of local conditions and of tropical agriculture. They were generally ignorant of the correct cultivation methods, the requirements and the diseases of the few crops that apparently offered possibilities as commercial ventures. Moreover, their knowledge of the peninsula away from the immediate environs of the British Settlements was minimal; the acquisition of land for agricultural purposes was restricted to British-controlled territories and was governed more by accessibility, and therefore proximity to the port-towns in these Settlements, than by considerations of suitable soil or topography. Before any degree of success could be achieved these early European settlers had to come to terms with a totally unfamiliar humid tropical environment inimical to the development of agriculture on the lines adopted by their contemporaries in western Europe.

The luxuriant growth of tropical vegetation persuaded the European settlers in the early British Settlements that local soils were extremely fertile and that once the jungle was cleared the land would yield an abundance of crops; as an observer remarked in 1836 'The soil is good,—the climate fine,—the situation excellent;—and nought is wanting but the hand of man to bring abundance to our own doors.'[1] It was some time before it was realized that the fertility of local soils had been grossly over-estimated and that agriculture in a humid tropical environment required completely different techniques from that in temperate countries. If the natural vegetation is cleared in a temperate region the fertility of the soil remains. The situation in a tropical forest is totally different. Decomposition of organic matter is very rapid, feeding roots are superficial and nutrients pass immediately from decayed matter into living roots. A very large part of the mineral reserves resides in the trees; if the luxuriant forest is removed, and the ground completely cleared, a surprisingly infertile soil remains. By using a shifting system of commercial crop production the pioneer Chinese overcame this problem. Not until late in the century, when they began to cultivate tree crops which created their own nutrient cycle, did the Europeans begin to achieve comparable success.

There was little in existing agricultural patterns to guide the European settlers in the development of export crop production, nor was there a pool of skilled agricultural labour on which they could rely. To a very considerable extent, therefore, the initial attempts to develop export-orientated agriculture were experimental in nature. In general they turned to non-indigenous crops for which a demand existed in Europe and which already were grown successfully for export in other parts of the world. Pepper was the first such crop to be tried in Penang in the early 1790's and a little later nutmegs and cloves were introduced. Some success was achieved with the former crop in the early years of the nineteenth century and nutmegs and cloves appeared to offer a bright future for a short while in the 1830's and 1840's, but neither proved permanent. During the 1830's the European settlers in the Straits Settlements experimented with many other commercial crops

[1] *S.F.P.*, 9 June 1836 quoted by P. Wheatley, 'Land use in the vicinity of Singapore in the Eighteen-thirties', *M.J.T.G.*, Vol. 2, 1954, 64, footnote 3.

— notably coffee, cotton, tea, tobacco and cinnamon—in their efforts to find an export staple, but the results proved unsatisfactory. Failure with these early attempts led them to turn to sugar cultivation, particularly in Province Wellesley, in the 1840's and 1850's, as the possibility of success with this crop had been demonstrated already by Chinese pioneers. When intervention opened up the Malay States to the European planter in the 1870's a similar process of experimentation began involving pepper, tea, tobacco and cinchona, and culminating in the 1890's in a concentration on coffee.

These early European ventures into commercial agriculture in Malaya differ in two important respects from the Chinese agricultural pioneering discussed previously. Firstly, almost all the crops chosen by the Europeans tended to have a long maturation period and could not be expected to produce economic returns for several years. Generally they were also crops that demanded relatively large inputs of capital and labour and that required specialized treatment in the hands of an experienced labour force. In contrast, the Chinese pioneers relied on crops that would grow almost anywhere with a minimum of care, that gave quick returns and that required a relatively small capital investment. It is therefore hardly surprising that the Chinese were more successful in the pioneer conditions of nineteenth-century Malaya.

Secondly, the European settlers regarded agricultural holdings as long-term investments that would provide a future source of income and an inheritance for their families; as such, they wanted legal title to the land in which they invested. To the Chinese pioneers, as temporary sojourners intent upon quick profits, land as such held little value unless it produced crops economically. They did not want titles to the land they cultivated and frequently operated as illegal 'squatters'; the Chinese planters had no hesitation in abandoning land once the returns diminished.

The European residents of Penang and Singapore in the first half of the nineteenth century regarded the Settlements more as permanent homes than do their present-day counterparts. Their returns to their homelands were infrequent and their connexions more tenuous. Many began to accumulate capital and sought a local investment, preferably one that they could supervise personally. Tin mining was as yet carried on only on a small scale and was undertaken in the virtually unknown wilderness of the Malay states. Landed estates producing crops for export to the home market seemed the obvious answer to these European settlers, coming as many did from a class in which capital invesment in land was a dominant interest. Moreover, commercial crop production was officially encouraged in the early days of the British Settlements as a means of financing their administration and protection. Thus, within a short while of the founding of Penang, European residents began to acquire 'estates' on the island, parts of which they planted with pepper. Pepper planting in early Penang therefore falls within the context of this form of commercial agriculture rather than that discussed in Part I. The temporary success of nutmegs and cloves induced many more to develop 'estates' in Singapore and Penang. In large measure these were the attempts of amateur European planters to develop export agriculture as a side-line to their other interests. They represent the beginnings of proprietary estate ownership in Malaya.

After the initial encouragement provided by the importation of pepper, nutmegs and cloves under Government aegis official support was generally withdrawn from these early attempts to establish commercial agriculture in the British Settlements and for almost half a century such development as occurred resulted from the enterprise of individual Europeans. Under the stimulus of considerable pressure from the planters the Government did introduce land regulations in the early 1840's which provided terms more suitable for the development of *permanent* plantations in Penang and Singapore, but in other respects little help was forthcoming. The last twenty years of the century, however witnessed a complete change in the official attitude towards commercial agriculture in Malaya.

The new political policy towards the Malay States indicated by intervention was accompanied by the appearance of an official desire to promote economic development. In particular the development of agriculture became a prominent feature of Government policy in each of the Malay States, and to the

British officials in charge the most satisfactory means of effecting such development was to encourage European planters. To this end, various measures were introduced to ensure the provision of the basic necessities for development—the first roads and railways were built with public money, suitable land regulations were quickly evolved, steps were taken to facilitate the introduction of immigrant agricultural labour, and loans were made to *bona fide* planters from Government funds. By 1888 Hugh Low could write in his report on Perak that

...it has always been the great desire of the Government to encourage European planters to settle in the State.... Large sums varying from $2,000 to $40,000 have been lent or promised to substantial planters, on condition of their providing similar amounts to be employed in opening estates of Liberian and Arabian coffee, sugar, tobacco and pepper.... It is obvious, however, that pioneers labour under special difficulties and the Government cannot do better than support such undertakings until the great advantages of soil and elevation in Perak become better known.[2]

Two other changes occurred during the nineteenth century that affected the character of European commercial agriculture in Malaya. The estates established in the early part of the century were owned and supervised by amateur planters; they were in the nature of part-time interests for European residents who had other full-time occupations in the Straits Settlements and who, for the most part, had had little or no previous experience of tropical agriculture. The first signs of change came with the arrival of a few sugar planters from Mauritius and Demerara in the 1840's; the advent of coffee planters from Ceylon in the 1870's and 1880's marked the emergence of a professional European planting community in Malaya.

Signs of more complex organization also began to emerge in the middle of the century in connexion with sugar planting in Province Wellesley where a large part of the acreage was held by a London-based owner who employed resident European managers to work his land. In the last two decades of the century the typical proprietary estate began to give way to ownership

[2] *A.R. Perak, 1888, S.S.G.G.,* 1889, No. 355, 1031.

by companies, a process very greatly accelerated after the turn of the century with the expansion of rubber planting. Corporate enterprise replaced individual enterprise and directly helped to strengthen and to promote European interest in commercial agriculture in Malaya.

The European ventures into export crop production in nine-teenth-century Malaya were as speculative in nature as were the ventures of the Chinese. Attractive market conditions aroused the initial interest and possibilities of considerable profit encouraged a rapid extension of the planted acreage. Falling prices produced dismay and despondency and, despite the heavy capital investment sometimes involved, resulted in a reduction of the planted area, and, in the case of pepper, nutmegs and cloves, complete abandonment. This section considers the most important of these European ventures in the pre-rubber era and attempts to elaborate the factors involved in limiting European success in the early nineteenth century and in promoting it later in the century.

6

EARLY PLANTATIONS IN THE
BRITISH SETTLEMENTS

EUROPEAN INTEREST IN PLANTATION AGRICULTURE in Malaya dates
from the establishment of British Settlements at Penang and
Singapore. These islands were acquired principally to facilitate
the East India Company's trade with China but the development of export crop production was favoured as one means of
covering administrative costs. Though inexperienced in tropical
agriculture, the early European residents proved extremely
willing to invest their capital in the cultivation of crops introduced by the local authorities. At this time pepper, nutmegs
and cloves were major items of export from South-East Asia to
Europe. Local officials arranged for seeds and young plants to
be brought to the new British Settlements and these crops formed the basis of the initial venture of Europeans into plantation
agriculture.

Pepper Planting in Penang

Pepper planting in Penang in the last decade of the eighteenth
and first quarter of the nineteenth centuries was the first type
of export-orientated agriculture to develop in a British Settlement in the Malay Peninsula. From the very beginning it was
a joint European-Chinese enterprise and differed in several
important respects from the pepper planting undertaken by
Chinese either in Singapore and Johore in the first half of the
nineteenth century or in Malacca, Negri Sembilan and Selangor
at a later date.

In the latter areas pepper was always grown in conjunction
with gambier; in Penang this joint cultivation never became
general. Certainly gambier was grown in Penang in the early
1790's and a Chinese established a gambier cauldron near Batu
Lanchang to process the product. In this instance, the planter
found that labour costs made his product more expensive than

the imported article and he therefore 'rooted out the [gambier] plants, and put pepper vines in their place'.[1] Thereafter, there is no evidence of gambier planting on the island. In fact, gambier did not become an important export from the Malay Peninsula to Britain until import duties were drastically reduced in the early 1830's (see Chapter 2). Before that time the gambier exported from Singapore was destined mainly for China and as noted later, Penang suffered firstly from a lack of space on ships going to China and later, from a restriction prohibiting Company China-bound vessels from calling there. Thus in the brief heyday of pepper planting in Penang there was little to encourage the associated cultivation of gambier in the manner in which these crops were planted in Singapore and Johore.

This fundamental difference may owe something to two other factors. As a joint European-Chinese enterprise pepper planting in Penang may have been influenced by the ideas of the European planters. Moreover, the method of pepper cultivation in Penang differed in at least one important respect from the methods employed by the Chinese in Singapore and Johore. In Singapore the vines were trained up hardwood posts; significantly, this method was also used by the Chinese in eighteenth-century Brunei. In Penang *dedap* trees were planted as supports for the vines.[2] This was a method widely used in Sumatra at the time and one which later in the century became associated with Achehnese immigrants in Malaya. This distinction in planting techniques probably reflects the fact that pepper planting spread to Singapore and Johore from Riau where gambier was grown together with small patches of pepper in the late eighteenth century. In contrast, pepper planting came to Penang from Sumatra where pepper was grown as a major export crop throughout the eighteenth century.

[1] W. Hunter, 'Plants of Prince of Wales Island', *JSBRAS*, No. 53, 1909, 73.

[2] Thomson, 'General Report on the Residency of Singapore', 137; T. Forrest, *A Voyage to New Guinea and the Moluccas ...*, London, 1780, 382; Sir George Leith, *A Short Account of the Settlement, Produce, and Commerce, of Prince of Wales Island in the Straits of Malacca*, London. 1804, 60.

Expansion and Decline of Pepper Planting in Penang,
1790-c.1835

The planting of pepper in Penang began soon after the establishment of the British Settlement. It was hoped that local production of an export crop would attract trade to the new
Settlement and thereby contribute to the cost of administration.
Initially pepper appeared a suitable choice because the demand
in Britain was not fully satisfied by the plantations of near-by
west Sumatra. Accordingly vines were introduced from Acheh
in 1790 by the *Capitan China* of Penang, Che Kay, with financial
aid from Francis Light. Planting probably began in the Sungei
Kluang area and was first undertaken by Chinese[3] (Fig. 19).

During the early 1790's the East India Company established
experimental pepper gardens at Sungei Kluang and Ayer Itam
and many of the European residents, including Light, planted
pepper on their newly-acquired estates. At the same time the
Chinese 'with characteristic industry' occupied and planted
comparatively small holdings in many parts of the island. By
1798 a total of 533,230 vines had been planted on Penang,
probably occupying between seven and nine hundred acres.[4]

Between 1798 and 1801 a further three-quarters of a million
vines were planted, bringing the total number in cultivation
to over one and a quarter million, and the planted area to
between 1,700 and 2,200 acres.[5] Pepper vines came into bearing
when about three years old so that production increased
markedly in the early years of the decade. In 1802 Penang
produced between sixteen and twenty thousand pikuls and
pepper was already 'the most important article of produce' on
the island.[6] Three years later output had risen to about 27,000
pikuls, three-quarters of which was considered suitable for the
European market, and for which the price obtained varied

[3] Leith, op. cit. 25 and 63; W. Hunter, 'Remarks on the Species of
Pepper, which are found on Prince of Wales's Island', *Asiatick Researches*, Vol. 9, 1807, 388; Hunter, 'Plants of Prince of Wales Island',
57.

[4] F.G. Stevens, 'A Contribution to the early history of Prince of Wales'
Island', *JMBRAS*, Vol. VII, pt. 3, 1929, 396. Jackson, op. cit. 9.

[5] Leith, op. cit. 30.

[6] Hunter, 'Remarks on the Species of Pepper', 385 and 389.

between ten and twelve Spanish dollars per pikul. The annual
yield of the Penang pepper plantations is believed to have risen
to as much as 30,000 pikuls by 1806.[7] Expanding production at
favourable prices aroused considerable optimism regarding the
future of pepper planting in the early years of the decade. This
wave of enthusiasm was short-lived, however, and affairs in
Europe quickly changed the picture.

Napoleon's Continental System, confirmed by the Decrees of
Berlin (1806), and Milan (1807), excluded Great Britain from
trade with Europe and consequently severely limited the market
for the produce of British overseas possessions. The Penang
planters suffered greatly because the bulk of their produce had
hitherto been shipped to Britain for sale to the European
markets. As demand on the London market declined, prices
fell drastically. The Penang planters found it uneconomic to
sell their pepper at less than eight or nine Spanish dollars per
pikul and in March 1806 good quality pepper was selling at the
latter price; thereafter prices fell below production costs.[8]

The Penang pepper planters asked for Government aid in
November 1808; $20,000 were advanced as a temporary relief
by the local authorities, but the Supreme Government deprecat-
ed such aid and the planters received no further financial
assistance. In fact, the East India Company already had such
large stocks of pepper in its London warehouses that there was
little justification for it to subsidize the depressed Penang
planters; indeed, in 1809 the Penang Government was urged to
discourage pepper planting on the island, and two years later
the Court informed the Governor that pepper growing on
Penang did not seem necessary to 'a supply of the Markets in
Europe'.[9]

China apparently offered an alternative market. In July 1807
over 12,000 pikuls of pepper were shipped from Penang to

[7] C.D. Cowan, 'Early Penang and the Rise of Singapore, 1805-32',
    JMBRAS, Vol. XXIII, pt. 2, 1950, 24 and 141; Low, *Dissertation on
    the Soil and Agriculture . . .* , 40.
[8] Cowan, op. cit. 5, 33 and 46; Hunter, 'Remarks on the Species of
    Pepper', 389.
[9] M. Stubbs Brown, *A History of Penang, 1805-1819*. Unpublished M.A.
    Thesis, University of Malaya, April 1963, 223 and 225; Cowan, op. cit.
    35-36, 38, 41 and 43.

Canton and part of the following year's crop was also dispatched to China.[10] But there was generally insufficient shipping space available to make China an important and regular market for Penang pepper and, in any case, the large quantities of pepper available in China, which was at this date also the destination for Benkulen produce, kept prices low there also.

The effects of this depression were clearly visible on the island. In many areas plantations were neglected or abandoned, and by 1810 'a large proportion of the Island formerly in high Cultivation [had] again reverted to its original state of Jungle'.[11] In mid-1814 Phillips reported that cultivation was in a 'lamentable state of deterioration' and that nearly half the land previously cultivated had been abandoned.[12] Production had declined to about 20,000 pikuls in 1810 and to between twelve and fourteen thousand pikuls in 1815.[13] There was, therefore, a marked decline of pepper planting in Penang between 1806 and 1815 and several planters showed a temporary interest in other potential export crops, notably coffee, cotton and hemp.

The depression was largely the result of external factors over which neither the Penang Government nor the planters could exert any control. In addition, over two-fifths of the vines in existence in 1801 were over three years old; by about 1810 many of these would have passed the stage of economic working at current prices.[14] Abandoned land could not be replanted immediately with pepper because young vines would not thrive 'on old worn out pepper land'.[15] Yet, low prices and the local Government's refusal to issue new land grants because of the confusion resulting from earlier land regulations, had acted as strong deterrents to new planting during the earlier part of the depression.

After the fall of Napoleon European markets were reopened to British trade and pepper prices rose from about seven Spanish

[10]Stubbs Brown, op. cit. 223.

[11] Cowan, op. cit. 41.

[12] Penang Consultations, 25 June 1814, Minute by Phillips, S.S.R. (IOL), Vol. XLIV, 1430 quoted by Stubbs Brown, op. cit. 204.

[13] Cowan, op. cit. 41 and 57.

[14] Leith, op. cit. 30.

[15] Low, *Dissertation on the Soil and Agriculture ...*, 43.

dollars a pikul in 1814 to about twelve Spanish dollars per pikul in 1817-18.[16] Interest in pepper planting in Penang revived and cultivation was 'again commenced with spirit'. Neglected plantations were improved and between 1816 and 1818 over 300,000 vines were planted, chiefly in the Telok Tikus, Sungei Tiram, Paya Terubong, Sungei Nibong and Ayer Itam districts. Almost one and three-quarter millon pepper vines, occupying between two and three thousand acres, had been planted in Penang by 1818 (Fig. 19).

Production increased accordingly and by 1818 was estimated at 'little less than 18,000 pikuls'.[17] This revival was short-lived however, for prices on the London market fell markedly after 1817; thereafter the produce of the Penang plantations went mainly to China, although a little went also to continental Europe and North America.[18] By 1823 Penang was estimated to produce between twelve and fifteen thousand pikuls annually, but it was becoming increasingly difficult for the Penang authorities to combat the restrictive regulations prohibiting the Company's China-bound ships from calling there.[19] Cut off from their main market and suffering the depredations of insects on their plantations, the Penang planters began to abandon pepper in the mid-1820's and by 1825 output was estimated to total only about 8,000 pikuls. Pepper prices continued to fall in the late 1820's and the increasing interest in nutmegs and cloves resulting from the first successes of the pioneer planters hastened the decline of the pepper plantations. By the mid-1830's production was less than 2,000 pikuls and 'the jungle [had] usurped the extensive tracts formerly under pepper'.[20]

[16] Cowan, op. cit. 141.

[17] Penang Consultations, 7 October 1818, S.S.R. (IOL), Vol. LXVII, 287, Enclosure in Report of Finance Committee quoted by Stubbs Brown, op. cit. as Appendix VIB.

[18] J. Bastin, The Changing Balance of the Early Southeast Asian Pepper Trade, Papers on Southeast Asian Subjects, Department of History, University of Malaya, No. 1, 1960, 50-53 and 58; Stubbs Brown, op. cit. 237.

[19] Cowan, op. cit. 30; Bastin, Changing Balance of the Early Southeast Asian Pepper Trade, 58.

[20] Low, Dissertation on the Soil and Agriculture . . . , 41.

Pepper Planting in Penang: A Joint European-Chinese Enterprise

In the early nineteenth century a European planter proposing to open a new plantation first employed a group of Malays to fell the jungle, paying them at the rate of $5 per *orlong* (1.3 acres). All subsequent work—digging out the roots and burning them, pulverizing and levelling the soil, and planting the vines and the trees to support them—was undertaken by Chinese labour invariably employed on a contract system.

It was usual to contract for the opening of a plantation, and for its maintenance until it came into bearing three years later, at the rate of $225 per 1,000 vines. This sum was paid to the contractor in instalments to enable him to pay his labourers. 'Something more than one third' was paid in the first year 'because the labour is then greatest'; about a quarter was reserved until the contract was completed and the plantation delivered to the owner. This contract price excluded the cost of cuttings which were supplied by the proprietor.[21] The vines came into bearing when they were three years old and when this initial 'caretaker' contract terminated it was the general practice to rent the plantation to a Chinese at a fixed amount of pepper per vine. Hunter maintained that this was the only way in which 'a very extensive plantation, or one whereon the proprietor [could] not bestow his whole attention [could] be managed to advantage'.[22] This contract system ensured the development of the European estates whilst leaving their owners free to engage in other activities; moreover, it placed the onus of acquiring and supervising the necessary labour force on the Chinese contractors.

The larger plantations, therefore, were generally developed with European capital by Chinese contractors employing *sinkheh* labour. The Chinese were, in fact, always the chief cultivators of pepper on Penang whether as labourers for con-

---

[21] Hunter, 'Remarks on the Species of Pepper', 385-6; see also Leith, op. cit. 65.

[22] In 1802 a plantation containing 3,000 bearing vines at Sungei Kluang was let for three years at a rent of 'seventy *picols* yearly, or at the rate of 2⅓ *cattis* each plant'. Hunter, 'Remarks on the Species of Pepper', 388-9.

tractors or as small-scale planters on their own behalf. Apart
from the larger European-owned plantations there were also
many smallholdings planted with pepper. These were probably
opened up by *sinkheh* labourers who had completed the period
necessary for the repayment of their passage money. As in so
many instances, the Chinese devised a method of financing the
impecunious *sinkheh* desirous of opening his own small pepper
plantation. A capitalist provided him with advances for building a house and for agricultural implements; he then received
'two dollars monthly to subsist on until the end of the third
year, when the estate or plantation [was] equally divided
between the contracting Parties'.[23] It was then usual for the
capitalist to rent his half share of the new plantation to his
cultivating partner for five years at a rent (in the early 1830's)
of thirty pikuls per annum. Once a pepper plantation was
established an average of one Chinese labourer was required
to care for two *orlongs* (i.e. 2⅔ acres) of vines. The small-hold-
ings established by individual Chinese under this system of
financing were probably of about this size.

Pepper cultivation was a labour-intensive form of agriculture.
The Penang plantations were clean-weeded and the soil was
turned twice annually during the first five or six years. When
the vines came into bearing two crops were obtained each year,
one in the period December to February and the other between
May and July. Harvesting was a delicate operation and the
quality of the pepper produced depended to a great extent on
the care taken in gathering and drying the crop. Operative
costs were high in Penang; they were, in fact, higher than in
Indonesia. The Penang vines, however, were extraordinarily
productive, yielding on average almost seven times as much
pepper per acre as did the vines at Benkulen.[24] It was the prospect
of large profits resulting from these high yields that produced
such optimism in the first decade of the nineteenth century
and that persuaded the planters to maintain their plantations
until the situation became hopeless in the mid-1820's.

[23] Low, *Dissertation on the Soil and Agriculture ...*, 42.
[24] Bastin, *Changing Balance of the Early Southeast Asian Pepper ɩ rade*,
55.

Nutmegs and Cloves at Penang: The Years of Doubt, 1796-c.1825

Nutmegs and cloves were of major interest to European traders in South-East Asia long before the founding of Penang, and to the Directors of the English East India Company in particular the Dutch spice monopoly was a traditional grievance. Nevertheless when the British Settlement of Penang was founded the spice trade was not regarded as of fundamental importance by the East India Company. In the first instance, the island had been acquired to facilitate trade with China. The agricultural development of the new Settlement was a secondary consideration, but it was hoped that such a development might help to cover administrative costs. Although pepper was introduced first nutmegs and cloves were also expected to form the basis of this development. These crops had for long been a traditional South-East Asian export to Europe and, in fact, few other crops were known that could be grown under local conditions and sold profitably in the home market.

In the early 1790's Francis Light had obtained, at considerable expense, a small number of clove plants from Mauritius, where they had been taken by the French, and these were unsuccessfully planted out in Penang.[25] The first British occupation of the Dutch Spice Islands in 1796 provided an excellent opportunity to supply Penang with nutmeg and clove plants in large numbers in a way which had been impossible under the Dutch monopoly. A botanist, Christopher Smith, was sent to the Moluccas to organize a supply of seeds, seedlings and young plants for the East India Company's possessions. At the same time private arrangements were made for the shipment of plants to Penang and a large quantity arrived in 1798 which were put up for public sale. Between 1798 and 1802 Smith shipped a total of 71,266 nutmeg and 55,264 clove plants from the Moluccas, chiefly to Penang. These were planted in a 130-acre Government botanical garden at Ayer Itam and on several

---

[25] H.R.C. Wright, 'The Moluccan Spice Monopoly, 1770-1824', *JMBRAS*, Vol. XXXI, pt. 4, 1958, 48; Stubbs Brown, op. cit. 24; Burkill, *Dictionary of the Economic Products of the Malay Peninsula*, Vol. 1, 962.

European-owned plantations, one of the earliest of which was the Glugor Estate; some were also planted on Chinese-owned holdings.[26] A very large proportion of these plants died 'owing at first to the shyness of cultivators, and the carelessness with which the newly arrived Plants were treated, and subsequently to the prevailing ignorance as to the proper method of cultivating these exotics'. It is estimated that by 1802 only 33,000 nutmeg plants remained alive on the island.[27]

Nevertheless in the early years of the century a golden future was prophesied for spice planting in Penang. Glowing reports from a series of officials testified to the 'thriving' nature of the plantations and to the expectation that in a few years' time Penang would satisfy the demands of the British market and also supply the European markets 'at full as cheap a rate as they can purchase elsewhere'.[28] The first nutmeg tree fruited in Penang in 1802; the following year the Court of Directors requested that every encouragement should be given to the Penang spice planters because it was stated, on authority, that the island was 'the most eligible spot of all the East India Company's possessions for spice cultivation'.[29]

Official policy towards spice planting wavered, however. Costs were high and the returns slow and the early enthusiastic support was quickly withdrawn. In October, 1805 the Government spice gardens at Ayer Itam were sold in lots for the 'inconsiderable' sum of $9,656, the chief purchasers being James Scott and Christopher Smith. This sale acted as a 'temporary stimulus to the private planter', but the prevailing ignorance of correct cultivation methods produced poor results and induced apathy among the planters. The abandonment of the

---

[26] Wright, op. cit. 49; Rev. K. Garnier, 'Early Days in Penang', *JMBRAS*, Vol. 1, pt. 1, 1923, 6; Hunter, 'Plants of Prince of Wales Island', 119.

[27] *Singapore Chronicle*, N.S., Vol. 4 No. 35, 28 August 1834; Thomson, 'General Report on the Residency of Singapore', 30.

[28] Leith, op. cit. 45; N. Macalister, *Historical Memoir relative to Prince of Wales Island in the Straits of Malacca and its Importance, political and commercial*, London, 1803, 11-12; 'Formation of the Establishment on Poolo Peenang', *Miscellaneous Papers Relating to Indo-China*, Vol. 1, 1886, 33-34.

[29] H.N. Ridley, *Spices*, London, 1912, 102.

Government gardens left the inexperienced private planters to experiment with spice cultivation unaided; they received very little further official encouragement until the 1820's.

Ignorance and apathy had reduced the total number of nutmeg trees on the island to about 13,000 by 1810, 'several *hundreds* of which only' were in bearing.[30] Moreover, up to 1812, apart from a few samples, no locally-produced spices had been sent to England. By this date however, more was known about cultivation methods and greater care was taken in selecting sites for and in tending new plantations.

A small group of European planters, notably David Brown, but also John Danbar and Thomas McGee, persevered with nutmegs and cloves despite the adverse circumstances and cultivation was quickly extended. In 1813 the Governor reported that the cultivation of nutmeg was extending yearly, 'that some hundreds of trees were in a state of bearing; and that the produce was in no way inferior in quality to that of the Moluccas'.[31] Three years later, in consequence of the anticipated improvement in prices with the restoration of the Moluccas to the Dutch and renewed hope for official encouragement and aid, including preferential treatment in the British market, cultivation was reported to be 'extending fast'. It was expected that the island would soon be in a position to export a 'considerable quantity' of nutmegs and the Governor noted that 'the Cultivators are Sanguine on this point, and are turning their full attention to the means of insuring it'.[32]

Although official encouragement was not forthcoming and prices in England fell sharply after 1816, a total of 78,910 nutmeg and 103,929 clove trees had been planted on the island by 1818. Of these only 6,910 nutmeg and 1,003 clove trees were in bearing, so that planting activities had been particularly energetic during the preceding five or six years. Over four-fifths of the nutmeg trees and almost all the clove trees were in the Sungei Glugor district where David Brown had his plantation, a plantation to which he had added by the acquisition of a considerable number of neighbouring small holdings previous-

[30] *Singapore Chronicle*, N.S., Vol. 4 No. 35, 28 August 1834.
[31] Wright, op. cit. 55.
[32] Cowan, op. cit. 65; Wright, op. cit. 95.

ly alienated to Malays and Chinese.[33] Smaller plantations also
existed in the Ayer Itam, Sungei Kluang, Ayer Rajah and Paya
Terubong districts and a few trees had been planted in several
other areas (Table 7).

During this period David Brown stood alone as a spice planter
on an extensive scale in Penang. He remained confident in the
future of the enterprise and after his death in 1825 his plantation was managed by his son George 'with a spirit and judgment
which finally overcame every difficulty, and displayed, for the
first time, after thirty years of perilous trial, the full value of
the pursuit'.[34]

The introduction of spice planting to Penang resulted from
official encouragement which was quickly withdrawn. The
success that the enterprise later achieved was based on the
initiative and perseverance of a small group of private European planters who continued to invest in spice cultivation when
the risks were great and the results doubtful.

The Expansion of Nutmeg Planting in Penang, c. 1825-50

In the early 1820's prices in London were extremely low and
the East India Company was reported to have 'an immense and
unsaleable amount' of spices in its warehouses.[35] Towards the
end of the decade however, the situation improved and the
pioneer efforts of planters such as Brown began to be favoured
with success; in consequence the enterprise 'commenced to show
results in the markets of Europe in 1830'.[36]

Renewed interest was shown in the planting of both nutmegs
and cloves, and in the case of the latter about 50,000 new trees
were planted between 1821 and 1834.[37] But the expansion that
characterized the 1830's and 1840's was concerned less with
cloves than with nutmegs. The loss of interest in clove planting
was attributed to 'the unfortunate result of the large plantations
formed on the Pentland range of hills, which died gradually

[33] Stevens, op. cit. 410.
[34] Low, *Dissertation on the Soil and Agriculture* ... , 20.
[35] Wright, op. cit. 97-98.
[36] Ridley, *Spices*, 139.
[37] *Singapore Chronicle*, N.S., Vol. 4 No. 37, 11 September 1834.

TABLE 7

NUTMEG AND CLOVE TREES IN PENANG, 1818

District	NUTMEGS			CLOVES		
	Trees in bearing	Trees not in bearing	Total Number of Trees Planted	Trees in bearing	Trees not in bearing	Total Number of Trees Planted
Sungei Glugor	—	65,000	65,000	60	101,000	101,060
Ayer Itam	1,540	4,230	5,770	255	442	697
Sungei Kluang	230	1,370	1,600	200	200	400
Telok Ayer Rajah	4,341	—	4,341	266	963	1,229
Paya Terubong	240	1,360	1,600	2	6	8
Sungei Nibong	300	—	300	23	—	23
Batu Lanchang	180	8	188	150	150	300
Kampong Penang	76	30	106	—	29	29
Telok Jelutong	3	2	5	20	21	41
TOTAL	6,910	72,000	78,910	1,003	102,926	103,929

Source: Penang Consultations, 7 October 1818, *S.S.R.* (IOL), Vol. LXVII, 287, Enclosure in Report of Finance Committee, quoted by Stubbs Brown, op. cit. as Appendix VIB.

before they attained the 15th year of their age, which had produced 3 crops or so', and the low prices at which cloves had been
selling.[38] By the 1840's an 'unfavourable opinion' had been
formed of clove cultivation; in some instances it had resulted
in total loss to the proprietors and in no case had it brought
profits.[39] The crop was avoided by almost all the Chinese planters
and by many of the owners of smaller plantations. In 1843 it
was largely restricted to European-owned plantations in Penang
of which twelve were in existence. In total cloves occupied a
mere 615 acres on the island and there were about half as many
trees as there had been in 1834 (Table 8 and Fig. 20). At the
same date only seventy-two acres were planted with the crop in
Province Wellesley.[40]

Concurrently, nutmeg prices were high and the success
achieved by the pioneer planters provided a strong incentive for
many others to follow their example. By 1838 nutmeg cultivation was extending rapidly in all parts of the island as new
plantations varying in size from less than an acre to several
hundred acres were established. So swift was the expansion that
the editor of the Penang Gazette wrote 'we would not be sur-
prised to see the whole of the Island become one vast Spice
garden' and he suggested that the enterprise already provided
a livelihood for a large proportion of the population including
Chinese, Malays and Indians.[41] During this boom period planting also extended into Province Wellesley and by 1834 over
thirty spice plantations had been estabished on the island and
its mainland appendage. Five of these were large plantations
containing between 4,000 and 20,000 trees; seventeen were much
smaller with between fifty and 2,000 plants each.[42]

This expansion of nutmeg planting in the 1830's and 1840's
was largely, although not entirely, European-sponsored (Table
9). At the same time however, a considerable number of very
small plantations were opened by Chinese 'squatters'. Thomson
remarked in 1849 that the success achieved by the European

---

[38] Penang Gazette, Vol. 1 No. 17, 28 July 1838.
[39] Thomson, 'General Report on the Residency of Singapore', 103.
[40] Penang Gazette, Vol. 2 No. 44, 11 May 1844.
[41] Penang Gazette, Vol. 1 No. 17, 28 July 1838.
[42] Singapore Chronicle, N.S., Vol. 4 No. 35, 28 August 1834.

TABLE 8

CLOVE PLANTATIONS IN PENANG, 1843

Plantations	Number of Plantations	Trees in Bearing	Total Number of Trees Planted	Percentage of Trees in Bearing	Planted Acreage (a)	Average Size of Plantations (acres)	Percentage of (a) over (b)
European-owned Plantations	12	24,772	60,702	40.8	509	42.4	82.8
Larger Chinese-owned Plantations	1	500	2,750	18.2	21	21.0	3.4
Larger Plantations owned by 'others'	1	700	1,000	70.0	9	9.0	1.4
Total Larger Plantations	14	25,972	64,452	40.3	539	38.5	—
Smaller Plantations	76	2,767	8,327	33.2	76	1.0	12.4
TOTAL	90	28,739	72,779	39.4	615(b)	6.8	100

Source: Penang Gazette, Vol. 2 No. 44, 11 May 1844.

TABLE 9

NUTMEG PLANTATIONS IN PENANG, 1843

Plantations	Number of Plantations	Trees in Bearing	Total Number of Trees Planted	Percentage of Trees in Bearing	Planted Acreage (a)	Average Size of Plantations (acres)	Percentage of (a) over (b)
European-owned Plantations	30	49,213	137,202	35.8	2,070	69.0	68.2
Larger Chinese-owned Plantations	10	6,717	15,517	43.3	210	21.0	6.9
Larger Plantations owned by 'others'	3	3,380	8,485	39.8	125	41.6	4.1
Total Larger Plantations	43	59,310	161,204	36.7	2,405	55.9	—
Smaller Plantations	374	5,592	46,889	11.9	630	1.7	20.8
TOTAL	417	64,420	208,093	30.9	3,035(b)	7.2	100

Source: Penang Gazette, Vol. 2 No. 44, 11 May 1844.

planters and by the pioneer Chinese who already 'occupied the few favourable localities offering rich soil' had induced a great many Chinese to clear and cultivate 'less favourable localities on the hills, where their attempts can hardly meet with success, if they do not end in total failure'.[43] So extensive was the clearance of jungle by Chinese on the steep slopes of the Penang hills during the 1840's that Logan expressed grave concern as to its probable effects and prophesied that since many of the clearings were on slopes 'too steep for any permanent cultivation' they would soon be abandoned.[44]

This extension of Chinese planting activities was undertaken mainly by individual 'squatters' dependent upon advances provided by the Chinese merchants and shopkeepers of George Town. In the first instance, the 'squatter' obtained an advance to enable him to clear a small patch of land on which he began by raising 'plantains, indigo, nilam and kitchen vegetables, which at once support[ed] him and [kept] his ground clean'. He also planted nutmegs. When the cultivation of these began to interfere with his other activities he obtained further, larger advances from his financier in town who also provided him with provisions. The risks involved for the merchants and shopkeepers were great for the plantations were unlikely to yield even a small quantity of nutmegs for the first six or seven years. The rates of interest charged on the advances were therefore high, generally varying between 18 and 24 per cent.[45] Using this system of financing, Chinese 'squatters' pushed nutmeg cultivation into the southern and western parts of the island (Fig. 21).

In both the island and the Province cultivation was therefore expanding in two ways. The greatest addition to the planted area occurred on the large plantations, the majority of which were owned by European residents. At the same time individual

[43] Thomson, 'General Report on the Residency of Singapore', 37-38; see also J. Low, 'Notes on the Progress of the Nutmeg Cultivation and Trade from the early part of the 17th century to the present day', *J.I.A.*, Vol. 5, 1851, 471.

[44] J.R. Logan, 'The Probable Effects on the Climate of Pinang of the Continued Destruction of its Hill Jungle', *J.I.A.*, Vol. 2, 1848, 534.

[45] *Penang Gazette*, 3 March 1855 quoted in *S.F.P.*, Vol. 22 No. 11, 15 March 1855.

Chinese 'squatters' financed in the traditional way by members of their own community, cleared and planted a multitude of small plantations; usually these were less than two acres in size and were worked by a single labourer. The cultivation of nutmegs, even on the European-owned plantations, was mainly in Chinese hands.

Almost invariably Chinese labour for European-owned estates in nineteenth-century Malaya was obtained on a contract system which placed the onus of providing, supervising and paying the labour force on a Chinese overseer or contractor who retained a proportion of the crop for his efforts.The nutmeg plantation owners adopted the contract system used earlier by the pepper planters. As many of the European plantation owners had other interests besides spice planting the contract system left them free to deal with these other interests with full confidence that their plantations would not be neglected.

By 1853 the area devoted to spices in Penang had increased to an estimated 9,430 acres and in Province Wellesley to 488 acres.[46] Seven years later the respective figures were given as 13,153 acres and 1,349 acres, the former figure representing almost 40 per cent. of the total estimated cultivated area of Penang Island.[47] Thus, the expansion of the 1840's was matched by a further increase in planting activities in the subsequent decade. By the 1850's however, prospects were no longer so encouraging and by the end of the decade the nutmeg had completely lost favour in Penang.

Nutmeg 'Mania' in Singapore

The development of nutmeg planting in the first half of the nineteenth century was not restricted to the northern Settle-

---

[46] *Penang Gazette*, Vol. 11 No. 46, 12 November 1853.

[47] Braddell, *Statistics*, 13. A different source gives 13,153 acres for Penang, but only 200 acres for Province Wellesley in 1860. *A.R.S.S., 1860-1*, Appendix VII. Elsewhere Braddell says that there were 433 acres planted with spices in Province Wellesley in 1858. T. Braddell, *Singapore and the Straits Settlements Described*, Penang, 1858, 2. Ridley quotes a figure of 14,500 acres for the area devoted to spices in Penang and Province Wellesley in 1860. H.N. Ridley, 'Spices', *Agricultural Bulletin of the Malay Peninsula*, No. 6, April 1897, 99.

ment. Nutmeg and clove plants and seeds were sent to Singapore from Fort Marlborough by Raffles in 1819 and were planted on the slopes of Fort Canning Hill. In the letter accompanying this consignment Raffles exhorted the Resident at Singapore 'to exert your utmost endeavours to establish the cultivation under your immediate authority'.[48] When Singapore was founded the spice planters of Penang were on the verge of success and it was hoped that by encouraging spice cultivation at both Settlements the British could break the renewed Dutch monopoly.

Little progress was made for over a decade, however, although spice planting was recommended in the press as a good branch of agriculture for the European residents and in 1827 the Government intimated that anyone wishing to try spice planting on the island would be supplied with young plants from the Company's Botanic Garden.[49] Nevertheless, some interest had been aroused for in February 1827 the Resident Councillor observed that many of the European landholders were 'preparing their Lands for the reception of spices, for which culture it appears the soil is not ill adapted', and he requested that supplies of young nutmeg and clove plants be sent to Singapore from Penang.[50]

During the 1820's however, the development of spice planting in Singapore was hampered by unfavourable land terms. Moreover, away from the immediate environs of the new town the island remained largely unknown to its European residents and in an almost totally undeveloped condition, with roads either poor or non-existent. Other discouraging factors were the inefficiency of the police, 'who could not guarantee the protection of isolated settlements', the frequency of reported attacks by

---

[48] T. Oxley, 'Some Account of the Nutmeg and its Cultivation', *J.I.A.*, Vol. 2, 1848, 658; Makepeace and others, op. cit. Vol. 2, 66.

[49] *Singapore Chronicle*, No. 76, 15 February 1827; ibid. No. 83, 24 May 1827; ibid. N.S., Vol. 3 No. 7, 14 February 1833. See also 'Report on the Honble. Company's Botanical Garden, Singapore, 1 February 1827' in T. Braddell, 'Notices of Singapore', *J.I.A.*, Vol. 9, 1855, 62-65.

[50] Cowan, op. cit. 174; W. Milburn, *Oriental Commerce* (revised by T. Thornton), London, 1825, 350.

tigers on the fringes of settlements, and the absence of a suitable labour supply.[51]

Cloves never proved successful at Singapore and after several abortive attempts to cultivate this spice by private individuals it was almost completely abandoned. Interest centred instead on the nutmeg. Some of the nutmeg trees in the Botanic Garden had borne fruit by the mid-1820's and the feeling became general that the soil and climate of Singapore were better suited to nutmeg cultivation than those of Penang. Enthusiasm for nutmeg planting mounted among the European residents in the late 1820's and early 1830's as the pioneer plantations began to show signs of success and as the agricultural development of the island as a form of investment became the common interest. By the beginning of 1837 'many [had] been led, who were previously very sceptical, to entertain more liberal opinions on the subject' of nutmeg cultivation.[52] Good returns from existing plantations, coupled with the very high prices quoted locally for nutmegs, turned this growing enthusiasm into an unthinking 'mania' in the late 1830's and early 1840's. In the words of John Cameron,

These were powerful inducements to hold out in a settlement whose residents had not only grown rich beyond measure, but who had grown attached to the land itself, and were ready and willing to embark in any enterprise that, while likely to be remunerative for the capital invested, tended further to develop its resources. Planting in Singapore now went on with a vengeance. A nutmeg mania seized upon all the landed proprietors. What had been flower gardens and ornamental grounds of private residences were turned over, and nutmegs planted to within a stone's throw of the house walls.[53]

In 1834 there were 'upwards of twelve' spice plantations on the island, most of which were recent and all of which were in the vicinity of the town.[54] Planting activities extended in the

---

[51] G.W. Earl, *The Eastern Seas*, London, 1837, 408-10; Wheatley, op. cit. 64.

[52] *Singapore Chronicle*, N.S., Vol. 7 No. 1, 7 January 1837.

[53] Cameron, op. cit. 168.

[54] *Singapore Chronicle*, N.S., Vol. 4 No. 20, 15 May 1834.

late 1830's following the establishment of an Agricultural Society in Singapore in 1836. The introduction of more favourable land terms in the early 1840's resulted in a doubling of the planted acreage between 1841 and 1848 (Table 10). Several European residents built themselves houses on the outskirts of the town and established nutmeg plantations around them. For the most part these plantations lay within a three- to four-mile radius of the town centre and particularly along the roads leading westwards where nutmeg planting began on the *lalang*-covered hills abandoned by the Chinese gambier and pepper planters in the Tanglin district (Fig. 22).

TABLE 10

NUTMEGS IN SINGAPORE, 1841-8

Year	Total Number of trees planted	Number of trees in bearing	Percentage of trees in bearing	Approx. acreage planted	Production (Number of nutmegs)
1841	25,000	?	?	550-600	? *
1843	43,544	5,317	12	600-750	842,328 †
1847	55,925	14,914	26	800-950	4,085,361 †
1848	71,400	20,821	29	1,190	7,616,105 †

* *S.F.P.*, Vol. 6 No. 47, 25 November 1841.

† Thomson, 'General Report on the Residency of Singapore', 30-31 and 219A.

Thomson maintains that in Singapore nutmeg trees were planted at a density of sixty per acre (ibid. 207); both Oxley op. cit. 657, and Ridley, *Agricultural Bulletin of the Malay Peninsula*, No. 6, April 1897, 104, give a figure of seventy trees per acre. These estimates take account of both these average figures.

Towards the end of the decade the Chinese, following the lead of those whom they supposed knew what they were doing, also began to take an interest in the enterprise. The crop was planted by Chinese at various places on the island and by 1848 there were fifty-eight nutmeg plantations of varying sizes in Singapore owned mainly by Europeans and Chinese.[55]

[55] Low, 'Notes on the Progress of the Nutmeg Cultivation and Trade', 471; Thomson, 'General Report on the Residency of Singapore', 31-32.

European planting activities had reached their peak by the end of the 1840's. The Chinese, having entered the field later, continued to plant nutmegs during the early 1850's in the various parts of the island in which they were also cultivating gambier and pepper. By 1855 over 36,500 nutmeg trees, of which 2,600 were in bearing, had been planted on Chinese holdings in Singapore.[56] By this time however, several adverse factors had served to dampen the early enthusiasm for nutmeg planting and a clear-headed review of the situation showed that it was not the promising enterprise that it was first thought to be.

Pepper, Nutmegs and Cloves in early Malacca

Mills maintained that the history of spice cultivation at Malacca 'can be dismissed in a few words: there was none'.[57] But Malacca was not entirely passed over by the developments occurring in the other Settlements. Pepper, nutmegs and cloves were grown on a small scale in the second and third decades of the nineteenth century, although admittedly with little success.

It is probable that pepper cultivation began in Malacca during the first British occupation of the Settlement between 1796 and 1818. In the early 1820's the crop was fairly widely cultivated by Chinese on the huge blocks of land held by the 'so-called Dutch Proprietors'. The labour force comprised recently-arrived immigrants who were organized as a 'fraternity' and many of the *sinkhehs* obtained 'fresh advances for forming pepper gardens' of their own after completing the period necessary for the repayment of their passage money.[58]

Planting centred particularly on Appa Katchee's estate at Batu Berendam, on J.B. Westerhout's estate immediately to the north-west of Malacca town and on de Wind's massive estate in eastern Malacca. Smaller plantations existed at several other places, including Bachang and Bukit Rambai. It was however, a short-lived enterprise. By the mid-1820's pepper prices were falling and continued to do so and the confused

[56] *S.F.P.*, Vol. 22 No. 20, 17 May 1855.
[57] L.A. Mills, 'British Malaya, 1824-67' (edited by C.M. Turnbull), *JMBRAS*, Vol. XXXIII, pt. 3, 1960, 220.
[58] A.H. Dickinson, 'The History of the Creation of the Malacca Police', *JMBRAS*, Vol. XIX, pt. 2, 1941, 261.

and uncertain situation regarding the Malacca land question only made matters worse.[59]

Pepper production in Malacca was already declining by 1826. In that year the Malacca plantations yielded approximately 6,000 pikuls; the following year this had dropped to some 4,500 pikuls. In the early 1830's annual production was estimated at about 4,000 pikuls.[60] The late 1820's were characterized therefore by a sharp decline in pepper planting in Malacca and many plantations were abandoned. Some pepper plantations still existed in the early 1830's and Malacca continued to produce a little pepper in the early 1840's. By the late 1840's, however, the crop had virtually disappeared from the state.

The cultivation of nutmegs and cloves never became widespread in Malacca although some interest was aroused in these crops when pepper prices fell in the late 1820's, an interest probably heightened by the success which the Penang spice planters were then beginning to achieve.[61]

By 1827 spice trees had been planted by some of the Chinese planters and in that year Lewis suggested that the large landholders should distribute spice plants among the householders on their estates and that the Government should supply clove plants to the people of Naning.[62] Both the Malacca Government's decision in 1828 to take over the land held by the 'Dutch Proprietors' and the Naning War (1831-2), interfered with these suggestions and spice planting at Malacca in the 1830's was restricted to a few small plantations.[63] Some nutmegs and cloves

[59] Malacca Diary, *S.S.R.* (IOL), 28 September 1826, Vol. 165, 171; ibid. 30 January 1828, Vol. 168, 47-59, W.T. Lewis' Report on the Malacca Lands; F.L. Baumgarten, 'Agriculture in Malacca', *J.I.A.*, Vol. 3, 1849, 707; Mills, op. cit. 118-36.

[60] The plantations at Batu Berendam were stated to have produced twice as much in previous years as they did in 1826. *Singapore Chronicle*, No. 75, 1 February 1827; *Malacca Observer*, 25 March 1828 quoted in *Singapore Chronicle*, No. 106, 10 April 1828; J.H. Moor, *Notices of the Indian Archipelago*, Singapore, 1837, 243.

[61] Malacca Diary, *S.S.R.* (IOL), 28 September 1826, Vol. 165, 171.

[62] Dickinson, op. cit. 264.

[63] *Singapore Chronicle*, N.S., Vol. 4 No. 20, 15 May 1834; Burkill, *Dictionary of the Economic Products of the Malay Peninsula*, Vol. 2, 1526.

were produced during the 1840's but the enterprise achieved
little success and by the end of the decade was hardly worthy
of note. All Cameron saw in the early 1860's was a single 'half-
forsaken' nutmeg plantation.[64]

This absence of spice plantations at Malacca to rival those
that developed at Penang and Singapore cannot be explained in
terms of the greater suitability of the soil and climate of the
latter Settlements. The fundamental inhibitive factor in the
case of Malacca was the intractable land question. When the
British took possession of Malacca in 1825 very large parts of
the territory were held by a small number of 'Dutch Proprietors'
who, for various reasons, had done relatively little to develop
their holdings agriculturally. Between 1825 and 1828 the situation regarding these large estates remained confused and uncertain whilst the British officials sought to ascertain the true
rights of the landholders. In 1828 the Government decided to
take over the land and compensate the proprietors financially.
Land laws were introduced in 1830 and in fact, had been in
force as a temporary measure since 1828. These laws however,
represented an attempted compromise between the English and
Malay tenure systems and merely served to cause increased
confusion during the 1830's and 1840's.[65] These circumstances
gave little encouragement to planters to indulge in the heavy,
long-term investment required to establish spice plantations.

Other factors militating against the development of spice
planting at Malacca included the relatively limited labour
supply available and the fact that Malacca had a very much
smaller European population than either Singapore or Penang.
At no time during the first three-quarters of the nineteenth
century did Malacca have an active, enthusiastic and enterprising resident European planting community either amateur or
professional of the type that appeared in the other two Settlements. Moreover, Malacca was of little commercial importance
by the early nineteenth century. It therefore did not offer the
scope for the accumulation of capital that could be invested

---

[64] Cameron, op. cit. 394.

[65] Mills, op. cit. 118-36. For the extent of these large holdings in Malacca
see the map facing page 246 in Moor, *Notices of the Indian
Archipelago*.

in spice planting that existed in its sister Settlements; indeed, in 1834 it was remarked that 'capital and energy seem wanting in order to raise any considerable quantity' of spices.[66] Malacca, in fact, shared few of the advantages of either Penang or Singapore as a centre of spice cultivation.

The Decline of Nutmeg Planting in Penang and Singapore

Nutmeg planting declined very rapidly both in Penang and Singapore during the 1850's. The conditions necessary for the success of this form of agriculture as a long-term venture were numerous and complex; from the very beginning the planters faced serious difficulties many of which in their ignorance they tended to discount. Eventually the problems reached such great proportions that the planters came to believe that neither the soil nor the climate of the Straits Settlements were suited to this branch of agriculture. By the 1860's it was the general opinion that the nutmeg had proved 'a most disastrous deception' to all who had engaged in its cultivation.[67]

To a large extent the expansion of spice planting in the Straits Settlements resulted from the efforts of a small group of European residents anxious that the development of export agriculture should provide them with a remunerative local investment. These people were mostly amateur planters and although many of them were 'of that class of lower English gentry accustomed to the management of land', in general they had very little experience of tropical crops or of agriculture under tropical conditions.[68] Nor for that matter was there a pool of local experience or an existing labour force with the requisite skills to which they could turn for guidance. As Dr. Little said in the late 1840's, 'all is novelty with us, there are no records of the past to guide us, while the recorded experience and science of the west is little else than a dead letter'.[69]

[66] *Singapore Chronicle*, N.S., Vol. 4 No. 20, 15 May 1834.

[67] C. Collingwood, 'On Nutmeg and other Cultivation in Singapore', *Journal of the Linnean Society (Botany)*, Vol. X No. 41, 1867, 48; *S.F.P.*, Vol. 27 No. 23, 7 June 1860; Cameron, op. cit. 164.

[68] Wheatley, op. cit. 64.

[69] R. Little, 'Diseases of the Nutmeg Tree', *J.I.A.*, Vol. 3, 1849, 679.

The development of the type of agriculture envisaged by the European residents of the British settlements in the first half of the nineteenth century was greatly inhibited by the official policy towards the granting of land. The European settlers did not look for quick returns in the manner of the Chinese pioneer planters; their intention was the long-term development of landed property which they could regard as their own and which would increase in value with time.[70] One of the attractions of nutmeg planting was that, as a long-term venture, it fitted their picture of an agricultural enterprise. Only later did they begin to realize that the value of agricultural land in Malaya was based on the 'permanently exportable products derivable from the durable plants and trees actually growing upon it. Divest the land of this permanency in its products, and the capital is lost'.[71] Land was only worth having whilst it could produce suitable returns, a fact clearly recognized by the Chinese pioneers.

A nutmeg plantation required a considerable investment and could be expected to yield satisfactory returns for more than twenty years. The planters therefore needed security of tenure for at least the economic life of the plantation. In Penang a large area of land was obtained by Europeans on favourable terms in the late eighteenth and early nineteenth centuries. In Singapore however, land was granted, for the most part, on short-term leases and the general uncertainty caused by the frequent changes in the regulations during the 1830's merely increased the exasperation of local planters. In the later years of the decade the Singapore planters agitated for longer leases, firm in the belief that an agricultural holding should be a permanent asset. In 1840 it was decided to grant land on twenty-year leases, renewable for a further thirty years on certain conditions. The planters were still not satisfied with these terms and, as a result of further complaints, in 1842 the acting Governor proposed the alienation in fee-simple of all agricultural land within two miles of the town limits at the rate of ten rupees per acre and of all land further away at five rupees

[70] See, for example, *Singapore Chronicle*, N.S., Vol. 7 No. 39, 30 September 1837.
[71] *S.F.P.*, Vol. 6 No. 47, 25 November 1841.

per acre. These proposals, which also affected Penang and Province Wellesley, were approved by the Government of India in 1843.[72] The introduction of these new land terms removed one of the major obstacles to the expansion of nutmeg planting in the 1830's and contributed directly to the thoughtless planting 'mania' at both Settlements that characterized the subsequent decade.

The land problem was solved but many other difficulties remained. Not the least of these was the need for a skilled labour force. Spice cultivation was labour-intensive for the plants needed to be carefully tended at every stage of their growth. Both nutmegs and cloves were planted initially in nurseries where they were watered and weeded frequently. After a minimum of six months they were planted out and a small *atap* shed was built to shade each seedling. In Penang cloves and nutmegs were often grown together on the same plantation and on the steeper slopes they were planted on terraces supported by granite boulders. Elsewhere cloves were of little importance and although the nutmeg trees were usually planted on hillsides to ensure adequate drainage the slopes were not such as to require terracing.

The labour force was continuously employed in caring for a plantation even after the seedlings had been transplanted and Oxley warned that the planter 'having set out all his trees must not deem his labours completed, they are only commencing'. Indeed, the trees had to be patiently watched and tended for at least a further ten years. One of the main tasks involved keeping the ground scrupulously free of weeds, a difficult job under humid tropical conditions. The young trees were also heavily manured by digging a trench around each one and filling it with cow dung, cut grass, pig manure, prawn dust, fish refuse or bat guano, depending on which was available locally. Moreover, it was considered necessary that during the first six years the plants should be 'trenched around three times, enlarging the circle each time', in order to loosen the soil to allow the roots to spread. Other recurrent tasks included removing the moss from the trunks annually, removing white

[72] *S.F.P.*, Vol. 5 No. 24, 11 June 1840; Makepeace and others, op. cit. Vol. 1, 310.

ants and all other insects and their eggs, and pruning to remove all perpendicular shoots and decaying branches.[73]

A large labour force was still required when the plants came into bearing. In the Straits Settlements nutmeg trees tended to fruit all the year round and once the nuts were ripe they had to be collected within a few days otherwise they fell off and began to deteriorate. On most plantations the nuts were collected daily, and this work had to be done by hand. Oxley maintained that once a nutmeg plantation had come into bearing an average of one labourer was required to care for every one hundred trees, 'provided there be some 4 to 5 thousand trees' on the plantation;[74] many European-owned plantations contained this many trees (Table 9). Labour costs therefore absorbed a major part of the investment needed to establish and maintain a spice plantation. In this respect the Straits planters faced a dual problem for on the one hand labour was expensive, the average monthly wage-rates in Singapore being two to three times higher than those paid in India and Java, and on the other hand there was a dearth of suitably skilled labour.[75] It was probably for these reasons that some European planters contracted with Chinese to work their plantations.

In contrast to cultivation and harvesting, processing the nutmeg fruit was a relatively simple and inexpensive matter. Within the husk the nutmeg was surrounded by a lace-work or aril known as the mace, the commercial nutmeg representing in effect, the kernel. When the nuts had been collected the mace was removed carefully, compressed and flattened on a board. It was then exposed to the sun for three or four days after which it was ready for export. The nutmeg itself required greater care. It was usually smoked over slow fires in a drying house for a couple of months to ensure that it was completely dry and then exported as quickly as possible. The nutmegs and mace produced in Penang were very highly regarded in the markets of Europe and this did much to encourage the expansion of planting in the 1840's.

Labour problems were not the sole difficulty facing the Straits

[73] Oxley, op. cit. 648 and 650-4.
[74] Ibid. 651.
[75] *Singapore Chronicle*, N.S., Vol. 7 No. 36, 9 September 1837.

planters. Dr. Oxley, himself a nutmeg planter, maintained that manure was 'beyond all other considerations the most important to the welfare of an estate; it is that which gives quantity and quality of produce, and without it a plantation cannot be carried on'. It is clear, in fact, that both nutmeg and clove trees remained 'stunted and almost unproductive, unless constantly cultivated and highly manured'.[76]

The Benkulen spice planters were recommended to keep herds of cattle to supply the large amounts of manure required on the plantations; indeed, the best manure for spice plantations was considered to be 'well rotted stable and cow yard manure mixed with vegetable matter'.[77] This type of manure was in short supply in the Straits Settlements and the planters turned to various alternatives. Extensive use was made of cut grass as a green manure and, in Singapore at least, it was fortunate that they had 'this never failing resource, since *cattle* manure could not be obtained in sufficient quantity or at a fair price'.[78] Oxley experimented with bat guano which he found unsuitable although it was used by some planters in Penang and the Province. The Chinese planters relied mainly on pig manure and night soil; prawn dust and fish refuse were widely used at the northern Settlement. In general, however, suitable types of manure were scarce, and as nutmeg planting extended in the 1830's and 1840's this scarcity became more acute. As a result the price of manure rose to very high levels thus increasing total operative costs.

The nutmeg tree is dioecious and only female trees produce nuts. It was impossible for the planters to determine which trees were female until they began to flower in their sixth or seventh year. Thus, the planters had to care for all the trees when they were young in the full knowledge that on average about half would prove to be male and therefore useless. Opinion differed as to the proportion of male trees that should be maintained in a plantation to ensure adequate fertilization. But whatever ratio was adopted it was necessary to remove many of the male trees

[76]Oxley, op. cit. 649; 'Agriculture of Singapore', *J.I.A.*, Vol. 3, 1849, 510.
[77] J. Lumsdaine, 'Cultivation of Nutmegs and Cloves in Bencoolen', *J.I.A.*, Vol. 5, 1851, 84; Oxley, op. cit. 649.
[78] *S.F.P.*, Vol. 6 No. 46, 18 November 1841.

when these began to flower and to replace them with new seed-lings, some of which would also ultimately prove to be male and have to be removed. A tremendous amount of time, money and effort was therefore required before a plantation was stock-ed with the desirable proportion of male and female trees. Indeed, Low considered that 'the originally contemplated number of bearing trees cannot well be established until the 20th or 25th year at least, after the plantation was begun'.[79] Chinese reaction to this problem was to cut out every tree that did not bear fruit.

The risks involved in spice planting were enhanced by the long period that the planters had to wait for their returns. Ordinarily neither cloves nor nutmegs began to fruit until they were between five and nine years old. The latter reached peak production in about their fifteenth year and could be expected to yield satisfactory returns for a further ten to twenty years, the amounts obtained depending very much on the degree of attention given to the plantation since its inception. As with all slow-maturing crops the planters had no guarantee that prices would stand at a remunerative level when their planta-tions began to yield. There seems little doubt that during the nutmeg 'mania' the planters, in their ignorance, minimized the risks involved. Indeed, in 1841 a contemporary observer warned that 'the chances of having the *capital* returned have scarcely ever been duly balanced by planters when beginning—for they seem to have acquiesced pretty generally in the delusion that two or three crops would repay both capital and interest'.[80]

Estimates of the rate of investment required to establish a nutmeg plantation in the 1840's and the probable returns that could be expected vary considerably, some being more optimis-tic than others. Specific income-expenditure figures exist how-ever, for W. Cuppage's plantation at Emerald Hill in the Claymore district of Singapore (Fig. 22). Work began on this plantation in mid-1837 and from then until December 1846, when it began to yield, it cost the owner a total of $4,200. This planter had to wait until 1848 before his annual income from

[79] Low, 'Notes on the Progress of the Nutmeg Cultivation and Trade', 482.
[80] S.F.P., Vol. 6 No. 47, 25 November 1841.

the plantation exceeded his annual expense in maintaining it, and he had to wait until 1852 before he made a net profit on the operation.[81] This plantation was not unusual and it would seem that generally the planters had to wait at least fifteen years before they realized a profit on the venture. The rate of investment was high, the returns far-off and uncertain.

TABLE 11

NUTMEG AND MACE PRICES QUOTED IN SINGAPORE, 1831-63

(Prices in Spanish Dollars per Pikul)

Date	Nutmegs	Mace
June 1831	65-70	70-80
January 1836	100-120	130-140
January 1837	100-120	120-130
January 1839	120-145	120-145
January 1840	75-105	100-120
January 1841	80-120	80-120
January 1844	80-90	90-100
January 1846	20-60	20-60
January 1847	65-85	60-65
January 1849	75	75
January 1851	56-63	44-45
January 1855	58	55
December 1858	45-47	42
January 1860	43	30
December 1863	38	19

Source: 'Prices Current' in the relevant issues of Singapore Chronicle, Singapore Free Press, Penang Gazette and Straits Times.

Although nutmeg and mace prices were exceptionally high in the late 1830's, they fell almost continuously during the next two decades (Table 11). Thus, the plantations established during the planting 'mania' came into bearing when market conditions were deteriorating. Much of the Straits produce was destined for the markets of Britain and Europe. The consumption of both nutmegs and mace in Britain increased markedly during the first thirty years of the nineteenth century; but, as supply began to exceed demand prices fell. By the mid-1840's the European market was glutted as a result of expanding pro-

[81] Thomson, 'General Report on the Residency of Singapore', 38-39.

duction in the Dutch Spice Islands and the stocks in hand in
Holland 'amounted to more than one year's consumption'.[82]
Production in Penang and Singapore soared at a time when
world demand showed few signs of increasing.

As early as 1837 Low warned the Straits planters that the
consumption of nutmegs and mace was unlikely to keep pace
with production but his warning was generally ignored.[83]
Twelve years later, when prices had fallen as he prophesied,
they were still sufficient to give the planter 'a fair and moderate
profit on his outlay'. But, it was now recognized that conditions
were worsening and the attitude of the British Government
towards the entry of Straits, Dutch and 'wild' nutmegs came
under heavy criticism.

In the early 1830's spices produced in British overseas possessions entered the home market at duties lower than those
charged on foreign produce. By the late 1840's, however, all
imported 'cultivated' nutmegs were subject to a duty of 2s 6d
per pound on entering Britain. This put both Straits and Dutch
produce on equal terms in the British market. The planters of
Singapore and Penang were confident that their produce was
superior to that of the Dutch Spice Islands; they felt, nevertheless, that they should be accorded some preference, not least
because nutmeg cultivation 'was at first undertaken at the
instance and with direct encouragement from Government, in
order to render Great Britain independent of the Dutch monopoly'.[84]

What worried them more, however, were 'the rapid strides'
that the 'wild' nutmeg was making in the British market for
the latter was subject to a duty of only 5d per pound on entering
Britain and could, therefore, be sold to the public at 2s 1d per
pound cheaper. As a result, sales of 'wild' nutmegs were increasing at the expense of the 'cultivated' type. Nevertheless, the
differential duty was maintained by the British Government
despite further protests from the Straits planters in the 1850's,
and despite the fact that there was a widespread and well-

[82] Thomson, 'General Report on the Residency of Singapore', 33-37.
[83] S.F.P., Vol. 2 No. 39, 28 September 1837.
[84] Singapore Chronicle, N.S., Vol. 4 No. 20, 15 May 1834; S.F.P., Vol. 14
No. 43, 26 October 1849.

founded belief that the so-called 'wild' nutmegs were not, in fact, uncultivated, but originated from the plantations in the Dutch Spice Islands.[85] At a time when market conditions became increasingly difficult the Straits planters received no help from the British Government.

All contemporary accounts lay most of the blame for the decay and rapid disappearance of the nutmeg plantations on the spread of disease. The 'nutmeg canker' first appeared in both Penang and Singapore in the 1840's. At that time however, most of the trees were still young and gave the impression of being in a flourishing condition, apparently promising good returns, for the disease had its most noticeable effects on bearing trees.[86] Thus, planting activities continued although the disease was already present. As an increasing number of trees came into bearing the 'canker' began to affect wider areas; apart from destroying trees, it also caused the nuts to open prematurely and since they were therefore unripe they were of little value. By the mid-1850's the disease had appeared on a large proportion of the trees in Singapore and in Penang

... disease [had] much spread amongst nutmeg plantations generally, while in several localities—as Bukit Gambier, Ayer Itam, Low's Pass, Bali Pulo and Telo Kumbar—it [had] affected considerable tracts, and many contiguous plantations ... [were] now in such a condition that no man of prudence and decision would hesitate to abandon their cultivation and replace them with some other plant.[87]

By the end of the decade every plantation was suffering from the ravages of this disease. In Penang the European planters were inclined to blame the Chinese 'squatters' for the problem, and the fact that almost all the smaller Chinese-owned plantations in the districts of Ayer Itam and Ayer Puteh were seriously affected by 1855 with, in several cases, more than a third of the trees destroyed, apparently supported their belief.[88]

[85] *S.F.P.*, Vol. 22 No. 5, 1 February 1855.
[86] *S.F.P.*, Vol. 14 No. 48, 30 November 1849; Little, op. cit. 679-80.
[87] *Penang Gazette*, Vol. 13 No. 21, 26 May 1855; ibid. No. 13, 3 March 1855.
[88] *Penang Gazette*, Vol. 13 No. 13, 3 March 1855; ibid. No. 38, 29 September 1855.

But the 'nutmeg canker' also spread rapidly on the European-owned plantations, both in Singapore and Penang; to a large extent this is attributable to the general ignorance of correct cultivation methods and to the inability of the planters to diagnose its cause.

Some suggested that the 'canker' was the result of over-manuring. Others believed that the trees died off 'because the soil did not extend deep enough, and the roots rotted away in the hard clay underneath it'. It was also suggested that the original stock introduced in the early nineteenth century had deteriorated and that 'an infusion of fresh seed from the parent soil might tend to rectify the evil'. Dr. Oxley was therefore sent to Banda in May 1855 to bring back a large supply of fresh seed nuts; since the diagnosis was wrong, the remedy proved ineffective.[89] Several other less credible theories were advanced, including a suggestion that the clearance of hill jungle had produced a change in climate which had damaging effects on the trees.

The nutmeg tree was subject to attacks by a variety of insects and Ridley confirmed earlier suspicions when he contended that the fatal 'disease' was actually the work of a small beetle, *Phloeosinus cribratus*.[90] It is highly likely, therefore, that the spread of disease in the 1840's and 1850's occurred in the following manner. During the planting 'mania' cultivation extended rapidly and many people entered the field with little or no agricultural experience. They were attracted by high prices and the prospects of a good investment. When prices fell and simultaneously trees began to die disappointment and apathy replaced the earlier enthusiasm. The full maintenance of a plantation was costly and many planters began to withdraw their attention. The lack of sufficient care caused plantations to deteriorate and so become increasingly prone to the attacks of this beetle, and the inability of the planters to diagnose the cause of the 'canker' greatly aided its extension. Ultimately, nutmeg cultivation failed because it was in the hands of inexperienced amateurs.

[89] *A.R.S.S., 1855-6,* 18.
[90] Ridley, *Spices,* 126-7.

By the early 1860's many of the plantations in Penang had been abandoned or replanted with other crops, including coconuts and fruit trees. In his report on Penang and Province Wellesley for 1860 the Governor, Cavenagh, noted that more than 6,000 acres had been 'thrown out of cultivation' and that large tracts in the hilly country had been 'totally abandoned'.[91] In Singapore the planters abandoned their plantations in disgust, in many cases while there were still many healthy trees, and the land reverted to the Government.

In other cases, where expensive bungalows had been built upon the estate, they were sold for a small proportion of the sums expended in building them, since they were, as a rule, too far from town to command any competition, and ceased to be conveniently situated. Many planters, both English and Chinese, whose whole estates were invested in nutmeg-plantations, were thus reduced to ruin, and absolutely penniless; and distress and disappointment everywhere prevailed.[92]

Spice planting was abandoned completely by the European residents at both Settlements. It was eventually revived on a smaller scale in Penang over a decade later by Chinese planters, chiefly Hakkas, and has continued to be of minor importance in the agricultural economy of this area to the present day.[93]

[91] A.R.S.S., 1861-2, 36; A.R.S.S., 1860-1, 20.

[92] Collingwood, op. cit. 48. By the later 1850's several of the European plantations in Singapore were offered for sale, some for building purposes. Straits Times, Vol. 12 No. 816, 28 October 1856.

[93] F.R. Mason, 'The Clove and Nutmeg Industry in Penang and Province Wellesley', M.A.J., Vol. 19, 1931, 4-8.

7

SUGAR PLANTING, 1820-67

WHEREAS THE EUROPEAN VENTURE into spice production in the early nineteenth century was destined to fail, considerable success was achieved by those planters who engaged in sugar growing in Province Wellesley. In the other British Settlements, however, sugar, as with spices, brought financial loss to those who desired to establish permanent agricultural estates. Unlike the spice cultivators of Penang and Singapore the European sugar planters of Province Wellesley adopted an agricultural enterprise whose potentialities had already been revealed by Chinese pioneers.

Chinese Pioneers in Province Wellesley, 1820-60

Chinese sugar estates may have existed on Batu Kawan Island before Province Wellesley was ceded to the British in 1800.[1] Clearly the Chinese initiated the sugar industry in this area, but its development dates principally from the third decade of the nineteenth century.

In 1875 J. Thomson noted that the Chinese were 'the first who reared the cane, and refined the sugar in quantities sufficient to make it a leading article of export'.[2] The American Consul in Singapore, writing after a visit to the Province Wellesley estates in 1896, maintained that the cultivation of sugar 'as a product of export was first commenced by *some Chinese from Swatow*, who ... settled in the central and southern portion of the Province of Wellesley'.[3]

---

[1] *Penang Gazette*, Vol. XIV No. 8, 23 February 1856; Purcell, *Chinese in Malaya*, 51 and 66; J. Low, 'An Account of the Origins and Progress of the British Colonies in the Straits of Malacca', *J.I.A.*, Vol. 3, 1849, 617 and Vol. 4, 1850, 378.

[2] J. Thomson, *The Straits of Malacca, Indo-China and China*, London, 1875, 27.

[3] *S.F.P.*, 3rd Series, No. 442, 14 January 1896. The italics have been inserted.

As in Thailand, estate sugar cultivation was probably introduced by Tiechius. There was, in fact, a traditional Tiechiu specialization in plantation agriculture and in the early nineteenth century this group were the agriculturalists and plantation workers *par excellence* throughout South-East Asia. Moreover, during the nineteenth century the Tiechiu region of south China was known for its production of sugar for export so that this dialect group had acquired the skills necessary for cane cultivation and processing.[4]

Most, if not all, the pioneer Chinese sugar estates in Province Wellesley were opened between 1810 and 1820 and probably in the later years of that decade.[5] The first estates were established on flat, very low-lying, mangrove-covered land in the northern part of Batu Kawan Island and immediately to the north of nearby Bukit Tambun (Fig. 23). That the industry gained a firm foothold and had begun to expand during the 1820's and 1830's is suggested by an increase of the Chinese population of the Province from 325 in 1820 to 2,259 in 1833. It was remarked in 1841 that

Before many years had passed a colony of petty planters was established, a plain of about 1,000 acres was cleared, on which a population of more than 2,000 Chinese settled, and sugar was manufactured to the extent of from 600 to 700 tons annually.... The prosperity of the planters, many of whom after a few years carried away a competent fortune to their native country, attested that the employment was lucrative in a high degree.[6]

With the advent of European planters during the 1840's further expansion of the Chinese-owned sugar estates was restricted. In 1858 they still comprised about 1,000 acres, yielding approximately one ton of sugar per acre, but no rum.[7] At this

[4] See G.W. Skinner, *Chinese Society in Thailand: An Analytical History*, New York, 1957, 46.

[5] *Penang Gazette*, 4 September 1841 quoted in *S.F.P.*, Vol. 6 No. 40, 7 October 1841; Thomson, 'General Report on the Residency of Singapore', 140; G.W. Earl, *Topography and Itinerary of Province Wellesley*, Penang, 1861, 32.

[6] *Penang Gazette*, 4 September 1841 quoted in *S.F.P.*, Vol. 6 No. 40, 7 October 1841.

[7] T. Braddell, *Singapore and the Straits Settlements Described*, Penang, 1858, 3.

time the traditional buffalo mills on the Chinese estates supplied
nearly all the sugar used for local consumption. In the 1850's
and 1860's Chinese-owned sugar estates continued to be located
principally in the areas in which they were first established.
Thus, there were Chinese estates in the northern part of Batu
Kawan Island, to the south of the village of Bukit Tengah there
were 'cane-patches belonging to Chinese establishments of old
standing', where there were about eighty Chinese planting
sugar in the mid-forties, and there were small Chinese sugar
estates at Badak Mati and along the road from Simpang Ampat
to Bukit Tambun[8] (Fig. 25A).

Early Chinese Methods of Cultivation and Processing

These early Chinese planters grew the *tebu kapor* or 'Selangor
cane'. Cultivation was labour-intensive and labour costs formed
the major part of the investment needed to establish and maintain an estate. Low estimated that in the mid-1830's it required
a capital outlay of 9,700 Spanish dollars to bring 100 *orlongs*
(i.e. 133⅓ acres) of cane to maturity in fourteen months. The
largest item of expenditure in his estimate comprised the wages
of fifty Chinese labourers paid at a rate of five Spanish dollars
each per month. One labourer was required to care for two
orlongs of cane which would eventually produce about forty-
eight pikuls of clayed sugar when the canes were ripe.[9]

In opening new lands for planting the Chinese cleared and
burnt the jungle and undergrowth and then removed the remaining roots and stumps. These were piled in heaps, covered
with earth and burnt, and the ashes and burnt earth were
scattered over the cleared land which was then 'dug and
thoroughly turned up' by hand-hoeing. Because of the location
of these estates on the low-lying and often flooded coastal
alluvium, trenches were dug around the cleared land to drain
it and 'at the same time to keep out all water from the adjacent

[8] Earl, *Topography and Itinerary*, 25; J.R. Logan, 'Journal of an Excursion from Singapur to Malacca and Pinang', *Miscellaneous Papers
Relating to Indo-China and the Indian Archipelago*, 2nd Series, Vol. 1,
1887, 19.
[9] Low, *Dissertation on the Soil and Agriculture*, 52-53.
[10] L. Wray, *The Practical Sugar Planter*, London, 1848, 41-42.

lands'. After a second *changkoling* (hoe-digging) the canes were planted out.[10]

As the plants grew trenches one to two feet deep were dug between the rows, and putrid fish, bat guano and prawn dust were applied as manure. On average there were about 2,500 bunches of cane per acre, each bunch containing five to ten canes. Usually the canes reached maturity in about fourteen months in the more favourable areas although it could take as much as sixteen to eighteen months in less favourable localities. The early Chinese planters did not allow *ratoons*[11] to grow and therefore after taking one crop they either planted new canes on the same land or, as was more usual, abandoned it and began again on fresh land.[12] Whilst April and May (the secondary rainfall maximum in this area) were generally regarded as the best months for planting, the Chinese planted cane throughout the year for, as Low observed in the mid-1830's they 'cannot afford to be regular, and were all the canes ripe at once, they would not have a sufficiency of mills to clear them off'.[13]

The Chinese watched the market very closely and produced clayed sugar when prices were high and a coarse black sugar when prices were low. In the mid-1830's, under favourable prices, 'the average quantity of clayed sugar, manufactured in the season of from 14 to 16 months, may be estimated at eleven thousand piculs on an average, or about 65.4 tons, and from four to five thousand piculs of coarse black sugar'.[14] Although this was insignificant in comparison with contemporary production in the West Indies, Low believed that it was nevertheless encouraging for it was the result of 'the labor, in a new country, of freemen whose tastes are even luxurious, on a tract of land, which, but a few years ago, was a wild forest.'[15]

At this time the Chinese were the 'sole sugar-makers' at the

[11] I.e. fresh shoots from the base of the harvested cane from which a further crop could be harvested.

[12] E.g. *A.R.S.S.*, *1857-8*, 75. In this report Moniot, the Surveyor-General, describes the Chinese sugar cultivators as 'petty planters who are satisfied with one crop from each spot they clear'.

[13] Low, *Dissertation on the Soil and Agriculture*, 51-52.

[14] Ibid. 49.

[15] Ibid. 50.

northern Settlement. Their processing methods were 'very imperfect and would by a West India planter, be thought rude, slovenly and inefficient'.[16] Significantly, the apparatus used by the Chinese in Malaya bears an unmistakably close resemblance to that used widely in south China during the nineteenth century.[17]

The Chinese sugar mill consisted of two granite or wooden vertical rollers some two feet in diameter resting on a wooden platform. These were driven by a pair of buffaloes working on a long crooked beam connected to a central axis. Six buffaloes were attached to each mill, and they worked in pairs in shifts. The canes were carried to the mill by labourers and were cut into convenient lengths so that one man could feed in the cane at one side of the rollers and another could remove the pressed cane at the opposite side. The inefficiency of the mills required that the canes be passed through three times before all the juice had been extracted. The resultant waste was usually used for firewood, especially when fuel prices were high, but in some cases it was used for pig-fodder. A barrel was sunk into the ground to receive the expressed cane juice.

The open shed covering the mill also contained the boiling apparatus which consisted of a brick and mortar fire-place and three iron boilers. The cane juice was carried in pails from the rollers to the boilers. No particular attention was paid to temperature during processing, 'the whole being *guessed*, by the force of practice', and if the juice appeared to boil too much, coconut oil was added. Processing by the early Chinese sugar planters was based therefore on skill and experience and not upon scientific method; the methods were traditional rather than primitive.

After being boiled and allowed to cool in each of the first two boilers the juice passed to the last boiler in which it was re-boiled with a little shell-lime and then poured into a cooler.

[16] Ibid. 50-51.

[17] See H.C. Prinsen Geerligs, *The World's Cane Sugar Industry, Past and Present*, Altrincham, 1912, 74, where the process used in China is described as follows: 'The cane is ground between two vertical wooden or stone rollers, which are turned by cattle, and the cane has to go through three times before being crushed sufficiently.'

Later, it was slowly drained off into conical porous jars, one layer being allowed partially to crystallize before a second was added. The jars were placed on a wooden platform and during the next twelve or fifteen days the molasses gradually drained off and were collected in a large barrel. Subsequently the surface sugar was scraped off every few days and placed in the sun to dry.[18]

These methods appear extremely inefficient when compared with the highly capitalized and complex factories used on the later European-owned estates. Nevertheless, it is probably the fact that they required relatively little capital investment which permitted the Chinese-owned estates to continue after the advent of European planters and which placed them in a comparatively stronger position when prices were low. Many Chinese returned from the sugar plantations to China 'with well-filled purses'.[19] Had they considered it financially worthwhile they would have adopted the processing methods employed on the European-owned estates at an earlier date than they did. In fact, it was not until the 1860's that they began to replace the traditional buffalo-driven mills with steam machinery.

Unsuccessful European Ventures in Singapore and Malacca

The high price of sugar at about the time of the emancipation of the slaves in the West Indies first induced European planters to attempt the cultivation of sugar cane in the Straits Settlements. The soil and climate were apparently suitable, labour was comparatively cheap and plentiful and there was the example of success, on a small scale, among the Chinese. Moreover, sugar appeared to offer a brighter future than most other crops had done so far.

The first European sugar estates were commenced in Singapore in 1836, in Penang in 1838 and in Province Wellesley in

---

[18] This account of early Chinese processing methods is based mainly on Low, *Dissertation on the Soil and Agriculture*, 49-53. Additional material has been taken from Cameron, op. cit 338-40.

[19] Low, *Dissertation on the Soil and Agriculture*, 58.

1840.[20] These early estates in the Straits Settlements were denied the preferential import duty accorded under the Sugar Act of 1836 to the sugar and rum imported into the the United Kingdom from other parts of the Empire. After agitation by the Penang planters this preferential duty was extended to the Straits Settlements with the exception of Singapore in 1846. The latter was excluded because it served as an entrepot for sugar from China, Java and Manila, and it was therefore impossible to distinguish locally-produced sugar from re-exports. The extension of this preferential duty to the Straits Settlements at a time when the nutmeg 'mania' was waning caused a very marked expansion of European sugar planting in Province Wellesley in the late 1840's and 1850's and also an abortive attempt to establish estates in Malacca. At the same time its exclusion of Singapore contributed directly to the failure of the estates on that island.

Singapore

Large-scale sugar cultivation was first commenced by two European planters in Singapore in 1836 at a time when a passion for agricultural development gripped its European inhabitants. William Montgomerie[21] began the Kallangdale Estate and Joseph Balestier[22] began the Balestier Estate on the low-lying clayey soils to the north and north-east of the town in an area labelled 'partly cleared for Sugar and Cotton plantations' on a map produced in the 1830's[23] (Fig. 24).

Sugar was produced by Chinese methods at Kallangdale in 1838, and on a large scale using West Indian methods in 1840. Locally-produced sugar appears to have been first exported from Singapore to Britain in 1841. Montgomerie persevered with Chinese contract labour on this estate and for a time achieved

---

[20] Thomson, 'General Report on the Residency of Singapore', 140; *Penang Gazette*, 4 September 1841 quoted in *S.F.P.*, Vol. 6 No. 40, 7 October 1841; Braddell, *Statistics*, 13.

[21] Dr. William Montgomerie, Senior Surgeon and formerly honorary Superintendent of the Singapore Botanic Gardens.

[22] American Consul in Singapore from 1836 to 1852.

[23] Coleman's Map, Buckley, op. cit. Vol. 1, opposite page 312.

a limited success, exporting sugar to Britain and Australia. The estate was worked by a contract system 'in which he gives the ground to the Chinese, who plant and cultivate the cane, at their own expense; on the manufacture of their crop, he pays them at the rate of $1\frac{1}{2}$ Spanish dollars per picul ($133\frac{1}{3}$ lbs.) for the Raw Sugar (that is sugar undrained of the molasses)'.[24] Montgomerie is reported to have obtained 55.8 pikuls of dry sugar from every 100 pikuls of raw sugar. This contract system is very similar to that employed by the European planters in Province Wellesley (see later), and the methods of cultivation adopted by the Chinese contractors were not unlike those used by their counter-parts in the Province. The estate had a water-power driven mill located to the east of a specially constructed canal linking the two arms of a meander of the Sungei Kallang, (Fig. 24); in 1847 it had an estimated planted area of 300 acres.[25]

Balestier was an ardent believer in the agricultural potentialities of Singapore. He invested large amounts of his own and borrowed capital in his estate, adopted all the most modern methods and equipment, and tried in every way to make it a showpiece of what an efficiently-run European estate should be. The Balestier Estate comprised a total of 1,000 acres of which 220 acres had been planted with sugar cane by 1848. It yielded an average of twenty to twenty-five pikuls of raw sugar per acre and two crops, one of planted canes and one of *ratoons,* were obtained in two years. Each 'field' was surrounded by a drainage ditch and these were connected to a canal, some two miles long, which ran through the whole estate and on which the canes were transported in boats to the mill (Fig. 24). The estate also contained a 'two-storey dwelling house for a large family', a house for the Superintendent and a well-equipped steam-power-ed factory and distillery. It was stocked with 'two Sydney horses and a young elephant used in ploughing; bulls and bullocks used to the plough and carts; carts and ploughs of various sizes'

[24] Thomson, 'General Report on the Residency of Singapore', 138-9; *Accounts and Papers,* 1849, Vol. L, C-351, *An Account of the Imports into the United Kingdom of Sugar, Molasses, Rum, Coffee and Cocoa, from the British West Indies, British Guiana, Mauritius, and the British Possessions in India for the Years 1831 to 1848.*

[25] Wray, *Practical Sugar Planter,* 125.

and numerous other aids to cultivation. The labour force consisted of both Chinese and Indians.[26]

Canes were introduced to Singapore from Mauritius by Joaquim d'Almeida in 1846. Like Balestier, d'Almeida believed that the soil and climate of Singapore were suited to sugar cultivation. He experimented with various types of cane in the late 1840's and imported 'China, Manila, Java, Siam, and Cochin-china canes but all . . . proved inferior (when grown in this climate) to the indigenous canes such as Tubu Liat [*tebu liat*], and Tubu Cappor [*tebu kapor*, the 'Selangor cane']'.[27] These experiments suffered the same fate as the two pioneer sugar estates on the island.

By the late 1840's the European sugar planters in Singapore were finding the preferential duties accorded to the Province Wellesley estates, but denied to them, inimical to further development. Balestier, with his highly capitalized estate which had 'swallowed up' his own money and much of that which he had acquired from Russell and Company of China, was facing financial ruin.[28] Nevertheless, he still waxed enthusiastic about the possibilities of sugar cultivation in Singapore. He claimed that the soil and climate of the island, if not ideal, were 'at least good', and that locally-produced sugar was 'in the London price current classed with that from Jamaica and obtaining in that market the same price.' It was his opinion that sugar planting in Singapore was 'stationary' because of the denial of the preferential duty and, ironically, because of 'the want of adequate capital to carry on the business on a large scale'.[29] Knowing that Balestier was in extreme financial difficulties when he made these comments, and that his estate was advertised for sale in April 1848, it is hard to believe that his optimistic claims were not backed by an ulterior motive. A few years later

---

[26] Based on an advertisement in the *Straits Times*, Vol. 4 No. 265, 8 April 1848. Much of the ploughing on this estate was done by a 5½-year old elephant, named 'Rajah', which could plough an acre in a day, an achievement that would have required at least fifty labourers. Wray, *Practical Sugar Planter*, 130.

[27] Thomson, 'General Report on the Residency of Singapore', 139.

[28] Buckley, *An Anecdotal History of Old Times in Singapore*, Singapore, 1902, Vol. 2, 483.

[29] Balestier, op. cit. 147-8.

J.T. Thomson, without a vested interest, observed that, even allowing for the preferential duty, Singapore presented 'a small field for this cultivation in comparison with the other Straits Settlements'. The soils suitable for sugar cultivation on the island, that is the low-lying alluvial soils, were of extremely limited extent, and 'can hardly exceed 3,000 acres'.[30]

It is unlikely that the area planted with sugar cane on the European estates in Singapore ever exceeded 600 acres. By 1849 the Balestier Estate had closed down. The Kallangdale Estate was advertised for sale in 1852; although it still functioned in 1860 it was only worked on a small scale.[31] Despite the extravagant claims made for the island, the two sugar estates opened by European planters using completely different methods of organization both resulted in financial loss for their owners.

Malacca

The extension of the preferential duty to the Straits Settlements, excluding Singapore, led to an attempt to introduce sugar planting on a large scale into Malacca in 1846-7. At this time there were a few Chinese planting sugar on a small scale in the state, and in March 1846 an advertisement was inserted in the *Singapore Free Press* by Chinese offering to contract to supply canes if a European would establish a factory in Malacca.[32] Soon after, applications were made by some wealthy Malacca Chinese and by several Europeans from Singapore and from Mauritius for about 20,000 acres of land for the purpose of sugar planting. Two large companies were proposed in addition to several private undertakings. One company, the Malacca Sugar Company, applied for a large tract of land on the Sungei Linggi. Another company was promoted by a planter with experience of the sugar industry in the West Indies, Bengal and the Straits. He selected 5,000 acres and 'prepared to follow the practice which had become usual in the cultivation of the crop'. This involved entering into contracts with Chinese, who cleared, planted and harvested the crop and then delivered it to the

[30] Thomson, 'General Report on the Residency of Singapore', 138.

[31] Braddell, *Statistics*, 18.

[32] *S.F.P.*, Vol. 11 No. 10, 5 March 1846.

entrepreneur's mills in return for a payment based upon the out-turn of sugar'.[33]

The local Government had long been plagued by land problems and was not prepared to entertain 'such extensive applications on the instant'; the matter was referred to the authorities in Bengal.[34] Grants on favourable terms were directed to be issued by the Bengal Government; the land was to be held rent-free for the first five years and thereafter at a rate of four annas per acre 'so long as there existed a sugar estate upon the land.'[35] But the land was never taken up because by the time that the reply was received from Bengal a fall in prices consequent upon 'the late mercantile distress in England' had altered the plans of the applicants.[36] Thus although the preferential duty was also applicable to Malacca, henceforth the interests of the sugar planters centred on the northernmost Settlement, and later on the adjacent parts of Perak.

Province Wellesley: Land of Promise

Europeans first made a successful entry into the sugar industry of the northern Settlement in the 1830's.[37] Initially they were involved only as processors when they opened two small water-power driven mills in the Water Fall Valley and the Ayer Itam district of Penang. A little later they also began to open estates. The first European sugar estate in Penang was the Otaheite Estate in the Ayer Itam valley commenced in 1838.[38] This experimental plantation was visited by planters from

[33] G.C. Allen and A.G. Donnithorne, *Western Enterprise in Indonesia and Malaya: A Study in Economic Development*, London, 1957, 107; see also Looi Sik Cheong, *The Sugar Industry in the Straits Settlements with special reference to Province Wellesley, 1840-1913*, B.A. Hons. Academic Exercise, University of Malaya (Singapore) 1961, 56-57.

[34] Braddell, *Statistics*, 18.

[35] *S.F.P.*, Vol. 11 No. 35, 27 August 1846.

[36] F.L. Baumgarten, 'Agriculture in Malacca', *J.I.A.*, Vol. 3, 1849, 707-8.

[37] An unsuccessful attempt was made to cultivate sugar cane on Penang soon after the founding of the Settlement. See Hunter, 'Plants of Prince of Wales' Island', 69.

[38] *S.F.P.*, 3rd Series, No. 442, 14 January 1896; *Penang Gazette*, Vol. XIV No. 8, 23 February 1856.

Mauritius and Bengal. Sugar of a 'better quality than had hitherto been produced in the Island was manufactured, sent to England and the report upon it was highly favourable and encouraging'.[39] Two years later the first European-owned sugar estate was opened in Province Wellesley and during 1841 over 6,500 acres of forest land in the Province was leased to Europeans for sugar planting. In that year it was maintained that the most fortunate result of the success of the Penang venture was that sugar planters in Mauritius were attracted to the Settlement; however, it was not until 1846 that cultivation was undertaken on a large scale on the mainland.

From the 1840's until the late 1870's sugar planting in Malaya concentrated almost entirely in the southern half of Province Wellesley. A combination of physical and economic advantages gave rise to this situation. The sugar produced on this strip of the mainland was accorded the preferential import duty when this was extended to the Straits Settlements in 1846 and it also lay in an advantageous position to export its produce to Britain via Penang.

For its successful cultivation sugar cane requires that 'a period of plentiful rain be succeeded by some months of dry weather, as otherwise the cane is unable to attain to full maturity'.[40] The northwest rainfall region of Malaya within which both Province Wellesley and Krian fall, is characterized by unusually low rainfall in December, January and February, following a period of maximum rainfall in October and November.[41] Moreover, the very flat, low-lying coastal alluvial soils of this area were of a type well-suited to cane cultivation. Balestier remarked that

... the natural fertility of the soil in Province Wellesley, which generally is level and little raised above the adjacent sea, assisted by abundance of fish, bat-guano and other manures, of which the Chinese avail largely, cause large returns from the land, amounting in some instances to three tons of raw sugar or gour per acre.[42]

[39] Penang Gazette, 4 September 1841 quoted in S.F.P., Vol. 6 No. 40, 7 October 1841.
[40] R.A. Quintus, The Cultivation of Sugar Cane in Java, London, 1923, 4.
[41] W.L. Dale, 'The Rainfall of Malaya, Part 1', J.T.G., Vol. 13, 1959, 35.
[42] Balestier, op. cit. 142.

Southern Province Wellesley also enjoyed topographic advantages for this area consists of very level, low-lying alluvium intersected by many rivers and streams. These facilitated drainage works. They also permitted the sugar planters to construct a complex network of canals upon which barges could be used to transport the bulky canes cheaply and quickly from the fields to the mills and from the mills to the place of shipment, thus reducing transport costs and minimizing loss by inversion. Canals were first constructed on the European-owned estates here in the 1840's; by the 1850's they had become a common feature.[43] A lengthy network of canals fed from the numerous rivers and streams was constructed on each estate; on the Prai Estate for example, there were nearly thirty-two miles of canals in 1908.[44] After processing at the factory the sugar and rum were conveyed along these canals to special shipping points from which they were dispatched to Penang for export.[45] The internal movement of harvested cane was a major difficulty on the estates in many of the world centres of sugar production in the nineteenth century; canal construction enabled the Province Wellesley planters to overcome this difficulty with ease.

The estates here were also favoured by an abundant supply of easily obtainable suitable fuel in the form of extensive mangrove forests along the coast (Fig. 25). This was in fact an important locational factor in the siting of new estates, and Earl prophesied correctly in 1860 that it was unlikely that sugar planting would extend much further inland 'as the cost of transporting fuel by land is very great, while near the coast the mangrove jungle furnishes an abundant supply which can be

---

[43] Wray, *Practical Sugar Planter*, 126; *A.R.S.S.*, *1859-60*, 17.

[44] A. Wright and H.A. Cartwright, eds., *Twentieth Century Impressions of British Malaya*, London, 1908, 369.

[45] E.g. on the Jawi Estate the shipping point was at Bagan Boya and on the Caledonia Estate at Sungei Daun. On the Batu Kawan Estate a special canal was cut from the factory to the Sungei Jajawi about half a mile above the Bukit Tambin ferry so that cargo boats could be loaded immediately from the factory. Earl, *Topography and Itinerary*, 28-29 and 33.

brought to the works by boats at a comparatively small expense'.[46]

Until the transfer of Government created problems in 1867, the estate owners in Province Wellesley did not suffer unduly from labour difficulties. The greater part of the planted area was worked by Chinese contractors with their own labour force (see later), and the Europeans could obtain sufficient Indian labour for the various factory tasks.

The marked concentration of sugar estates, both European- and Chinese-owned, in the southern half of Province Wellesley also reflects local settlement history. In the area to the north of the Sungei Juru, and particularly to the north of the Sungei Prai, Malays had already established extensive padi-fields prior to the arrival of the first European planters. Many of these padi-planters were refugees from Kedah who had fled from their homes at the time of the Siamese invasion in the early 1820's. Some of these were prepared to sell their land at low rates to European planters in the 1840's so that they could return to Kedah now that the Siamese had withdrawn. But the very fact that these northern areas were already occupied by padi-planters hindered the establishment of large sugar estates. It was Logan's opinion on his visit to the Province in the mid-1840's that it would take so long to arrange to buy up a large enough block of land to establish a sugar estate from the multitude of land-owners amongst whom the padi-land was subdivided as to make it virtually impossible to open an estate in northern Province Wellesley.[47] On the other hand, in the southern half of the Province, apart from the existing Chinese estates, there were large areas of easily obtainable unoccupied land; it was to these that most European planters were drawn.

Twenty Years of Expansion and Improvement

In 1846 there were five European-owned estates at work in the northern Settlement. The preferential duty was extended to Straits-produced sugar in that year and caused 'a sudden

[46] Ibid. 30.
[47] Logan, 'Journal of an Excursion from Singapur to Malacca and Pinang', 18-20.

impetus . . . to the cultivation of sugar-cane, which had hitherto been carried on at a great disadvantage'.[48]

In the twelve months ending in June 1846 eight new estates were opened in southern Province Wellesley.[49] Most of these were created from jungle but despite the difficulties some planters 'seemed inclined to purchase paddy-lands for making sugar plantations, rather than clear waste tracts for that purpose'.[50] By June 1846 eleven estates had been established in the southern half of the Province; three years later thirteen European-owned estates were at work in Penang and on the mainland, although two of these—the Otaheite Estate in Penang and the Labu Meriam Estate in the Province—were abandoned before 1860.[51] This expansion in the number of estates was accompanied by a marked increase in the exports of sugar from Penang to which the importation of sugar was prohibited in 1845. In 1843-4, 12,800 pikuls of locally-produced sugar were exported; by 1850-1 this had risen to 44,700 pikuls and to 68,300 pikuls in 1854-5 (Fig. 26).

Eleven large European-owned sugar estates existed in Province Wellesley in 1858. They occupied a total of 10,720 acres, of which about 4,500 acres were planted with cane, and produced annually about 4,000 tons of sugar and 200,000 gallons of rum.[52] Most of the sugar was exported to the United Kingdom, although occasionally large consignments were dispatched to China. The rum, which was an important source of revenue for the Province Wellesley planters, was mainly destined for neighbouring British colonial possessions, particularly Burma and India.

By this date the sugar industry had become a European-controlled enterprise. Most of the planted area and that held in reserve lay on European-owned estates, and the largest Chinese-owned estate in 1860 had about 500 acres under the cane.[53]

[48] Ibid. 18.
[49] Ibid. footnote on page 20.
[50] Ibid. 18.
[51] Braddell, *Statistics*, 13.
[52] Braddell, *Singapore and the Straits Settlements Described*, 2.
[53] Earl, *Topography and Itinerary*, 30.

Control of these European estates was almost equally divided between two different types of owner. On the one hand, there was a small group of local European residents for many of whom sugar had provided a welcome alternative to nutmegs and cloves and whose numbers had been augmented by the arrival of a few experienced planters from other sugar-producing areas, notably Mauritius. On the other hand, a block of estates comprising a total planted area of over 2,700 acres was owned in 1856 by the Right Honorable Edward Horsman, Member of Parliament and Privy Councillor, who never visited the Straits and employed resident European managers on these estates.[54] Horsman provides an early example of the London-based control of European-owned estates which became so widespread in the later years of the nineteenth century and the first two decades of the present century.

During the first half of the 1860's a severe drought caused output to decline and expansion was halted temporarily. By the mid-1860's, however, fresh tracts of mangrove forest were cleared in the southern parts of the Province and along the Sungei Prai. The area in the hands of the planters had increased to an estimated total of about 13,500 acres by 1866 and exports again began to increase.[55]

Many of the estates in Province Wellesley were opened or managed by Europeans who had learnt sugar planting before their arrival. Thus, Thomas Braddell, who went to Demerara to learn sugar planting in 1840, arrived in Penang in 1844 to manage the Otaheite Estate and Leopold Es. Chasseriau and Joseph Donadieu, both Frenchmen trained in sugar planting in Mauritius, opened estates in the Province during the 1840's.

It has been claimed that Europeans commenced sugar planting in Province Wellesley in the 1840's 'with very little knowledge of the capital required or the quality of soil needed'.[56] It is clear however, that some of those involved brought with them a knowledge of the methods used in established sugar-producing areas in other parts of the world, and in this respect the development of European interest in sugar planting differed

[54] *Penang Gazette*, Vol. XIV No. 6, February 1856.
[55] *A.R.S.S., 1863-4*, 30; *A.R.S.S., 1864-5*, 54; *A.R.S.S., 1865-6*, 45.
[56] *S.F.P.*, 3rd Series, No. 442, 14 January 1896.

from all their previous ventures into agriculture in Malaya. The arrival of professional planters, with experience of up-to-date methods and in contact with technical developments elsewhere, helped to put the industry on a sound footing and its success is at least partly attributable to their efforts.

The Otaheite cane (i.e. *tebu telor*), was grown on the first European estate in Penang, but this cane 'did not pay to manufacture into sugar' and it was mainly used for eating. The initial European estates in the Province followed the lead of the existing Chinese estates by planting the 'Selangor' cane. The advent of planters from Mauritius in the 1840's, however, heralded the introduction of the 'Mauritius' cane which was quickly taken up by all the European estates and by the 1880's had 'quite superseded the Selangor cane'.[57]

Much effort and money were expended in making the European-owned estates as up-to-date and efficient as possible and the planters freely adopted new techniques developed elsewhere. By 1859 the southern half of the Province was 'studded with sugar factories, superintended by European gentlemen, and furnished in many instances with expensive machinery of the newest description'.[58] The following year it was noted that 'improvements are being continually effected both in the system of manuring, etc., in the field, and in the machinery in use in the Factories',[59] and Earl observed that the European estates were all supplied with excellent machinery, including 'centrifugals' for drying the sugar, and 'all modern improvements short of vacuum pans, which are only now being introduced, the first being in the course of erection at the Caledonia estate on the Krian'. Some consideration had also been given to the health of the labour force for by 1860 there was a hospital on the Jawi Estate 'for the treatment of the sick coolies belonging to the different estates'.[60]

The expansion of sugar planting in Province Wellesley between the 1840's and the 1860's was characterized by the

---

[57] J.M. Vermont, 'List of Sugar-Canes known in Province Wellesley, Straits Settlements', *A.R. Penang, 1881*, Appendix No. 2.

[58] *A.R.S.S., 1859-60*, 17.

[59] *A.R.S.S., 1860-1*, 20.

[60] Earl, *Topography and Itinerary*, 27-28.

growth of European control and by the associated introduction of new ideas and techniques, particularly with regard to processing. Many of these originated in Mauritius or Demerara and the industry in the Province had connexions with these areas through planters who had learnt the industry there. This was a period during which the unoccupied tracts of southern Province Wellesley were acquired by newly-formed European sugar estates, and a period marked by the transformation of a small-scale, traditionally organized, pioneer Chinese enterprise into a highly capitalized, European-controlled estate industry with a flourishing export trade.

Dichotomy in the Sugar Industry: Cultivating and Processing

Sugar cultivation was labour intensive and on the Province Wellesley estates an average of one labourer was required to care for every two and a half acres of cane. Indigenous labour was considered unsuitable for work on the estates and Indian labour was not available in sufficient quantities, so that the Chinese had a 'monopoly of field work' in the sugar industry of the Province.[61] As the industry became increasingly European controlled a marked division occurred between cultivating and processing. The traditional Chinese methods of processing were ignored by the new arrivals who introduced vastly improved techniques from elsewhere; within a short while most of the exports consisted of sugar that had passed through the European-owned factories. In contrast, the early European estate owners adopted the existing Chinese system of cultivation. A situation arose in which cultivation depended upon longstanding Chinese methods based on the intensive use of hand labour and was almost always under Chinese direction, whereas processing was supervised by experienced Europeans using the most up-to-date equipment.

This division between cultivation and processing was not peculiar to the sugar industry of Province Wellesley for it reflected two inter-connected facts. Cultivation required a large labour force which was not always fully employed throughout

[61] *Penang Gazette*, Vol. XIV No. 10, 8 March 1856.

the year and suitable labour was neither particularly cheap nor easy to obtain. Factory operation, on the other hand, if it was to make use of new techniques, necessitated a heavy capital outlay, but required a very much smaller labour force, running costs were low and it was generally considerably more profitable than cultivation. Throughout the nineteenth century in all parts of the world attention was focussed on improving processing methods and the cultivation of the cane was more or less casual and usually left in the hands of tenants or contractors.

Local conditions in the Straits Settlements merely served to enhance the more general reasons for this dichotomy. Generally speaking, the Chinese, although the originators of the sugar industry in this area, had neither the capital available nor the desire to establish the large mechanized factories introduced by the Europeans; yet by using their traditional processing methods they were unable to compete in the export market with cane that had passed through these large modern factories. For the most part the factory labour employed by the Europeans consisted of Indians and Javanese 'who bound themselves to serve for a specific period'.[62] Although several Chinese planters continued to use the old buffalo mills, the numbers of which declined very rapidly in the late 1880's, they were mostly content to remain the cultivators of sugar cane, either as contractors or independent growers, and allowed processing to become a European-dominated preserve. Thus, as in the case of Java, the introduction of technical improvements was accompanied by a deeper penetration of Western enterprise into the industry.[63]

The Europeans believed that Chinese labour could not be profitably employed unless the individual had a direct financial interest in the work and also that Chinese labourers worked most satisfactorily under the direction of their own countrymen. Under these circumstances cultivation of the estate was best left in the hands of Chinese contractors for such a system ensured a regular supply of canes to the factory at a fixed price and made the contractor liable for any loss involved in producing the canes. The Chinese found this arrangement satisfactory,

[62] O. Cavenagh, *Reminiscences of an Indian Official*, London, 1884, 280.
[63] Allen and Donnithorne, op. cit. 79.

despite the lower profits made from cultivation, because they were in direct contact with a large supply of cheap labour in the form of new immigrants and because the truck system operated by the contractors enabled them to make profits out of cultivation of a magnitude denied to non-Chinese without requiring a large capital investment.

Almost invariably Chinese labour was employed on a contract system of a type also used on the Chinese estates and often termed the *rumah kechil* system. From the very beginning the European estates were worked by the contract system because it was considered to be 'decidedly the most advantageous whether the manufacturer employs it upon land of his own, or merely erects a mill and contracts with the cultivators for their Cane'.[64] Under the *rumah kechil* system the cultivated area of an estate was divided into sections. Each of these was let out to a Chinese contractor who was obliged to sell the resulting crop at a fixed price to the estate owner. Although in many cases the contractors probably supplied the labour, heading *kongsis* formed for the purpose, frequently the estate owner obtained the *sinkhehs* who were distributed among the contractors.

Under a typical agreement the contractor took up twenty-five to fifty *orlongs* of land. He was obliged to fell, clear and burn the jungle and undergrowth, plant the canes, which were supplied by the owner, and care for them until they reached maturity. They must then be harvested, tied into bundles and laid on the roadside or put into the canal boats for conveyance to the mill. The contractor was also responsible for digging all main drains and cross-drains within the contract area and for their upkeep. Usually he employed a total Chinese labour force equal to the number of *orlongs* in the contract area and was paid by the owner a fixed sum ($3 in 1847), for each labourer working a full month. On agreeing to the contract he was given an advance to cover equipment, the building of labourers' quarters, provisions, etc., and when the cane produced in his section was processed the owner paid the contractor at a fixed

[64] *S.F.P.*, Vol. II No. 10, 5 March 1846.

price per pikul ($1.25 in 1847), after the advances had been deducted.[65]

It was unusual on the European-owned estates to allow the canes to grow further than first *ratoons* and 'as planted canes are from twelve to fourteen months before they are ripe and ratoons from ten to eleven in the Straits, the planter gathers two full crops in two years'.[66] Contracts for particular sections of an estate were probably therefore of about two years' duration, during which time the contractor obtained two crops. Usually the land was then allowed to remain fallow whilst new contract areas were worked.

Wray obviously approved of this contract system for it allowed estates to be 'cleared and brought into cultivation in the most regular, systematic, and satisfactory manner possible'.[67] Nevertheless, the fact that the European estate owners and managers were more or less completely removed from the actual cultivation of cane and concentrated their interests on the processing side of the industry probably explains why the methods of cultivation changed so little throughout the nineteenth century. Thus, the average yield of dry sugar per *orlong* on Horsman's estates in 1856 was very much the same as the average yields obtained on the Chinese estates over twenty years earlier.[68] In effect, by divorcing cultivation from processing and by relying to a very large extent on Chinese contractors to undertake the production of cane, the European estate owners allowed a pattern of organization existing among Chinese immigrants throughout nineteenth-century Malaya to make its imprint upon sugar cultivation in Province Wellesley.

[65] Wray, *Practical Sugar Planter*, 126-9.

[66] Balestier, op. cit. 142.

[67] Wray, op. cit. 129-30.

[68] Low, *Dissertation on the Soil and Agriculture*, 52-53 and *Penang Gazette*, Vol. XIV No. 6, 9 February 1856.

8

SUGAR PLANTING, 1867-1913

IN THE LAST THREE OR FOUR DECADES of the nineteenth century the sugar industry of Province Wellesley developed into a highly capitalized European-controlled enterprise. Huge factories incorporating the latest machinery were constructed and for these to attain maximum efficiency an assured supply of cane was essential. There was a marked tendency therefore, for the European estate owners and managers to seek a greater degree of control over cane cultivation than the Chinese contract system allowed. In most cases this was achieved by the employment of indentured Indian labour. In this later period the industry developed new characteristics; it was also a period during which the Province Wellesley planters faced an increasing number of problems.

Province Wellesley, 1867-1904

In the late 1860's the canes on many estates in the Province were badly affected by disease. Many planters began to replace the 'Mauritius' cane with the old stand-by, the 'Selangor' cane, while others attempted to introduce cane from Java. About 1866 Lawrence Nairne introduced the 'Striped Bourbon' cane from Mauritius. This proved immune to the disease currently affecting the estates; it also ripened in only ten months and gave high yields. Consequently, it was quickly adopted by the planters and by the early 1880's was extensively planted. Several canes were also introduced from the West Indies during the 1870's but few arrived in good condition and they did not thrive in Province Wellesley.[1]

The spread of disease was not the only factor halting the expansion of sugar planting in this area. Between 1867 and the 1880's the European-owned estates here faced serious labour

[1] Vermont, 'List of Sugar-Canes...', *A.R. Penang, 1881*, 192-3.

problems associated with temporarily restricted immigration from India, high death-rates and large-scale desertions. Shortly after the transfer of the Straits Settlements from the Government of India to the Colonial Office in 1867 objections were raised in India to unrestricted emigration to the Straits Settlements chiefly, it would seem, because of a fear that estate labourers were ill-treated, the men physically and the women morally. This emigration was forbidden without further inquiry in 1870, leaving Province Wellesley in a worse position than any other sugar-producing colony in regard to its labour supply, for many of the estates had come to rely increasingly on indentured Indian labour for cultivation as well as for factory work. The immediate reaction of the estate owners was to display great reluctance to invest further capital in the industry until their labour difficulties were solved.

In practice, however, the prohibition was not strictly enforced, and immigration was allowed to resume in 1872 following an assurance given by the Straits Settlements Government that it would provide adequate protection to immigrants. During the 1870's there were continuous reports of bad living conditions and ill treatment on the Province Wellesley estates and legislation was passed by both the Governments of India and the Straits Settlements in an attempt to improve the situation. This was replaced by the Indian Immigration Ordinance passed by the Straits Settlements Government in 1884.[2]

Nevertheless, the supply of Indian labour was not equal to the demand. Moreover, the expense of obtaining labour from India was heavy and wages were rising gradually. The planters were faced with the necessity of obtaining new labour to replace those whose contracts had expired and to augment the total labour force so that extensions could be made to the cultivated area. They also had difficulty in preserving the existing labour force. That they did not achieve much success is revealed by a decline in the number of Indians employed on the sugar estates from 5,590 at the end of 1884 to 4,600 at the end of 1888, and

[2] Kernial Singh Sandhu, 'Some Preliminary Observations of the Origins and Characteristics of Indian Migration to Malaya, 1786-1957' in K.G. Tregonning, ed., *Papers on Malayan History*, Singapore, 1962, 64; R.N. Jackson, *Immigrant Labour* ... 59-61 and 99.

by the retraction of the planted acreage which occurred in the 1880's[3] (Table 12).

Although there was a hospital on the Jawi Estate by 1860, and others were built on the Prai, Golden Grove and Batu Kawan Estates in the late 1870's, death-rates were very high among the immigrant Indian labourers, the chief scourge being malaria. Conditions apparently improved in the early 1880's for the average death-rate among the Indian labourers employed on the sugar estates fell substantially between 1881 and 1884; by the later years of the decade, however, mortality on most estates was again very high.[4]

Bad living and working conditions contributed largely to these high death-rates, but many Indian immigrants were not physically equal to the work required of them. Dr. McClosky, Colonial Surgeon, Province Wellesley, described the arrivals in 1886 and 1887 as 'poor in physique and unused to fieldwork'.[5] This had long been the case and it was said of the recently-arrived immigrants in 1879 that before arriving they had 'in nine cases out of ten, never had a changkol in their hands before ... they [had] been principally weavers before coming here'.[6] In the last quarter of the nineteenth century the sugar estates were operated with labour poor in quality as well as deficient in numbers; in a labour-intensive enterprise such as sugar cultivation problems of this type assumed tremendous significance.

During the 1870's and 1880's the Indian labour force on many sugar estates was also depleted by desertion. Although British protection was extended to Perak, Selangor and Sungei Ujong in 1874, the restriction making it illegal for Indians to emigrate to the Malay States remained in force. Consequently in order to

---

[3] *Accounts and Papers*, 1884-5, Vol. LII, C-4583, *A.R.S.S., 1884*; *A.R. Penang, 1888*, 21.

[4] The average death-rate among the Indian labourers on the sugar estates fell from 36.8/1,000 in 1881 to 18.0/1,000 in 1884. *Accounts and Papers*, 1884-5, Vol. LII, C-4583, No. 23, *A.R. Penang, 1884*. However, in 1887, for example, the death-rate was 93.1/1,000 on the Caledonia Estate and 62.9/1,000 on the Byram Estate. *A.R. Penang, 1887*, 15.

[5] *A.R. Penang, 1887*, 13.

[6] *S.S.G.G.*, 1879, 961.

attract labour the pioneer planters in these States found it
necessary to pay higher wages than those paid in Province
Wellesley.[7] The Government of India was asked to remove this
restriction in 1878, and it eventually did so in 1883, but the wage
differential tended to remain. 'Crimping' on behalf of Sumatran
planters was also common in Province Wellesley during the
1880's. There was, therefore, a continuous flow of labour from
the sugar estates to neighbouring states.[8]

These difficulties with Indian labour were exacerbated in the
late 1880's by a shortage of Chinese labour. At this time there
were increasing opportunities on the rapidly expanding sugar
estates of Krian and there was a large demand for labour on
the part of the Sumatran tobacco industry. By 1889 there were
general complaints from planters regarding the difficulty of
getting Chinese labour and 'considerable tracts of land, especially in the South of the Province [were] reverting to jungle from
want of labourers to cultivate the soil'.[9] Further problems arose
in 1894 when there was a temporary cessation of Chinese immigration because of an outbreak of bubonic plague in the ports
of south China and a simultaneous reduction in the supply of
Indian labour.[10] Clearly these labour difficulties played an important part in the recession experienced by the sugar industry
in Province Wellesley in the 1880's and early 1890's (Table 12).

The expansion that characterized the Malayan sugar industry
up to the 1870's had been reversed by the early years of the
subsequent decade. The 1880's were marked by a general world
depression, particularly apparent in the case of agricultural
products. After 1880 the price of sugar began a secular decline
which had serious effects in the world cane-producing areas,

[7] It was observed in 1883 that 'the great demand for labour in Perak,
where wages rising to 35 cents a day for an ordinary cooly, as against
12 cents given in Province Wellesley, continues to entice large numbers
of contract coolies from the estates'. *A.R. Dept. of Indian Immigration, 1883, S.S.G.G.*, Vol. 8, 1884, 498.

[8] In 1883, for instance, 567 Indian labourers were reported to have
deserted to Perak. *Accounts and Papers*, 1884-5, Vol. LII, C-4404,
No. 18, *A.R. Penang, 1883*.

[9] *A.A. Penang, 1889, S.S.G.G.*, Vol. 14, 1890, No. 407, 1409.

[10] *A.R. Penang, 1894*, 16.

effects enhanced by the expansion of beet cultivation, frequently under the protection of high tariffs, in many European countries. The worsening economic situation merely increased the difficulties of the Province Wellesley planters, although the depreciation of silver in the Colony in the late 1880's gave them some advantage over other producing areas using a different monetary standard.[11]

At least one new European estate and one new Chinese estate were opened in the Province during the 1870's, the latter being the property of Koh Bu Ann in Trans-Krian, the area added to Province Wellesley when its southern boundary was extended by the Pangkor Treaty of 1874[12] (Fig. 25B). Exports of sugar from Penang increased by about 78 per cent. between 1872 and 1879; there was a sharp decline in 1880-1 and during the 1880's the quantity exported fluctuated noticeably (Fig. 27). These figures include re-exports, however, and the effects of depression and labour problems were more clearly reflected in the reduced area devoted to sugar cane during the 1880's (Table 12).

By the early 1890's the situation had improved considerably. In 1891 for the first time for many years some of the European estates made a large profit, 'principally owing to economical management and improved machinery'.[13] Between 1892 and 1896 the area devoted to sugar in the Province reached a record total of 15,650 acres (Table 12), and peak production was registered in 1897. Although there was a temporary decline in the planted acreage in the last four years of the century, the total area under this crop in the Province rose to about 15,000 acres in the early years of the twentieth century (Table 12). By this time sugar estates occupied almost the whole of the Southern District with the exception of the higher land in the east and the padi-fields in the south-western corner (Fig. 25B). During the same period there was an increase in European interest in sugar planting in the neighbouring state of Perak.

[11] *A.R. Penang, 1888*, 21. The average price of sugar on the London market fell from 23s 1½d per cwt. in 1881 to 12s 1½d per cwt. in 1887.

[12] *Accounts and Papers*, 1874, Vol. XLIV, C-882, No. 21, *A.R. Penang and Province Wellesley*, 1872.

[13] *A.R. Penang, 1891*, S.S.G.G., Vol. 26 No. 344, 1822.

TABLE 12

SUGAR CANE IN PROVINCE WELLESLEY, 1865-1904

Year	Acres
1865	13,500
1871	13,500
1877	13,500
1880	10,000
1884	10,000
1887	10,000
1889	10,950
1892	15,650
1896	15,650
1897	11,000
1900	9,600
1901	15,051
1904	14,675

Source: The figure for 1865 is taken from *A.R.S.S.*, *1865-6*, 45; all other figures are from the *Straits Settlements Blue Books* for the relevant years.

This renewed expansion of planting operations in the Province during the 1890's reflected an amelioration of the labour situation. Wages were trending upwards and improvements were effected in living and working conditions as Government supervision became stricter. The flow of Indian immigrants to both the Straits Settlements and the Malay States increased with the introduction of the steamship subsidy in 1887, with the opening of an emigration depot at Negapatam in 1890, and with the Indian Government's withdrawal of all restrictions on emigration in 1897 and its agreement in 1900 to facilitate the free flow of migrants to Malaya.[14]

Chinese Expansion into Perak, 1877-1901

The suitability of the adjacent parts of Krian District for sugar planting was recognized at least as early as the 1860's but the continuous disturbances that plagued Perak until after British intervention in 1874 prevented any extension in this

[14] Jackson, op. cit. 99-100; Kernial Singh Sandhu, 'Some Preliminary Observations of the Origins and Characteristics of Indian Migration to Malaya', 49-51.

direction. At that time, apart from a few Malay padi-planters and several Chinese fishermen, Krian remained 'a roadless jungle'.[15] Nevertheless, it shared all the physical advantages enjoyed by Province Wellesley as a potential sugar-producing area: flat, low-lying coastal alluvium intersected by numerous rivers and streams suitable for the construction of canal networks, abundant supplies of fuel in the extensive coastal and riverine mangrove forests, proximity to Penang, and vast tracts of virgin land. All the 'eligible cane lands in Penang and Province Wellesley' had long been occupied,[16] and the planters were not slow to take advantage of the newly available land in Krian once peaceful conditions returned to Perak.

The movement of sugar planters into Krian was begun by the Chinese in 1877. They were encouraged by the policies of the third British Resident of Perak, Hugh Low, who took up his appointment in 1877; and by his energetic and enterprising European officer in Krian between 1877-81, Noel Dennison: for among other attractions the pioneer sugar planters arriving in the District between 1877 and 1881 were granted land rent-free.

Although Wong Ah Kong of Parit Buntar, who opened his estate in 1879, was hailed on his death in June 1898 as the 'pioneer sugar planter in Krian, and, indeed in the State',[17] he was in fact preceded by several others. The first sugar estate in Krian was opened by Goh Eng Chow in 1877 and in the following year two more estates were established, one by Koh Su Toh and the other by Tan Weng Cheang and Wong Ah Meng.[18] By the end of 1879 there were already five Chinese sugar estates in the District (Table 13), and Hugh Low, commenting on Krian that year, noted that 'settlers for padi and sugar-cane planting are flocking into the place, so that soon but little jungle will be left in accessible places'.[19] Until 1880 sugar planting concentrated along the Sungei Krian above Parit Buntar, but in that year

[15] F.A. Swettenham, *About Perak*, Singapore, 1893, 42.

[16] Wray, *Practical Sugar Planter*, footnote, page 125.

[17] *M.R. Krian*, June 1898, *P.G.G.*, Vol. 11, 1898, No. 524, 562.

[18] *A.R. Krian*, *1888*, *P.G.G.*, Vol. 2, 1889, No. 53, 81.

[19] *Accounts and Papers*, 1881, Vol. LXV, C-3095, Encl. 1 in No. 1, *A.R. Perak*, *1879*.

TABLE 13

CHINESE SUGAR ESTATES IN KRIAN DISTRICT, 1877-88

Year	Number of estates in existence	Total area occupied (acres)
1877	1	102
1878	3	1,936
1879	5	3,059
1880	8	8,379
1881	12	10,105
1882	15	11,301
1883	15	11,301
1884	16	14,159
1885	18	14,705
1886	20	16,157
1887	20	16,157
1888	21	16,414

Source: A.R. Krian, 1888, P.G.G., Vol. 2, 1889, No. 53, 81.

Heah Jin Wee (one of the most influential early Chinese sugar planters in Perak) and Low Chu Seng opened estates along the Sungei Kurau and in 1881 Tan Ah Pow established an estate at Bagan Tiang[20] (Fig. 28).

By 1881 there were twelve Chinese-owned sugar estates in Krian, occupying in total over 10,000 acres (Table 13). In that year Low observed that many estates had been opened 'by the *enterprising Chinese merchants of Penang*, and it is expected that steam machinery will be erected on some of them during the current year'; he continued, 'the opening of the new road through Larut to Krian and of the new port [Port Weld] will probably result in a further extension of this industry'.[21] Within a few months the completion of this road was being followed by a population 'which is cutting down forests and covering the land with sugar and other cultivation'.[22] Until 1883 the sugar

[20] A.R. Krian, 1888, P.G.G., Vol. 2, 1889, No. 53, 81.
[21] Accounts and Papers, 1882, Vol. XLVI, C-3428, Encl. 1 in No. 5, A.R. Perak, 1881. The italics have been inserted.
[22] Accounts and Papers, 1884, Vol. LV, C-4192, No. 15, Weld to Earl of Derby, 15 December 1883, 'Report of Visit to Perak and Province Wellesley, November, 1883'. See also General Map of the District of Krian and Kurau Showing Divisions of Districts Surveyed by H.L. Pemberton, 1881-1883. National Archives of Malaysia, Petaling Jaya.

industry in Krian was entirely in Chinese hands and that year witnessed the first export of sugar.

Despite labour difficulties 'in consequence of the inflow of Teow Choo Sink-Kehs having been practically stopped by the authorities in China', the Chinese planters extended their operations during the 1880's.[23] New land was cleared and planted on existing estates which were enlarged by the purchase of adjacent padi-land from Malays. Between 1883 and 1888 six new Chinese estates were opened in Krian, the largest of over 2,800 acres being the Sungei Bogak Estate belonging to the most influential Chinese planter in the adjacent part of Province Wellesley, Koh Bu Ann (Fig. 28). In 1888 there were twenty-one Chinese estates in the District occupying a total of 16,400 acres, of which about 6,200 acres were actually planted. Almost 10,800 acres had been alienated to Chinese sugar planters along the Sungei Krian, nearly a third of which had been planted, about 5,400 acres had been alienated along the Sungei Kurau, of which almost 2,500 acres were cultivated, and 254 acres at Bagan Tiang 68 acres of which had been planted. Altogether there were thirty-five sugar mills on these estates in 1888, five being steam-driven and the remainder the traditional type using buffaloes; they all produced basket or brown sugar. With the exception of Heah Jin Wee's estate which employed seventy-one Tamils, these estates were dependent entirely on Chinese labour and gave employment to 2,990 Chinese, a labour ratio of approximately one labourer for two acres of cultivated land. Two years later Indians were also employed on the Sungei Bogak Estate. As a result of the expansion of sugar planting in Krian during the 1880's, the total number of Chinese in the District rose from 3,339 in 1879 to 5,749 in 1889.[24]

Sugar prices varied during the 1890's, occasionally falling very low as in 1890 and 1894-5, but rising in the later years of the decade. Moreover, the estates were not free from labour difficulties. Nevertheless the planted acreage on Chinese-owned estates in Krian continued to increase and Chinese sugar plant-

---

[23] *A.R. Krian, 1888, P.G.G.*, Vol.2, 1889, No. 53, 80.

[24] *A.R. Krian, 1888, P.G.G.*, Vol. 2, 1889, No. 53, 80-81; *A.R. Krian, 1889, P.G.G.*, Vol. 3, 1890, No. 167, 224; *P.G.G.*, Vol. 2, 1889, No. 101, 220.

ing gradually extended into neighbouring areas. This was also a period during which an increasing number of Chinese planters erected steam mills to replace the less efficient buffalo mills; apart from adopting European manufacturing methods several of the Chinese planters in Krian also built canals for drainage and transport purposes.[25]

In 1890 there were twenty-one Chinese sugar estates comprising a total alienated area of 21,700 acres. Late in the following year when prices had improved applications were received for an additional 3,000 acres, of which 1,000 acres were granted to Tan Kang Hock for an estate on the Sungei Kurau.[26] As the area available for further extension in Krian diminished and local supplies of firewood decreased as the mangrove was cleared, the Chinese began to take an interest in the adjacent and equally suitable areas in Matang District.

The first application by a Chinese for sugar land in this District was made by Teoh Ah Ngoh in 1893. He applied for 1,000 acres at Kalumpang, and although this time he was unsuccessful because the land in question lay within the boundaries of a concession already applied for by Stewart and Kennedy (see later) his application presages Chinese extension into Matang. It may also reflect increasing competition for the available land nearer to the existing Krian estates. Teoh was finally granted 1,000 acres at Kalumpang, bordering the Stewart and Kennedy concession, in 1896 and immediately began clearing.[27] Two years later Treacher remarked that Chinese planters had 'acquired extensive areas for this cultivation in Matang, and [were] also buying up padi land from the natives'.[28] By 1899 there were two Chinese sugar estates in mukim Selinsing totalling 1,660 acres of which about 450 acres had been planted;

[25] E.g. a new steam mill arrived from England for Koh Bu Ann's Sungei Bogak Estate in February 1889. *M.R. Krian*, February 1889, *P.G.G.*, Vol. 2, 1889, 258; Wright and Cartwright, op. cit. 423.

[26] *A.R. Land Dept., Perak, 1890, P.G.G.*, Vol. 4, 1891, No. 250, 340; *M.R. Krian*, December 1891, *P.G.G.*, Vol. 5, 1892, No. 38, 41; *M.R. Krian*, May 1892, *P.G.G.*, Vol. 5, 1892, No. 226, 355.

[27] *A.R. Matang, 1883, P.G.G.*, Vol. 7, 1894, No. 328, 238; *A.R. Matang, 1896, P.G.G.*, Vol. 10, 1897, No. 410, 428.

[28] *A.R. Perak, 1898*, 15.

extensions were being made to these estates by the purchase of adjacent 'small native holdings'. By the same date a tapioca planter, Goh Hooi Chew, had also acquired a 1,000-acre concession for sugar planting at Temerloh, Sungei Tinggi, although work on this land had yet to start. In 1900 Tan Ho Heong applied for 5,500 acres for sugar in mukim Selinsing and this extension of Chinese sugar planting into Matang continued until 1901.[29]

In 1899, however, it was Rodger's opinion that it was unlikely that the area then alienated for sugar in Matang would be largely increased, 'as most of the available sugar land has been included in an irrigation area, in connection with the cultivation of rice';[30] within a short while sugar planting in Perak in general began to decline.

While Chinese sugar planting was extending into Matang small-scale additions were made to the existing estates in Krian, either by the acquisition of small additional blocks of new land from the Government or by the purchase of neighbouring padi-land. The Chinese planters required additional land not only because they wished to extend their operations, but also because the system of cultivation employed necessitated fallow periods. During 1895 about 1,200 acres were newly acquired for sugar planting, during 1896 460 acres and during 1899 a further 2,668 acres. By this time, however, most of the applications for new land in Krian were unsuccessful, and 'owing to the area of land available being restricted to lands outside the irrigation area' there was 'no more land available in the district for this class of cultivation'.[31]

This restriction on expansion in Krian was a major cause of the extension into Matang and was eventually to prove an important cause of the decline of sugar planting in this area (see below). Nevertheless, it did not immediately prevent further extension in Krian. In 1900 the planters had not 'appreciably ceased endeavouring to extend the boundaries of their estates

[29] A.R. Matang, 1899, 3; A.R. Perak, 1900, 3.

[30] A.R. Perak, 1899, 19.

[31] A.R. Land Dept., Perak, 1895, P.G.G., Vol. 9, 1896, No. 252, 239; A.R. Lands and Mines, F.M.S., 1896, P.G.G., Vol. 10, 1897, No. 198, 191; A.R. Krian, 1899, 3.

by the purchase of neighbouring *padi* lands'. Even within the proclaimed irrigation areas the process of buying out small agriculturalists continued; however it was 'but seldom that really good *padi* land [was] sold to sugar planters'.[32] In 1899 there were twenty-five Chinese sugar estates in Krian, occupying a total area of about 26,000 acres; four of these estates exceeded 2,000 acres each.[33]

Labour on the Chinese Estates

With few exceptions these Chinese-owned estates relied entirely upon Chinese labour. It was usual for part of an estate to be worked under the direct supervision of the owner or his representatives using *sinkheh* and *laukheh* labour and for the remainder to be worked on the contract or *rumah kechil* system. Certainly every Chinese estate utilized the *rumah kechil* system, although it was relatively more important on some estates, notably those using steam-powered mills. Grey, the acting District Magistrate in Krian, remarked in 1896 that although the *kongsi*-houses on the Chinese estates were generally in good order, and the *sinkhehs* housed in them were 'as a rule, well treated', on every estate there were

... some isolated huts called *rumah kechil*, where a tenant of the proprietor lives, who cultivates a certain amount of land, receiving advances from the proprietor, which are repaid, together with a percentage for land-rent, crushing and other expenses, when the sugar is sold. These sub-tenants employ free coolies, but in many cases they also obtain the transfer of sinkhehs from the big *kongsi*-houses to their huts, and these sinkhehs frequently undergo ill-treatment at the hands of their headmen, who are generally themselves members of the coolie class.[34]

In 1899 the estates in Krian employed a total of 4,121 Chinese labourers of whom 587 were *sinkhehs*, 1,598 *laukhehs* and 1,936 *rumah kechil* men.[35] Undoubtedly much of the ill-treatment which raised a stream of complaints about conditions on the

[32] *A.R. Krian, 1900*, 3.
[33] *A.R. Krian, 1899*, 8.
[34] *M.R. Krian*, December 1896, *P.G.G.*, Vol. 10, 1897, No. 70, 59.
[35] *A.R. Krian, 1899*, 8.

Chinese estates in Krian in the 1890's resulted from this dual system of cultivation. Although the Chinese estate owners did improve the lot of the labourers directly in their employ, they had no control over the *rumah kechil* labourers, and the contractors, necessarily wishing to keep costs as low as possible, had no desire to incur the additional expense required to improve conditions.

Province Wellesley and Perak came within the sphere of influence of the Penang Chinese who, to a large extent, financed and controlled Chinese sugar planting and processing in these areas. Several of the estate owners in Krian also had an interest in the sugar industry of the Province, and in both areas most of the Chinese estate labourers were Tiechius, as were most of the estate owners.[36] In general, the expansion of Chinese sugar planting into Perak in the last quarter of the nineteenth century reflected the difficulty of acquiring land in sufficient quantities in the Province at a time when the more enterprising Chinese planters were themselves beginning to adopt European processing methods.

European Interest in Perak, 1883-1905

European participation in sugar planting in Perak dates from the early 1880's and with the exception of one estate, achieved little success until the following decade. As early as 1874 some European planters from Province Wellesley visited Krian, but decided against establishing estates there. In 1883 A.G. Morrison (the agent and attorney of the late Edward Horsman) applied for a block of 6,000–8,000 acres for sugar planting between Kota Stia and Sitiawan. In his application he stated that he was of the opinion that 'within a line drawn from the Sungei Lumut to Kota Stia, there are the materials for large sugar cultivation'. Within a short while however, the price of sugar fell and he abandoned his plans.[37] At the same time an abortive attempt

---

[36] Thus, of the 2,986 *sinkheh* contracts registered in Krian in 1901 and 1902 approximately three-fifths concerned Tiechius. *A.R. Krian, 1901,* 5, and *A.R. Krian, 1902,* 4.

[37] *M.R. Lower Perak,* June 1891, *P.G.G.,* Vol. 4, 1891, No. 322, 621; 'Notes on the Acting Resident's Tour Through Kuala Kangsar, Kinta, Batang Padang and Lower Perak Districts', *P.G.G.,* Vol. 5, 1892, 682.

was made to establish a sugar estate on the mangrove-covered island of Pasir Hitam in Matang District, but the scheme was abandoned in 1884 'from want of funds' before any planting had been done.[38] The only successful venture into this field during the 1880's was made by W.V. Drummond of Shanghai. He acquired 6,000 acres between the Sungei Kurau and Sungei Gula in 1882 and this became known as the Gula Estate (Fig. 28). It was to be worked by a company, the Perak Sugar Cultivation Company Limited, incorporated in 1883 and with its head office in Shanghai.[39]

The first mill was erected on the Gula Estate in 1884 and the estate was laid out on the lines of the 'celebrated Prye estate' in the Province where Parkinson, the manager in the 1880's, was formerly employed.[40] A canal network was constructed for drainage and transport purposes and a hospital was built during the 1880's. As late as 1908 the Gula Estate included some fifty miles of canals fed from the Sungei Kurau on which there were 120 punts or barges of an average capacity of three and a half tons each for transporting the canes.

Initially Chinese contract labour was employed, but before the end of 1883 the estate also employed Tamils, Malays and Javanese; thereafter, except for short periods, it relied almost exclusively on Indian labour for estate work.[41] Despite the fact that in 1890 sugar planters were 'much handicapped chiefly by increased prices and scarcity of labour, also by reduced market value for their produce', the Perak Sugar Cultivation Company Limited remained confident that sugar planting had a bright future and development proceeded rapidly on the Gula Estate. In 1892 the estate was described as 'exceedingly well cultivated and free of weeds', and $30,000 worth of new machinery had

---

[38] *M.R. Matang*, January 1889, *P.G.G.*, Vol. 2, 1889, No. 72, 118.

[39] Wright and Cartwright, op. cit. 396; *Accounts and Papers*, 1884, Vol. LV, C-4192, Encl. 1 in No. 13, *A.R. Perak, 1882* and Encl. 1 in No. 21, *A.R. Perak, 1883. Gula* is the Malay word for sugar.

[40] *Accounts and Papers*, 1888, Vol. LXXIII, C-5566, Encl. 1 in No. 5, *A.R. Perak, 1887.*

[41] Thus, in 1888, when 853 acres had been planted, the estate labour force comprised 1,303 Indians (of whom 1,103 were indentured immigrants), together with 25 Malays who were employed in house-building, repair work, etc. *A.R. Krian, 1888, P.G.G.*, Vol. 2, 1889, No. 53, 82.

recently been erected. Two years later a new rum distillery and a new hospital had been built and generally the estate showed signs of 'prosperity and progress'.[42]

Almost all the white sugar exported from Perak in the 1890's was produced on this estate. By the end of 1894, when the price of white sugar had reached 'a figure the sterling value of which [was] lower than [had] been known before', over 2,000 acres had been planted on the Gula Estate and 1,600 acres were already yielding a crop. The price of white sugar almost doubled between 1895 and 1899 by which time the estate comprised a total of 9,512 acres. Sugar continued to be of major importance on this estate until the end of the first decade of the twentieth century; in 1906 it produced 73,000 pikuls of sugar.[43]

The operations of the Perak Sugar Cultivation Company Limited were frequently hampered by labour problems during the 1890's. Tamil labour was preferred for most of the estate work but it was difficult to acquire a sufficient number to satisfy the growing needs of the Company which also suffered depletion of its Indian labour force as a result of frequent desertions and high death-rates. At various times different methods of overcoming these problems were attempted. In the early 1890's they unsuccessfully experimented with the employment of discharged Chinese labourers from the Sumatran tobacco estates and part of the estate was sub-leased to a Chinese on the *rumah kechil* system in 1894. Later in the decade the estate was more successful in supplying its labour requirements, and the total number of Indians it employed rose from 1,500 in 1894 to 1,913 in 1898. Nevertheless, as late as 1902 it was maintained that 'a great difficulty with which sugar planters have to contend is the inadequate supply of Indian labour'.[44]

Earlier European interest in Matang and Lower Perak as

[42] *M.R. Krian*, November 1890, *P.G.G.*, Vol. 3, 1890, No. 639, 808; *M.R. Krian*, January 1892, *P.G.G.*, Vol. 5, 1892, No. 70, 97; *M.R. Krian*, June 1894, *P.G.G.*, Vol. 7, 1894, No. 434, 394.

[43] *A.R. Krian, 1894, P.G.G.*, Vol. 8, 1895, No. 333, 406; *A.R. Krian, 1899*, 8; Wright and Cartwright, op. cit. 396.

[44] 'Inspection of Krian District by the Protector of Chinese, January, 1893', *P.G.G.*, Vol. 6, 1893, No. 86, 123; *A.R. Krian, 1894, P.G.G.*, Vol. 8, 1895, No. 333, 406-7; *A.R. Indian Immigration Department, 1898, P.G.G.*, Vol. 12, 1899, No. 211, 173; *A.R. Krian, 1902*, 2.

potential sugar-producing areas was revived in the early 1890's
when a prospective planter from Province Wellesley, John
Turner, made a reconnaissance visit to the area between Telok
Anson and Sitiawan, and when Kennedy made known his
intention of applying for several thousand acres for sugar
planting near Kalumpang in Matang. At the same time Stewart
and Stephens visited the site of the estate on Pasir Hitam island
which had been abandoned in 1884.[45]

The immediate result was that in 1893 Stewart and Kennedy
applied for a concession of about 5,000 acres for sugar at Kalumpang in mukim Selinsing and Drummond applied for the whole
of Pasir Hitam island. Stewart and Kennedy were apparently
granted land adjoining the Gula Estate but during 1894 when
only a little jungle felling had been done, this was taken over
by the Perak Sugar Cultivation Company Limited. The following year Stewart and Kennedy acquired about 2,500 acres in
mukim Selinsing, and clearing began early in 1896[46] (Fig. 28).

During 1893 Turner of the Caledonia Estate in Province
Wellesley bought 1,854 acres of land in mukim Selinsing from
the Perak Sugar Cultivation Company Limited on behalf of
Sir T.H. Ramsden of the Straits Sugar Estates Company; he
also purchased 'other adjacent land from the native occupiers,
presumably padi land'. This became known as the Gedong
Estate (Fig. 28). By the end of 1899 about 1,200 acres had been
planted with sugar cane at an average cost of $90 per acre. This
estate was worked by both Indian and Chinese labour, the latter
on the *rumah kechil* system. By 1900 it was equipped with the
'finest' factory in Perak, lit by electricity and formally opened
on 28 December 1900. Expansion into Matang District continued and in 1901 Turner acquired a further 1,570 acres in
mukim Selinsing on behalf of the Straits Sugar Estates
Company.[47]

[45] *M.R. Lower Perak*, December 1892, *P.G.G.*, Vol. 6, 1893, No. 67, 92;
M.R. Matang, March 1893, *P.G.G.*, Vol. 6, 1893, No. 227, 303; *M.R.
Matang*, July 1893, ibid., No. 452, 765.

[46] *A.R. Matang, 1893*, *P.G.G.*, Vol. 7, 1894, No. 328; 238; *A.R. Krian,
1894*, *P.G.G.*, Vol. 8, 1895, No. 333, 407; *A.R. Matang, 1895*, *P.G.G.*,
Vol. 9, 1896, No. 247, 210.

[47] *A.R. Lands, Mines and Surveys, F.M.S., 1898*, 9; *A.R. Matang, 1899*,
3; *A.R. Matang, 1900*, 1; *A.R. Matang, 1901*, 2.

In May 1898 Turner again visited Lower Perak in connexion with the selection of land for sugar planting and in June he applied for two blocks of land covering a total area of 21,000 acres on either side of the Sungei Perak. Later in the year he was granted 11,000 acres on behalf of the Straits Sugar Estate Company and this became known as the Rubana and Nova Scotia Estates. By 1900 over 1,000 acres had been cleared on these estates and much had been planted with canes. As on the other European-owned estates the most modern processing equipment was installed; in 1900 machinery valued at $160,000 was in the course of erection and a further $40,000 worth of plant, including electric lighting equipment, had been ordered. The factory here was opened in September 1901, by which time 1,350 acres had been planted with canes.[48]

In 1901 sugar planting in general in coastal Perak continued to 'prosper, flourish and extend' and the estate owners continued to buy adjacent land from Malay padi planters. Rodger observed that 'the cultivation of sugar is at present the most successful planting industry in Perak'.[49] The following year 'new and extended plantations of sugar-cane were opened, both by Europeans and Chinese, in coast districts; the largest plantations being those of the Straits Sugar Company in Krian and Lower Perak, and of the Perak Cultivation Company in Krian'.[50]

The expansion of sugar planting, both within Krian and outwards into Matang and Lower Perak during the 1890's was reflected in a very marked increase in the total exports of sugar from Perak, rising from 84,400 pikuls in 1890 to 278,160 pikuls in 1900. As the new estates in Matang and Lower Perak came into production total exports rose to over 420,000 pikuls in 1902. After 1905 however, exports of sugar fell rapidly; by the beginning of the second decade of the twentieth century sugar planting in Perak was of limited importance and had virtually disappeared as a large-scale enterprise before the first World War (Fig. 29).

[48] *M.R. Lower Perak*, May and June 1898, *P.G.G.*, Vol. 11, 1898, Nos. 466 and 467, 507; *A.R. Perak*, *1898*, 15; *A.R. Perak*, *1899*, 19; *A.R. Lower Perak*, *1900*, 2; *A.R. Lower Perak*, *1901*, 2.

[49] *A.R.F.M.S.*, *1901*, 2; *A.R. Perak*, *1901*, 3.

[50] *A.R. Perak*, *1902*, 3.

This expansion of European sugar-planting operations in Perak was a Company-sponsored, large-scale venture. The two concerns involved, the Perak Sugar Cultivation Company Limited and the Straits Sugar Estates Company, acquired between them about 25,000 acres of land in coastal Perak for the purpose of sugar planting during the 1890's and early 1900's. This was divided into very large estates, centrally organized, worked to a considerable degree with indentured Indian labour, but European managerial and technical staff were employed in relatively large numbers. In the early years of the present century for example, the Gula Estate employed a European manager trained in sugar planting in Demerara and Brazil, together with an engineer, medical officer, accountant and seven assistants.[51] In general indentured Indian labour was preferred on these estates for it allowed the whole estate to be worked under single management; Chinese contract labour under the *rumah kechil* system was only utilized when shortages of indentured Indian labour made it absolutely necessary. Each estate was equipped with a huge factory containing the most up-to-date machinery of a type comparable with those existing in any other sugar-producing area in the world.

During the same period the wealthier Chinese planters also began to adopt modern processing methods, in some cases employing European engineers in the factories. By 1899 ten of the twenty-six sugar estates in Krian already possessed steam mills and two others were about to erect them.[52] At the same time indentured Indian labour became more common on the larger Chinese-owned estates, although most continued to rely on the *rumah kechil* system of contracting with cultivators for the supply of canes to their factories. In fact, during the 1890's a clear distinction emerged between the large, heavily capitalized Chinese-owned estates in Perak, such as the Jin Heng and Sungei Bogak Estates which closely resembled the Company-owned European estates, and the smaller Chinese-owned estates, some of which continued to employ the obsolete, traditional buffalo mills. Others had begun to send their cane for processing in the factories on the European estates either in Perak or in

[51] Wright and Cartwright, op. cit. 396.
[52] *A.R. Krian, 1899*, 8.

the Province. Indeed, the political boundary separating the Malay state of Perak from the British Settlement of Penang and Province Wellesley had little meaning in the context of the sugar industry which, in effect, straddled the boundary-marker, the Sungei Krian. Koh Bu Ann owned estates immediately on either side of this river, the Straits Sugar Estates Company held a considerable area of land distributed between southern Province Wellesley and the Districts of Krian, Matang and Lower Perak and several of the small-scale Chinese planters sent their cane across the boundary for processing.

By the beginning of the twentieth century the sugar industry of Perak and Province Wellesley had become a highly capitalized and efficiently organized plantation venture, very similar to the type of large-scale agricultural enterprise that characterizes present-day Malaya. At the turn of the century, when the industry here reached its zenith, over 65,000 acres had been granted to sugar planters and total exports were in the order of 600,000 pikuls, or 35,700 tons per year, representing more than twice contemporary Jamaican exports and more than a third of those of British Guiana. In 1905 total exports of sugar from Perak alone were valued at over $2 million. For a matter of thirty years sugar was the most important agricultural produce exported from Perak and second only to tin amongst all exports. It was the staple crop on the estates in the Province for almost a century.

The Restriction and Decline of Sugar Planting in Perak and Province Wellesley

Sugar planting declined very rapidly in both Perak and Province Wellesley after about 1905. In the Province the area devoted to sugar cane fell from 14,700 acres in 1904 to a mere thirty-one acres in 1913 in which year the last sugar factory was closed (Tables 14 and 15). In the Federated Malay States the total area planted with this crop, which was heavily concentrated in the Krian District, declined from 7,100 acres in 1909 to 2,100 acres in 1911, and much of this was interplanted with rubber and other crops;[53] exports of sugar from Perak had

[53] *A.R.F.M.S., 1910*, 10 and *A.R.F.M.S., 1911*, 10.

virtually ceased by 1914 (Fig. 29). This rapid decline was the result of a complex set of factors associated with changing circumstances at both the local and world levels, the effects varying from area to area and estate to estate. In all cases however, the *coup de grâce* was the growing profitability of rubber planting.

It has already been shown that the sugar estates, whether European- or Chinese-owned, were frequently plagued by labour difficulties in the last quarter of the nineteenth century. Because sugar cultivation was highly labour intensive these difficulties proved an important factor in limiting expansion. With the rapidly growing demand for labour of all types as the country was speedily opened up the problems facing the sugar planters were intensified for the increasing competition for the available labour caused wages to rise markedly.

At the turn of the century it was observed that the estates had 'for a long time past been very much undermanned, owing to the difficulty, from a variety of causes, of obtaining sufficient labour from China and India', and in 1902 there were further complaints about 'the inadequate supply of Indian labour'.[54] Although the European sugar planters provided a partial solution to their difficulties by inaugurating a planters' bureau to superintend the introduction of Javanese labourers, the labour problem remained basically intractable. Already by 1899 it had become necessary to pay 'double and sometimes treble the wages current a few years ago'.[55] Admittedly, increasing numbers of Indian labourers arrived in Malaya during the first decade of the twentieth century but most took up other forms of employment, particularly on estates devoted to different crops and on various Government-sponsored schemes. Indentured Indian labour was preferred by the sugar planters, not least because it tended to be less expensive, and the abolition of the indentured system of immigration in 1910 merely served to

[54] *A.R. Krian, 1899*, 8; *A.R. Krian, 1902*, 2. Thus, the Prai Estate in the Province applied for 1,000 Indian immigrants during the year commencing 1 November 1903 but by 29 February 1904 had received only twenty-seven and the Straits Sugar Estates Company, which had asked for 2,000, received only twenty-nine. *A.R.F.M.S., 1903*, 14-15.

[55] *A.R.F.M.S., 1899*, 5.

increase their difficulties. Problems of labour supply and rising wages reduced the relative profitability of sugar planting at a time when other less labour-demanding crops, notably rubber and coconuts, promised a brighter future.

The availability of cheap, plentiful and easily accessible supplies of firewood in the form of coastal and riverine mangrove forests was an important stimulus to the establishment and expansion of large-scale sugar planting in this area. By the end of the nineteenth century supplies were diminishing, partly because much of the remaining mangrove lay within special Forest Reserves and partly because the supplies previously obtained from lands within or adjacent to the estates had been exhausted. This caused the price of firewood to rise, and the high prices charged in 1903 were said to bear 'so heavily on the owners of the small estates, who do not use modern machinery, as to induce them to abandon sugar cultivation in favour of coconuts, tapioca or indigo'.[56]

Most of the smaller Chinese-owned estates had ceased production by 1905. Apart from the rising cost of firewood, their early demise was also related to the 'old fashioned and wasteful system of planting adopted by most of the Chinese planters, especially on the Krian river', few of whom made use of manure, and to the obsolete manufacturing methods based on the traditional buffalo mill, still employed on many estates.[57] Those Chinese planters who had not adopted the technological improvements in processing introduced on the European estates and who still processed their own cane produced sugar of inferior quality. When local prices declined in the early 1900's the returns they received for their produce made it uneconomical to continue with sugar cultivation. The last buffalo mill closed in the Province in 1905 (Table 14) by which time only the larger, more efficient Chinese estates in Perak remained under sugar. At this date only one of the 'old style Chinese Baba Estates' continued to function in Matang and generally, Chinese sugar planting in Perak had retreated to the initial centre of concentration in Krian.

[56] *A.R.F.M.S., 1903, 13.*
[57] *A.R. Larut and Krian, 1905, 6.*

TABLE 14

SUGAR AND RUM FACTORIES IN PROVINCE WELLESLEY, 1887-1913

Year	Sugar factories		Rum factories
	Steam	Buffalo	
1887	11	21	5
1890	12	13	4
1893	11	5	4
1896	10	4	4
1899	8	3	3
1902	7	1	3
1905	8	1	2
1908	5	—	2
1911	2	—	1
1913	1	—	1

Source: *Straits Settlements Blue Books* for the relevant years.

An important cause of the decline of large-scale sugar planting in Malaya in general and in Krian in particular was the change that occurred in official policy towards agriculture during the 1890's. The arrival of the pioneer sugar planters in the Province and in Perak was welcomed for it heralded the clearance of virgin jungle and introduced a new source of revenue. In both areas the planters acquired land on very easy terms, the pioneers in Krian being exempt from paying rent in an attempt to encourage others. By the 1890's, however, one of the aims of Government policy in the field of agriculture, at least in the Federated Malay States, was to extend the area planted with padi by financing irrigation schemes in order to reduce the rapidly increasing rice imports needed to feed the growing population. The most suitable areas for large-scale irrigation schemes to provide for extended padi cultivation in Perak tended to coincide with the very areas selected by the planters themselves as being most favourable for sugar cultivation, namely the low-lying coastal alluvium of Krian, Matang and Lower Perak.

The largest irrigation scheme undertaken by the Federated Malay States Government in this period was that in Krian, first suggested in 1889 by Welman, the acting District Magistrate.

After much discussion and several reports on the proposed scheme work began in the mid-1890's. Construction proceeded slowly and hesitantly partly because of labour difficulties and questions of finance, and the scheme was finally completed in 1906 at a total cost of $1.6 million. Having invested so much public money, the Government no longer looked with favour on sugar planters whose land lay within the area that could now be irrigated.[58]

As early as 1896, when construction work had only just commenced, Grey, acting District Magistrate in Krian, wrote

I would again impress on the Government the advisability of separating, as far as can now be done, the sugar cultivation of the district from the *padi*. Experience has already shewn in Krian that when a sugar planter establishes himself among *padi growers* he, so to speak, crowds them out, and if attention is not paid to this subject the Government will find itself in the curious position of providing an expensive system of irrigation for *padi* cultivation while that cultivation is gradually decreasing throughout the the district.[59]

Two years later, when sugar cultivation was still expanding in coastal Perak, it was suggested that further extension should be so regulated 'as to prevent the possibility of its superseding or reducing an equally important industry or of rendering fruitless the contemplated expenditure of public money'. At the same time, Burnside, acting District Magistrate in Matang, felt that no time should be lost in deciding 'how far sugar-cane cultivation should be allowed to extend further southwards' in his District.[60]

These pleas for a restriction on the further extension of sugar planting in the areas that it was hoped would benefit from the irrigation scheme culminated in the Irrigation Areas Enactment, 1899.[61] Under this enactment two large 'Irrigation Areas' were proclaimed in Krian and one in Matang within which it was assumed that only padi would be cultivated, except on land

---

[58] A.R. Perak, 1895, 21; A.R.F.M.S., 1906, 8.

[59] A.R. Krian, 1896, P.G.G., Vol. 10, 1897, No. 309, 310.

[60] A.R. Lands, Mines and Surveys, F.M.S., 1898, 9; A.R. Matang, 1898, 4.

[61] P.G.G., Vol. 12, 1 September 1899, No. 596, 624.

already held by sugar planters (Fig. 28)· Although it was officially believed that no more land was available for sugar planting
in Krian as a result of this enactment, it was several years before
the planters ceased to acquire additional land for sugar.

The Government in fact had no means of preventing this
until it introduced a special cultivation clause stipulating that
padi must be planted on all land newly alienated within the
'Irrigation Areas', for no such special clause existed in the case
of land already alienated. In the early 1900's planters in Krian
were still buying adjacent Malay padi land and Willis, writing
in 1905, noted that land within the 'Irrigation Areas' was falling
into the hands of 'Chinamen and others who find sugar a much
more profitable crop, and who, in order to drag their sugar
barges about, dam up the canals, thus interfering with the
proper irrigation of the rice crop in other parts of the land'.[62]
Nevertheless, the establishment of the 'Irrigation Areas' and
Government encouragement of padi planting soon began to
limit the possibilities of further extension in Krian and Matang
and once the land unaffected by the special cultivation clause
had been absorbed further expansion was impossible.

The completion of the Krian Irrigation Scheme in 1906
therefore played a major part in the decline of sugar planting
in the area, for once it began to function properly it severely
restricted the area of land available for sugar planting. In these
circumstances, a change in Government agricultural policy
eventually added to the already burdensome troubles of the
sugar planters.

By the end of the century large-scale sugar planting in Malaya
was faced with growing competition from producing centres
in other parts of the world where, for various reasons, very
much greater profits could be achieved. Increasing production
of beet sugar, particularly in Europe, and the rising importance
of certain other cane-producing areas, notably Cuba, where
production more than quadrupled between 1899 and 1907, and
also nearby Java, added to the problems facing the planters. By
the early 1900's many had begun to turn to other crops relatively more remunerative under local conditions. The crops claim-

[62] J.C. Willis, *A Report Upon Agriculture in the Federated Malay States*, Kuala Lumpur, 1905, 17.

ing most of their attention were rubber and coconuts, both of which required very much smaller labour forces and were currently commanding increasing prices, while some of the smaller Chinese estates were planted with tapioca or indigo.

By early 1903 coconuts had replaced sugar cane on many estates and by 1906 sugar cane was mainly serving as a catch-crop for rubber or coconuts throughout both Province Welles-ley and coastal Perak. It was reported that in Krian in that year '7,000 acres formerly under sugar is now planted with rubber' and the majority of the sugar remaining in Matang was merely a catch-crop. In Lower Perak 'the Sugar Estate Nova Scotia (6,526 acres) owing to the fall in the price of sugar which appears permanent, is now being turned into a rubber estate, as its sister, Rubana Estate (4,667 acres) has long been'.[63]

TABLE 15

PROVINCE WELLESLEY : ACREAGE OF SUGAR AND RUBBER, 1905-14

Year	Sugar	Rubber
1905	11,233	?
1906	7,916	4,009
1907	6,285	4,833
1908	6,480	7,894
1909	4,594	14,166
1910	5,319	15,501
1911	5,100	?
1912	2,890	30,530
1913	31	34,766
1914	6	35,554

Source: Straits Settlements Blue Books for relevant years.

In the later years of the first decade of the present century there was a sharp decline in the acreage devoted to sugar and a very rapid increase in the area planted with rubber (Table 15). At the same time there was a continuous decline in the number of sugar mills in operation both in Province Wellesley and Perak, and by 1914 they had all been closed (Table 14). During this period many of the former sugar estates passed into the

[63] A.R. Lands and Survey, F.M.S., 1906, 7; A.R. Lower Perak, 1907, 3.

hands of newly-formed rubber planting companies such as the Kalumpang Rubber Company Limited, the Straits Settlements Bertam Rubber Company and the Isseng Rubber Company Limited.

This replacement of sugar cane by other crops was clearly in accord with the changed Government policy, for the Chinese estates in particular were no longer viewed with favour. Hale, the District Officer of Larut and Krian, expressed the opinion in 1908 that it was perhaps 'the most satisfactory item of progress in the district, that these sugar estates, held for the most part by old-fashioned Penang Chinese, should pass into the hands of energetic rubber planters'. He continued that even if, as in many instances, the enterprise had to be bolstered up by Government loans, 'I still live in hopes that the few remaining estates, which—although practically abandoned, are able to protect themselves behind their very old titles, without cultivation conditions—will ultimately pass into abler hands'.[64] Although the smaller and less efficient estates turned quickly to other crops, the larger modernized estates, such as the Gula, Gedong, Kalumpang or Jin Heng Estates in Perak or the Prai Estate in the Province continued to produce sugar for a few years longer. Several Chinese planters who held land lying either within the 'Irrigation Areas' or in areas which could be irrigated easily turned to padi planting in the late 1900's.[65]

The process by which sugar planting in Province Wellesley and Perak gave way to rubber and coconut cultivation was accompanied by a modification of the *rumah kechil* system. In 1908 Heah Swee Lee's Jin Heng Estate was 'mostly worked by Chinese squatters, who grow the canes under advances and sell them to the proprietor'. These men also contracted to keep the newly-planted rubber clean 'and in this way it is possible to run the estate much cheaper than could be done by employing day labour'.[66] At the same date Chinese 'squatters' were employed on other former sugar estates which were turning to rubber

[64] *A.R. Larut and Krian, 1908,* 6.

[65] Heah Swee Lee, for example, acquired the Bagan Tiang Estate in 1909 and planted it with padi. *A.R. Perak, 1909,* 7.

[66] Wright and Cartwright, op. cit. 428.

cultivation.[67] In due course this developed into a contract system for utilizing Chinese labour on rubber estates. Today, this system and the surviving canal networks are the sole relict features of the extensive plantation sugar industry that formerly characterized the coastal plains of Province Wellesley and Perak.

[67] E.g. on the Isseng Rubber Estate in Perak and on the Bertam Estate in the Province. Ibid. 419 and 377.

9

EUROPEAN COFFEE ESTATES

THE POTENTIALITIES OF SUGAR PLANTING had been revealed already by Chinese pioneers before Europeans took an interest in the industry. Coffee, on the other hand, was a European introduction and the development of coffee estates in late nineteenth-century Malaya was based almost entirely on the efforts of European planters. In general these estates were established in areas that had not been affected by other forms of commercial agriculture. Moreover, they were opened by newly-arrived European planters for whom this was the first venture into agriculture in Malaya. Coffee grew to importance in western Malaya at the same time as several other export crops. This did not result in competition however, for the coffee industry appeared in different areas, relied to a large extent upon a different type of labour, and was the interest of a different group of planters. In effect, coffee planting was the penultimate stage in the development of modern commercial agriculture and served as the prelude to the domination of Malayan agriculture by large-scale corporate European enterprise.

Coffee Prospectors and the Pioneer Estates, 1877-90

Several unsuccessful attempts were made to establish coffee estates in the Straits Settlements in the first half of the nineteenth century. It was not until the last quarter of the century however, that large-scale coffee planting gained a firm foothold in the peninsula. The industry was developed successfully in the Malay States of Selangor, Negri Sembilan, Perak and Johore, it never grew to prominence in the Straits Settlements where large areas were already planted with other profitable crops and where land was not so easily acquired. The successful introduction and expansion of estate coffee cultivation, which reached boom proportions in the mid-1890's, was related to developments both in Malaya and in other world coffee-producing centres, notably Ceylon and Brazil.

In 1869 the fungus *Hemileia vastatrix* appeared on the coffee estates of Ceylon; it spread rapidly, causing considerable devastation, and within a matter of twenty years had destroyed the Ceylon coffee industry. During the 1870's several Ceylon planters began to show interest in opening new coffee estates in Malaya. Their attention was attracted in particular to the states of Perak, Selangor and Sungei Ujong to which British protection was extended in 1874 and in which vast areas of apparently suitable virgin land existed. Johore also aroused some interest, chiefly because of its accessibility from Singapore and the attitude of its ruler towards agricultural development.

This new-found interest in the potentialities of these areas for large-scale coffee planting was stimulated by the numerous contemporary writings of both official and non-official observers, all of whom extolled the virtues of these parts of the peninsula from the point of view of agricultural development now that peace had been restored. In 1874 for example, Birch wrote of Perak that 'it is believed that the land on the eastern side of the Gunong Bubo [Bubu] range of hills would prove admirably adapted for its [i.e. coffee] cultivation'.[1]

European planters first showed interest in opening coffee estates in Perak in 1877 and in the subsequent two years several Ceylon planters visited the interior parts of the state, mainly in search of suitable hilly land on which to open estates of Arabian coffee (*Coffea arabica*), the type most widely grown in Ceylon. Some however, were more attracted to Liberian coffee (*Coffea liberica*) which had been introduced recently into both Ceylon and Malaya.

In August 1878 two such planters, Christie and Handyside, visited the Kinta District. Later in the year Handyside began his first clearing on the slopes of Gunong Bujang Malaka by the side of the Sungei Kampar. He was attracted to the place 'not so much by the soil as by the facilities afforded by a navigable river at the foot of the hill' (Fig. 30). By the beginning

[1] *Accounts and Papers*, 1874, Vol. XLV, C-1111, No. 65, 'Report of the Visit of the Colonial Secretary to the Native States, 1874'.

of 1879, however, this pioneer venture in Perak had proved a 'miserable failure', and Handyside's ignorance of local conditions was chiefly to blame. He employed twenty newly-arrived Chinese labourers, but no interpreter; moreover, using his Chinese labourers and a few Malays and aborigines he cleared eight to ten acres in the height of the wet season which made burning impossible. By January 1879 the solitude of his life and the semi-mutiny of his labourers had produced in him a 'most desponding state of mind'. Soon afterwards he sold out to another visiting coffee prospector, Percy Lionel Smith.[2]

Smith's attempts to open coffee estates in Perak, at least for a short while, proved more successful. In mid-1879 he visited the valley of the Sungei Geliting in Ulu Slim and was 'simply in raptures about the soil, which he compared to that of Ouva, the best coffee district in Ceylon'. Here, in conjunction with Innis Mitchell, Smith began to plant Liberian coffee and cocoa (Fig. 30). By 1881 their attempts had made progress and the following year were reported to be 'brilliantly successful as regards Liberian coffee'.[3] But when Smith died in the later 1880's the coffee he had planted here was neglected and the estate ruined, although for many years the diminishing crop continued to be harvested by a small group of Chinese working under Khoo Sow Chin of Penang.[4] Inaccessibility was one of the major causes of the failure of this attempt to establish coffee planting in Perak; Rathborne, writing with the benefit of hindsight in the late 1890's, felt that Smith had had little chance

---

[2] H.W.C. Leech, 'About Kinta', *JSBRAS*, No. 4, 1879, 25-27. Isabella Bird, who was in Perak in 1879, noted that 'an enterprising son of an Edinburgh "Bailie" has been trying coffee-planting beyond the Perak, but has got into difficulties with his labourers, and is "getting out of it" '. Isabella Bird, *The Golden Chersonese and the Way Thither*, London, 1883, 357.

[3] H.W.C. Leech, 'About Slim and Bernam', *JSBRAS*, No. 4, 1879, 36 and 39; *Accounts and Papers*, 1882, Vol. XLVI, C-3428, Encl. 1 in No. 5, *A.R. Perak, 1881*.

[4] *M.R. Lower Perak*, August 1889, *P.G.G.*, Vol. 2, 1889, No. 345, 767; *A.R. Batang Padang, 1889*, *P.G.G.*, Vol. 3, 1890, No. 168, 226; *M.R. Batang Padang*, August 1892, *P.G.G.*, Vol. 5, 1892, No. 373, 89.

of success 'not realizing what the difficulties of transport were'.[5]

Apart from a small plantation of Arabian coffee and cinchona opened by Captain Schultze at Gapis and the Government-owned Waterloo Estate, both in Kuala Kangsar District, no other attempts were made to open coffee estates in Perak until the late 1880's[6] (Fig. 30). Thus although interest was shown by Ceylon planters in taking up land in Perak for coffee cultivation in the late 1870's and early 1880's, this interest did not bear fruit. Most of the prospectors were in fact, discouraged by the unsatisfactory land terms offered by the British administration; the early enthusiasm waned and the attention of coffee planters was diverted elsewhere. Despite the introduction of more favourable land regulations and the growth of an official policy designed to attract European coffee planters to the state there was a noticeable tendency for prospective planters to shy away from Perak until the boom period of the 1890's.[7]

In the late 1870's coffee prospectors from Ceylon were also attracted by the possibilities of the other two Protected Malay States, Selangor and Sungei Ujong. The first two estates were opened in Sungei Ujong in 1879. One at Rantau, known as the Linsum Estate was the property of Thomas Heslop Hill and was planted with Liberian coffee, Arabian coffee and cocoa. The other, at an elevation of over 1,500 feet on the western slopes of Bukit Berembun and known as the Antoinette Estate was apparently initially the property of C.E. Kay and was planted with Arabian coffee, cinchona and tea[8] (Fig. 30). In

---

[5] Rathborne, *Camping and Tramping in Malaya*, 175. This transport problem is best illustrated by the fact that in 1892 supplies for the Chinese then working this estate were brought by boat up the Sungei Sungkai to Kuala Geliting, whence they were carried about two miles overland; as a result a bag of rice cost about $7.50 delivered to the estate.

[6] *Accounts and Papers*, 1884, Vol. LV, C-4192, Encl. 1 in No. 13, *A.R. Perak, 1882; A.R. Superintendent of Government Plantations, Perak, 1888*, P.G.G., Vol. 2, 1889, No. 151, 354.

[7] See Swettenham, *British Malaya*, 237.

[8] *Accounts and Papers*, 1881, Vol. LXV, C-3095, Encl. 3 in No. 1, *A.R. Sungei Ujong, 1879* and No. 4, Weld to Kimberley, August 1880, *Report of a Tour Through the Straits Settlements, Protected Malay States and Kedah*.

the early 1880's this latter estate passed into the hands of Hill and Rathborne, the most important coffee-planting pioneers in Malaya.[9] At first this estate proved an unqualified success but at the beginning of 1884 it was abandoned temporarily and lapsed into secondary jungle, apparently because of the continued delay in the passing of legislation for the introduction of Tamil labour into the Malay States.[10] Although it was decided to re-open the estate at Bukit Berembun at the end of 1885, it was not on the hills of interior Sungei Ujong that the future of European coffee planting in Negri Sembilan lay but on the lower undulating land between Seremban and the coast, particularly along the Linggi road.

The year 1879 also witnessed the first European attempt to open coffee estates in Selangor although these were quickly abandoned. At the time Swettenham remarked that the two estates started by Europeans on the Damansara road had been abandoned 'owing, I cannot but think, to the inexperience of those entrusted with their management'.[11] The first success in Selangor was achieved slightly later by R.B. Downall from Ceylon, who was granted a 194-acre block of land on the north-eastern outskirts of Kuala Lumpur in February 1881 (Fig. 30). This he named the Weld Hill Estate and he planted it experimentally with Liberian coffee, tea, pepper and cocoa.[12] Within a matter of months this estate became the property of Hill and Rathborne and Liberian coffee became the major crop.

In 1884 Hill and Rathborne also acquired a large block of land at Batu Caves, a little to the north of Kuala Lumpur, on which small amounts of Liberian coffee and tea were planted;

---

[9] Hill was granted an agricultural lease for land at Bukit Berembun by the Dato' Klana of Sungei Ujong in July 1880. *N.S.S.F, Land 4012/1905.* During the early 1880's Hill and Rathborne also opened the Siliau Estate and acquired a 560-acre block of land, known as the Jerah Estate, in Sungei Ujong. Work never began on the latter estate. *N.S.S.F., Land 1471/92* and *Land 1472/92.*

[10] *A.R. Sungei Ujong, 1884, S.S.G.G.,* 1885, No. 171, 392.

[11] *Accounts and Papers,* 1881, Vol. LXV, C-3095, Encl. 1 in No. 2, *Audit Report on the Selangor Accounts, 1879.*

[12] *Selangor Journal,* Vol. 1 No. 18, 19 May 1893, 292. Weld Hill is still known to many older Chinese in Kuala Lumpur as *kopi san* i.e. 'coffee hill'.

the following year they were granted a lease for 2,500 acres on the slopes of Ginting Bidai to the north-east of Kuala Lumpur near the Selangor-Pahang boundary on which Arabian coffee was to be planted (Fig. 30). This latter attempt to establish coffee planting in the higher reaches of Ulu Klang soon failed. The estate was 'quite abandoned before any results could be obtained' and the lease was surrendered in 1890. The Government had incurred the expense of constructing a bridle-path to this estate with Hill and Rathborne as contractors and although Hill claimed that the estate was abandoned because the Government failed to maintain this bridle-path, many other factors were probably involved, including the difficulty of keeping labour on an estate 'some 23 miles from Kuala Lumpur in the heart of the jungle'.[13] Although several European pepper estates were opened in Klang District during the early 1880's, the relatively small-scale activities of the coffee planters in Selangor remained concentrated in the immediate vicinity of Kuala Lumpur town.

Coffee prospecting and the opening of pioneer estates in the late 1870's and early 1880's was not confined to the Protected Malay States. That peripatetic coffee prospector from Ceylon, Thomas Heslop Hill, paid a three-month visit to Johore in late 1878 and early 1879 to investigate the agricultural possibilities of the state and in particular to examine the hilly areas around Gunong Pulai, Gunong Panti, Gunong Blumut and Gunong Muntahak.[14]

Liberian coffee was first planted in Johore 'from pots in November [18]76' and in 1879 Hill opened a coffee estate on Pulau Ubin in the Johore Strait.[15] The Johore ruler was quick to appreciate the advantages to be gained from encouraging European planters to enter his state and expressed the hope that Johore would become an important coffee-producing centre. Several coffee estates were established in Johore during the early 1880's, some for Arabian coffee, such as that opened by Dew and McKenzie on Gunong Pantai, but most for Liberian

[13] *A.R. Selangor, 1890*, Appendix F; *Selangor Journal*, Vol. 1 No. 15, 7 April 1893, 238.
[14] T.H. Hill, *Reports on Johore*, 1879.
[15] Ibid. 16.

coffee as were the Pioneer Estate on Gunong Pulai and the Castlewood Estate at Tebrau.[16]

Most of the early coffee estates in Johore were in the southern part of the state, generally lying at the most twenty miles from the Johore Strait. The attraction of Johore lay in its proximity to Singapore, coupled with the belief that should large tracts be opened the Sultan would 'give every assistance reasonably to be expected in the way of roads'. Certainly the land terms offered to planters in Johore were not particularly more favourable than those offered in the Protected Malay States.[17]

European coffee planting grew in importance in Johore during the 1880's. By 1888 there were estimated to be about 1,500 acres planted with Liberian coffee on European-owned estates, and this acreage was reported to be increasing annually; a few Chinese had also planted small areas with the crop in southern Johore.[18] By this time the planting of Arabian coffee was declining rapidly 'owing to the poorness and unsuitability of the soil, the elevation of the hills (only a few hundred feet in height), the difficulties of labour supply, and the unhealthiness of the climate'.[19] Henceforth the planters concentrated their attention on Liberian coffee, almost exclusively in the Johore Bahru and Batu Pahat Districts.

Coffee prices on the London market, the intended destination of the produce of the new European estates in Malaya, declined noticeably during the early 1880's, and in 1885 were over 40 per cent. below the average price in 1876. This dampened the desire of European planters to open further estates in the Malayan wilderness. No new coffee estates were opened by Europeans in the Protected Malay States between 1885 and

[16] Winstedt, 'History of Johore', 117; S.F.P., N.S., Vol. 2 No. 5, 31 January 1885; S.F.P., N.S., Vol. 1 No. 12, 20 December 1884 and Vol. 3 No. 3, 18 July 1885.

[17] Hill, op. cit. 3. In Johore planters could apply for blocks of forest aggregating 1,000 acres, to be taken up in separate blocks of not less than 300 acres each, on 99-year leases. Ibid. 17.

[18] S.F.P., 3rd Series, No. 58, 31 August 1888.

[19] Rathborne, op. cit. 15-16.

1888, although in 1886 Sir Graeme Elphinstone did buy the part-planted Waterloo Estate from the Perak Government.[20]

Improved market conditions, coupled with the example of success on the part of the pioneer planters and growing Government concern to encourage European planters to open estates produced a marked expansion of European coffee planting in the late 1880's, particularly in Selangor. At the same time one estate was opened in Perak, but no further development occurred in Negri Sembilan. Meanwhile, a few Chinese in Malacca had planted Liberian coffee, usually on abandoned tapioca land.[21]

In 1888 in recognition of his work in pioneering European estate agriculture Hill was granted rent-free a 10,000-acre agricultural concession in Kuala Kangsar District. This became known as the Kamuning Estate, part of which was planted with Liberian coffee and a small amount of pepper[22] (Fig. 30). The granting of this land to Hill reflects the growing desire of Government officials in Malaya to attract more European planters, for in 1887 the Governor, Sir Frederick Weld, had given permission for Hill to be supported by a loan of public money to enable him to develop this new property. Weld's successor, Sir Cecil Smith, was apparently prepared to extend the same 'indulgence' to others but no other new European coffee estates were opened in Perak until the following decade.

The most marked extension of European coffee planting in the late 1880's occurred in Selangor. In 1888 Dougal, Toynbee and Currie acquired three blocks of land aggregating 1,500 acres in the Setapak valley to the north-east of Kuala Lumpur; these they named the Hawthornden, Lincoln and Roslin Estates. The following year R.S. and C. Meikle opened the Wardieburn Estate near-by (Fig. 30). The major crop on all these estates was

[20] A.R. Superintendent of Government Plantations, Perak, 1888, P.G.G., Vol. 2, 1889, No. 151, 354.
[21] For example, Chee Hoon Bong and Chee Lim Bong had planted coffee at Batu Berendam and Tan Hun Guan had a 'splendid estate' of Liberian coffee on a former tapioca plantation at Durian Tunggal. Malacca Weekly Chronicle, Vol. 1 No. 1, 7 January 1888 and Vol. 1 No. 6, 11 February 1888.
[22] A.R. Superintendent of Government Plantations, Perak, 1888, P.G.G., Vol. 2, 1889, No. 151, 356.

Liberian coffee, although small amounts of pepper were also planted. In 1889 H. Huttenbach acquired two small blocks close to Kuala Lumpur town which had already been planted with Liberian coffee, one by a former member of the Land Office staff and the other by a group of Javanese; these he named the Selangor and Batu Estates respectively. A year later a new estate, The Mount, was opened in this same area by the Glassford brothers who had had experience of coffee planting in southern India.[23] by 1890 ten European coffee estates had been opened in Selangor, although one, that at Ginting Bidai, had been abandoned and the land surrendered. These estates were restricted to the immediate environs of Kuala Lumpur town, and especially to the Gombak and Setapak valleys (Fig. 30). It is unlikely that their aggregate planted area exceeded 350 acres.

This marked regional concentration of European coffee estates immediately to the north and north-east of Kuala Lumpur town requires special explanation. Clearly the sites chosen were both accessible and convenient in relation to the near-by town. This was an important consideration at a time when suitable roads were few in Selangor, but it takes on a new significance when it is noted that many of the estate pioneers were involved in other activities besides planting, and in particular frequently acted as road and railway contractors, as did Hill, Rathborne and Toynbee. Consequently, they chose sites for their estates that permitted them to live in or close to Kuala Lumpur so that they could supervise the work on their estates and keep up their other business interests.[24] Moreover, in selecting land in this area they took into account the fact that at that time mining activities centred on the flatter land to the east and south of the town in a zone extending from Ampang to Petaling. There appeared to be little fear of competition arising between mining and planting interests if they took up land in the undulating area on the northern and north-eastern periphery. Finally, the success already achieved on the Weld Hill Estate

[23] *A.R. Selangor, 1889*, 18; *Selangor Journal*, Vol. 1 No. 15, 17 April 1893, 238-9.

[24] See for example 'Interviews with Celebrities—F.A. Toynbee', *Selangor Journal*, Vol. 3 No. 13, 8 March 1895, 209.

provided a strong motive for establishing new estates in the same general area.

General Features of the Pioneer Phase

Before passing on to a discussion of the boom period of the 1890's it is desirable that some of the general features of this pioneer stage in the establishment of the coffee industry in Malaya should be considered. The most important point to bear in mind is that the cultivation of Liberian coffee was 'as yet in an experimental stage... and it was still uncertain whether it would take kindly to the soil and climate, or become the failure it afterwards was in Ceylon'.[25] The original estates in Ceylon were planted with Arabian coffee, a crop particularly suited to hilly terrain. When the fungus struck these estates it was the Arabian coffee bushes that it devastated. In 1872 Sir Joseph Hooker directed attention to Liberian coffee as a substitute believed to be more resistant to the fungus, and during the 1870's trial plantings of this variety were made in Ceylon. Although it has been suggested that a Frenchman, Leopold Es. Chasseriau, introduced Liberian coffee to Malaya, it is more usual to attribute this introduction to Leonard Wray, the so-called 'Father of Coffee-Planting in Malaya'. Whoever deserves the credit Liberian coffee seeds first arrived Malaya in 1875.[26]

The circumstances outlined above explain the variety of crops grown on most of the pioneer European coffee estates. Their unhappy experiences in Ceylon and their limited knowledge of local conditions made most of the planters cautious in the development of their new estates. Some planted Arabian coffee on high-level estates, but many others preferred Liberian coffee, believing it to possess a greater immunity to disease. They all planted parts of their new estates with crops other than coffee, including cocoa, tea, cinchona and pepper, so that if their experience in Ceylon was repeated they would have something to fall back on.

[25] Rathborne, op. cit. 46.
[26] J. de Morgan, 'Historique de la Presqu'ile Malaise', footnote 1, page 15, in J. de Morgan, Exploration dans la Presqu'ile Malaise (Royaumes de Pérak et de Patani), Paris, 1886; S.F.P., 3rd Series, No. 489, 8 December 1896.

Coming from the lower areas of the west coast of Africa Liberian coffee was well-suited to the lowlands of Malaya. It produced lower yields than Arabian coffee and gave seeds 'rather too large to find favour in markets which prefer a small bean; and they were rather variable in appearance' and apparently less fragrant.[27] Nevertheless, by the late 1880's the Malayan industy was becoming increasingly based upon Liberian coffee which was now giving successful results and for several reasons the cultivation of Arabian coffee was declining. The experience of the planters in Ceylon, where their major crop had been Arabian coffee, generally seems to have predisposed them to prefer inland, hilly locations for the pioneer estates and European-owned Liberian coffee estates were not opened extensively on the coastal plains of western Malaya until the 1890's (Figs. 30 and 31).

A final point worthy of note is the very limited interest shown by the Chinese in coffee planting. Apart from nutmegs and cloves, this was the first type of plantation agriculture to appear in Malaya that did not owe much of its early development to Chinese enterprise. One reason for this situation is the fact that Chinese planters were already involved in the cultivation of several other remunerative crops. Moreover, coffee was basically different from the crops currently in favour with the Chinese planters and merchant-financiers in that it involved a relatively heavy capital investment that would give very little return until at least the fifth year.[28] In other words, coffee planting was a long-term investment and one which the Chinese had yet to be convinced was really likely to produce higher profits than their existing crops. The short-term investment involved in tapioca, gambier and even sugar planting, which either produced quick returns or allowed rapid replacement by other crops, was better suited to the requirements and methods of financing of Chinese in nineteenth-century Malaya. In the long run the cautious

---

[27] Burkill, *Dictionary of the Economic Products of the Malay Peninsula*, Vol. 1, 624 and 627.

[28] 'Liberian Coffee', *Kew Bulletin*, No. 47, November 1890, 248; Isabella Bird estimated that a capital of £2,500 to £3,500 was needed to open a coffee estate in Malaya. Bird, op. cit. 248.

attitude of the Chinese towards coffee planting proved to their advantage.

Labour Problems in the Pioneer Phase

The growing desire of Government officials to attract further European planters to open estates has already been noted. But the granting of land on easy terms was not alone sufficient; prospective planters also required an assured supply of labour. Coffee planting was comparatively labour intensive; between forty and sixty labourers were required to work 100 acres of land already planted with coffee or pepper on the early Selangor estates.[29] Liberian coffee has relatively shallow roots and is therefore susceptible to weed competition; the estates were therefore clean-weeded. Other labour-demanding tasks included pruning and harvesting. The coffee berries were gathered by hand and, although the main cropping seasons were May to June and December to February, smaller crops ripened all the year round.

The labour problems facing the planters during this pioneer phase were pin-pointed by Swettenham in 1889 when he observed that

... the native of the country works little for himself and absolutely refuses to hire himself out as a labourer on any terms that a planter could accept. The mines absorb the attention of the Chinese, who prefer failure there to steady work and steady wages on an estate, and the planter's only chance of a labour force on which he can rely depends on the natives of Southern India, whom he must import into the State on certain conditions for a term of months.[30]

During the 1880's the number of Indian labourers coming to Malaya was always insufficient; their quality as labourers was often poor; and the cost of recruiting and importing them was heavy; moreover, the coffee planters had to compete with other large-scale employers, particularly the Government, for the limited Indian labour available.

Initially many of the pioneer coffee planters overcame this shortage of Tamil labour by employing Malays, Javanese or

[29] J.C. Jackson, 'Population Changes in Selangor State', 47.
[30] *A.R. Perak, 1889, P.G.G.,* Vol. 3, 1890, 468.

Chinese. Thus, the Castlewood Estate in Johore was opened with Javanese labour and Paul noted in his report on Sungei Ujong for 1882 that a great deal had been done by the planters there 'towards utilizing Malay labour, and large numbers of coolies come from the adjacent small states to procure work both at Pantai and Rantau'.[31]

There can be little doubt however, that having come from Ceylon most of the pioneer coffee planters preferred Tamil labour, and that as more land was planted and came into bearing the labour shortage became critical. It was in fact the major restriction on the further expansion of European coffee planting during the 1880's. The closure of the Bukit Berembun Estate in the early 1880's has been attributed to this cause, and on the Selangor estates of Hill and Rathborne the crop 'was lost in 1884, 1885, 1886 and 1887 *from want of labour*'. Although the Linsum Estate was extended during 1888, 'the difficulty of procuring labour prevented greater extensions', and in 1890 parts of the Kamuning Estate 'for want of labour were temporarily abandoned'.[32]

Some Government officials considered that claims of labour shortages were merely excuses put forward by land speculators who had failed to cultivate the required proportion of land alienated to them for agricultural purposes within the specified period. The examples quoted above, however, are not isolated cases and the expansion of the 1890's is directly related to an improvement in the labour situation.

The Coffee Boom, 1891-6

Slavery was abolished in Brazil in May 1888, temporarily dislocating the coffee industry in the world's major producing centre. Prices began to rise and reached a peak of over $40 per pikul in 1894 and 1895.

In the meantime, the Governments of the Protected Malay

---

[31] *S.F.P.*, N.S., Vol. 1 No. 12, 20 December 1884; *Accounts and Papers*, 1884, Vol. LV, C-4192, Encl. 3 in No. 13, *A.R. Sungei Ujong, 1882*.

[32] 'Liberian Coffee in the Malay Native States', *Kew Bulletin*, No. 71, November 1892, 279; *A.R. Sungei Ujong, 1889, S.S.G.G.*, 1889, No. 357, 1091; *M.R. Kuala Kangsar*, January 1891, *P.G.G.*, Vol. 4, 1891, No. 87, 98.

States continued to do their utmost to attract European planters. In April 1891 the Perak Government issued a special *Notice to Planters* offering attractive terms to the first ten approved applications for large blocks of agricultural land. This produced a quick response and towards the end of 1891 it was replaced by a new circular stipulating that the Perak Government was prepared to grant a further limited number of approved applications for land on special terms.[83]

These moves on the part of the Perak Government are a practical reflection of the view expressed by Treacher in 1891 that 'to raise Perak to the position of a planting state, such for instance as Ceylon, the introduction of European planters and planting companies is a *sine qua non*'. It was his opinion that the Government should continue to offer the most attractive terms possible to *bona fide* European planters who could show that they possessed or could raise the necessary capital. 'Planting' he maintained, 'stands in need of at least all the support and fostering encouragement that has in the past been bestowed upon mining'.[34] Similar views were current among Government officials in Selangor and Sungei Ujong and in 1894 the Sungei Ujong Government issued a *Circular to Planters* inviting applications for land on terms that were much the same as those offered in Perak.[35]

But high prices and increasing Government encouragement were not sufficient to produce the boom of the mid-1890's; before large-scale expansion could occur the labour situation had to be improved. The granting of a steamship subsidy in 1887 and the opening of a depot at Negapatam to examine intending migrants in 1890 helped in this direction. Moreover, wages rose as demand grew. As a result, the number of immigrants began to increase and their quality improved. Most of the coffee planters preferred to employ 'free' Tamil labour rather than the indentured immigrants common on the sugar estates and the number of 'free' Tamil labourers arriving in Selangor more than doubled between 1891 and 1893. In the latter year Treacher reported that he was informed by one of

[83] *P.G.G.*, Vol. 4, 1891, No. 171, 205; ibid. No. 344, 1114.
[34] *A.R. Perak, 1891, P.G.G.*, Vol. 5, 1892, No. 243, 414 and 417.
[35] *Sungei Ujong Notifications*, 1894, No. 68, 45.

the leading European planters that 'the difficulty in procuring Tamil labour, not statute [i.e. 'free'] is decreasing annually'.[36] The improving labour situation permitted the planters to take full advantage of Government encouragement and rising coffee prices; the result was a rush for land and a rapid expansion of the acreage planted with coffee on European estates.

In response to the special terms now offered the Perak Government received twenty-two applications for land from European planters during 1891 and by mid-1892 'several hopeful applications for Liberian coffee land' had been received from Ceylon planters.[37] Nevertheless, the immediate effects of the special terms were not encouraging. Little work had been done on the large grants given to the approved applicants and it is probable that less than 400 acres of Liberian coffee had been planted on European estates in Perak by the end of 1892.

The coffee boom began to have its most noticeable effects in Perak, as elsewhere in Malaya, in 1893 and 1894. In 1893 the Government Plantation at Padang Rengas, formerly mainly under pepper, was acquired by Lutyens who immediately began to plant Liberian coffee.[38] The next year the expansion of European coffee planting into coastal Perak was initiated by F.A. Stephens who obtained 500 acres in Matang which he named the Jebong Estate. He was followed by several others, including C.G. Ogilvie of Ipoh who was granted 640 acres near Simpang and C.L. Gibson who selected two blocks totalling 820 acres near Kampong Dew on behalf of Monsieur Chambre. During the same year applications were approved for several large concessions for coffee planting between Ipoh and Gopeng in Kinta; by 1896 there were seven coffee estates in this District and negotiations were pending for the granting of several other concessions. During 1895 and 1896 European planters continued to show interest in acquiring land in Matang and Larut and new estates were commenced near Jebong and Sungei Tinggi.

[36] A.R. Selangor, 1893, 16.

[37] A.R. Land Department, Perak, 1891, P.G.G., Vol. 5, 1892, No. 205, 295; Report of State Commissioner of Lands, June 1892, P.G.G., Vol. 5, 1892, No. 320, 720.

[38] M.R. Kuala Kangsar, October 1893, P.G.G., Vol. 6, 1893, No. 678, 983.

By the end of 1895 however, coffee had been planted out on only one estate, the Jebong Estate, in Matang District.[39]

The acquisition of new land for coffee by Europeans in Perak was not restricted to Matang and Kinta. In 1895 land was granted for coffee near Tanjong Malim and early in 1896 additional land was granted for the same purpose in Batang Padang. New estates were also opened in Kuala Kangsar by Sir Graeme Elphinstone. European coffee planting first extended into Lower Perak in January 1896 when a block of land known as the Cecily Estate was granted to the Lower Perak Planting Company. During this same period a number of Chinese holdings, usually twenty to fifty acres in size, were planted with coffee in Perak, and coffee planting also became widespread among the Malay population. By the end of 1896 over 35,000 acres were in the hands of European coffee planters in Perak, and European coffee estates had been commenced in every District of the state except Upper Perak; a total of over 1,500 acres was planted with Liberian coffee on these estates.[40]

The extension of European coffee planting in Selangor in the late 1880's continued in the early years of the following decade. By the end of 1892 there were seventeen European-owned estates in the state, with a total area of 9,464 acres, of which about 1,400 acres were planted with coffee; a year later there were nineteen European-owned estates totalling 12,300 acres, and Liberian coffee had been planted already or was in the process of being planted on 2,150 acres.[41] These estates were still confined to the Klang and Kuala Lumpur Districts; although the crop had been planted on most of the former pepper estates

[39] M.R. Matang, June and October 1894, P.G.G., Vol. 7, 1894, No. 442, 549 and No. 761, 643. A.R. Land Department, Perak, 1894, P.G.G., Vol. 8, 1895, No. 174, 165; A.R. Lands and Mines, F.M.S., 1896, P.G.G., Vol. 10, 1897, No. 198, 189; A.R. Matang, 1895, P.G.G, Vol. 9, 1896, No. 247, 209.

[40] M.R. Tanjong Malim, August 1895, P.G.G., Vol. 8, 1895, No. 601, 848; M.R. Batang Padang, February 1896, P.G.G., Vol. 9, 1896, No. 205, 185; M.R. Kuala Kangsar, September 1896, ibid. No. 597, 680; M.R. Lower Perak, January 1896, ibid. No. 110, 104; A.R. Perak, 1896, 9.

[41] A.R. Selangor, 1892, 10; A.R. Selangor, 1893, 16.

in Klang, interest in the opening of new coffee estates remained focussed almost entirely on the Kuala Lumpur area (Fig. 31). W.E. Maxwell had not always been well-disposed towards the planting community, but his successor as British Resident in Selangor, E.W. Birch, adopted a different view. He noted in 1892 that

... it has been said, and with much reason, that as coffee planting is now established in Selangor the same arguments do not exist, as formerly, for extending to the planters Government assistance in the way of loans ... [but] it should be remembered that it is still to the interest of the State to attract planters, and that no inducement will prove so attractive as the success of those who first ventured.[42]

His assessment proved correct for in the subsequent four years European coffee planting extended very rapidly into every District of the state.

In 1892 one planter expressed the view that the soil of the Klang District was 'more suitable for coffee than any other district in the state', and European coffee planting on new estates began in this District in 1893. In the next two years large areas were acquired by European planters in Klang, which rapidly became 'the most important planting district in the state'.[43] The year 1894 also witnessed the extension of European coffee planting into Ulu Selangor, Ulu Langat and Kuala Langat, and in the following year the first estates were commenced in Kuala Selangor (Fig. 31). The number of European-owned estates in Selangor increased from thirty-five in 1894 to seventy-two, aggregating about 47,000 acres, in 1896; half of these estates were located in the Klang District and a quarter in Kuala Lumpur District.[44] The Malayan coffee boom had found its greatest expression in the Klang District of Selangor.

This replacement of Kuala Lumpur by Klang as the main centre of European coffee planting in Malaya is one of the most interesting geographical features of the boom period of the mid-

---

[42] A.R. Selangor, 1892, 10.

[43] Selangor Journal, Vol. 1 No. 10, 27 January 1893, 157 and Vol. 2 No. 15, 6 April 1894, 230; A.R. Selangor, 1894, 9.

[44] A.R. Selangor, 1894, 10 and A.R. Selangor, 1896, 3.

1890's. Liberian coffee was well-suited to the coastal plains of Selangor and the switch of interest to these, as to the coastal areas of Perak at the same time, possibly reflects the recognition of this fact. Interest in this area may also have been aroused by the success of Haji Mahomed Tahir who had planted Liberian coffee near Klang in the 1880's and also by that achieved by the European pepper planters who had turned to coffee cultivation.[45]

The main cause of this new concentration however, was the current Government policy of spatially separating mining and planting activities in the state. It was stated in 1895 that

... it has been the policy of the Government to direct planters to the coastal districts, as much as possible, leaving the inland districts practically free for miners, since, although it is probable that planting land in the latter is as rich as in the former districts, tin deposits ... are seldom found to be payable in Selangor, except within a few miles of the hills, and it is most undesirable that cultivated land should be disturbed by mining.[46]

Accessibility also helped to make Klang the most favoured of the coastal districts in the eyes of the coffee planters.

The rush for coffee land began in Negri Sembilan in 1893 when W. Dunman obtained a 1,000-acre grant at Senawang and A. Braddon was granted a similar block at Paroi. The following year with the assistance of further capital from relations at home Dunman opened the Terentang and Gadut Estates. Expansion was marked in 1895, particularly along the railway line where the newly-formed Port Dickson Coffee Company took up 2,000 acres and J. Burt and P. Sharpe, both of London, were each granted 500-acre blocks.[47] By this date more than 1,000 acres had been planted with Liberian coffee on European estates in Negri Sembilan.

European coffee planting here concentrated almost entirely in the Seremban and Coast Districts. But Chinese were also

[45] *Selangor Journal*, Vol. 2 No. 24, 10 August 1894, 400.
[46] *A.R. Selangor, 1895*, 11.
[47] W. Dunman, *Tales of Malaya*, Singapore, 1931, 32; *N.S.S.F., Land 1173/93, P.D. 1456/95* and *P.D. 1437/95; A.R. Sungei Ujong and Jelebu,* 1893, S. Ujong Notifications, 1894, No. 78, 67; *A.R. Negri Sembilan, 1895,* 51.

taking to the crop in Negri Sembilan during the 1890's, sometimes on smallholdings averaging twenty to fifty acres, and sometimes on much larger concessions, and this activity extended into every district of the state, as did coffee planting by Malay smallholders.[48]

Land Speculation and the 'Klang Fiasco'

It has been shown that rising prices, attractive land terms and an improving labour situation produced an increasing demand for land from European planters in the late 1880's and early 1890's. Generally speaking this development was heartily welcomed by the Governments concerned, although occasionally fears were expressed that some of the acquisition was little more than land speculation. The accusation made by Maxwell in 1890 that the alleged scarcity of labour would continue 'to furnish the land-speculators an excuse for not opening tracts of forest land obtained on easy terms from Government, ostensibly for agricultural purposes' was not, in fact, entirely unfounded.[49] In 1887 a 5,000-acre block of land was granted to Sword and Muhlinghaus in Klang. No attempt was made to open this land and in 1890 the Senior District Officer expressed the view that its acquisition was 'a mere land-speculation in view of an expected rise in the value of land on the opening of the Klang Railway'.[50]

Such examples, however, are rare because agricultural land was granted on terms designed to discourage this type of speculation. The terms stipulated that a *bona fide* commencement must be made on the land within one year and that at least one quarter of the total area granted must be cultivated within the first five years; if these terms were not complied with or the land was abandoned for three consecutive years then it reverted to the Government.

---

[48] E.g. a 25-acre block was planted with coffee by a Chinese at Kuala Panting, Kuala Pilah, in 1896, *M.R. Kuala Pilah*, February 1896, *N.S.G.G.* Vol. 1, 1896, No. 62, 101, and Wee Yong planted coffee on a 300-acre block in mukim Rasah granted to him in 1897. *N.S.S.F., Land 1340/97.*

[49] *A.R. Selangor, 1890, 13.*

[50] Ibid. Appendix F.

The rush for land, particularly in Klang in 1893 and 1894 caused considerable optimism in Government circles. By 1894 it was felt that coffee planting in Selangor had passed beyond the experimental stage and 'may fairly be considered an assured success, not merely in Klang, although planters have recently shown a special predilection for that district, but in every district of the state'.[51] This culminated in a feeling among Selangor Government officials that coffee planters no longer required special encouragement and that the time had come for the Government to receive a return on the money it had invested in the industry. This new outlook made itself felt in two different ways.

In the first place in 1894 it was decided that the annual rent on land taken up for coffee planting in Klang should be increased from twenty-five cents to fifty cents per acre. Secondly, it was recommended in 1892 that in future agricultural land should be granted in 320-acre blocks.[52] The planters were unanimously against this proposal; Thomas Heslop Hill believed that a block of this size was quite insufficient for economical working, and in his opinion 'any man wishing to open for coffee should be entitled to take up a block of 1,000 acres'.[53] Although the British Resident tended to agree with the planters, the proposal was adopted in 1895. At the same time it was decided that in future agricultural land in Klang and Kuala Selangor Districts and within a five-mile radius of Kuala Lumpur could only be alienated after being offered for sale by public auction. During 1895 twenty-four blocks were sold by public auction, twenty-two in Klang and two in Kuala Lumpur; although no auction was held in Kuala Selangor, twenty blocks had been surveyed and were shortly offered for sale.[54]

The terms of sale offered at these auctions necessitated accurate and complete surveys and this tended to slow down the process of alienation. In combination with rising coffee prices this caused a rapid increase in land values, particularly

---

[51] *A.R. Selangor, 1894*, 21.

[52] E.A. Watson, 'Scheme for Government Plantations in the State of Selangor', 8 July 1892. *N.S.S.F., C.S. 1513/92*.

[53] *Selangor Journal*, Vol. 3 No. 8, 28 December 1894, 129.

[54] *A.R. Selangor, 1895*, 11 and 20.

in Klang, where in some instances land planted with coffee ranging from two and a half to four and a half years old was changing hands at between $350 and $650 per acre.[55]

The introduction of these new regulations had a disastrous effect on the reputation of Selangor as a 'planting state'. Land immediately to the south of Klang town sold at auction in February and August 1895 was described as 'thickly timbered flat country very rich soil' on the official map issued for the sale (Fig. 32). It was discovered to consist mainly of peat 'on which no coffee could possibly grow'; it was, in fact, the contemporary belief that 'damp soils are unfit for coffee'; although Liberian coffee was well-suited to the coastal districts, it was intolerant of water-logged conditions.[56] Two planters from Ceylon, T.N. Christie and W. Forsythe, were most affected by this discovery for they had acquired several blocks in the area concerned at both auctions (Fig. 32). The District Officer of Klang, W.W. Douglas, considered that they were wrong in their belief that even if this peaty land was drained it would not grow coffee. Nevertheless, by May 1896 Christie and Forsythe had decided to abandon the land, known as the Dato Dagang, Sempang and Lanka Estates, which they had acquired between Jalan Kebun and the Langat Road (Fig. 32).

This so-called 'Klang Fiasco' considerably undermined the confidence that planters, both in Malaya and in Ceylon, had felt hitherto in the Selangor Government. A commentator in the *Singapore Free Press* in March 1896 observed that the planting reputation of Selangor was 'seriously endangered by the fiasco at Klang, to which indeed Government has made itself an accessory by its efforts to boom the district and inflate the price of land by having it put up to auction'. He continued, 'as a field for planting enterprise Selangor needs a fostering policy rather than a bleeding policy'.[57]

News of the 'fiasco' spread rapidly. By March 1896 *The Times of Ceylon* carried an article accusing the Selangor Government

[55] *S.F.P.*, 3rd Series, No. 449, 3 March 1896.

[56] *S.F.P.*, 3rd Series, No. 450, 10 March 1896; F.W. Dafert, 'On the present condition of the culture of coffee in Brazil', lecture given at Amsterdam, 18 March 1898. *N.S.S.F.*, *N.S. 3095/99*.

[57] *S.F.P.*, 3rd Series, No. 450, 10 March 1896.

of 'fostering a little boom'; henceforth many in Ceylon would be wary of investing in this state. This was the effect feared most both by established planters and Government officials. The District Officer of Klang was afraid that 'very exaggerated ideas of the now supposed worthless Klang land will ... spread far and wide, and be the cause of keeping away many intending investors of capital'. E.V. Carey pointed out that because the land involved in the 'fiasco' had been found to be peaty it should not be taken to indicate that the whole of Klang District was similar. The editor of the *Singapore Free Press* suggested that the Selangor Government should 'make for itself a decent name amongst the holders of planting capital elsewhere' by giving the planters involved the option of taking up other land in the state. But the damage had been done, and when signs of a fall in coffee prices appeared in 1898 European interest in acquiring land in Klang faded quickly.[58]

Clearly the 'Klang Fiasco' reflected badly upon the Selangor Government which must shoulder responsibility for much of the blame. It should be borne in mind, however, that the planters and their supporters were more vociferous in their complaints than the Government was in its defence, not least because the Government had little desire to publicize the event. Undoubtedly, the introduction of public auctions for blocks of 320 acres indicates a desire on the part of the Government to capitalize on the current rush for land. In view of the short-lived nature of the coffee boom they perhaps changed too quickly from a policy of encouragement and easy terms. But the main share of the blame attaching to the Government relates to its offer, on what must be regarded as almost false pretences, of blocks of 'supposed coffee-land' at public auction. Blame must also fall on the shoulders of the planters and their backers not least because the boom had made them incautiously land hungry.

In many instances investors in Ceylon relied upon planters resident in Malaya as intermediaries for the acquisition of land. If the buyers or their intermediaries did not inspect the land prior to the auction simply because the Government was

---

[58] *S.F.P.*, 3rd Series, No. 451, 17 March 1896; No. 453, 31 March 1896; and No. 458, 5 May 1896.

offering it for sale as 'coffee-land' then they are clearly to blame.
Yet there is evidence to show that Forsythe, one of the principal
buyers, 'inspected his selections prior to the sale by auction,
and on the date of the sale sent instructions by telegram for
certain blocks (included in those abandoned) to be purchased'.[59]
Signs that the price of coffee was likely to fall appeared early
in 1896 and there is the possibility that the buyers were indul-
ging in some form of speculation; however, Christie's position as
the planters' representative on the Ceylon Council would appear
to make this unlikely.

In the context of the present work the importance of the
'Klang Fiasco' lies in the fact that it shows that whereas Government policy did much to stimulate the expansion of European
coffee planting, and in particular caused the noteworthy concentration in Klang District, a change in that policy could just
as easily turn the attention of planters elsewhere. European
planters and Government officials formed two distinct and very
different groups in late nineteenth-century Malaya. At this time
the former, with their incipient but as yet largely ineffective
associations, had little means of influencing Government policy.
Changes could occur in agricultural patterns as much because
a new Government policy was introduced as because other conditions had altered.

The Decline of Coffee Planting

In 1894 and 1895 the price of coffee reached a peak of over
$40 per pikul. By the early months of 1896 it was clear that a
fall in prices was imminent and at the beginning of August
1896 the price on the Singapore market stood at $32 per pikul.
The effects were apparent immediately. Swettenham remarked
that the price of Liberian coffee fell so low in 1897 that 'the
hitherto bright prospects of the industry were overclouded; and
some of the planters who were working on a small capital were
unable to contend against the altered condition of the market'.[60]
In January 1898 the price of coffee fell below $20 and declined
further to $15.50 per pikul in August 1899. The effects were so

[59] *S.F.P.*, 3rd Series, No. 458, 5 May 1896.
[60] *A.R.F.M.S.*, *1897*, 3.

disastrous that in 1899 the Federated Malay States Government decided to suspend the export duty on coffee whilst the price remained below $19 per pikul. During the early years of the twentieth century coffee prices wavered around $20, but in 1904 rose to such a level that many estates on which coffee was inter-planted with rubber obtained sufficient income from the sale of coffee to cover all the expenses incurred in the maintenance of both crops.[61]

The year 1906 must be regarded as the final turning point in the history of the Malayan coffee industry. Although as a result of valorization in Brazil, prices had risen to a level which allowed a good profit, the events of the preceding decade had given rubber a magnetic attraction in the eyes of local planters. Sir William Taylor observed that had it not been for this fact the cultivation of coffee would probably have been on the increase 'in place of being wiped out as will shortly be the case'.[62] By 1906 the time had passed when a rise in coffee prices was sufficient to cause a widespread revival of the industry; the *coup de grâce* had already been effected by rubber planting.

The decline of coffee prices on the world market in the late 1890's resulted from greatly increased production in Brazil consequent on an inflow of immigrant peasant labour in the early years of the decade; the situation was aggravated by the price manipulations of the so-called 'Coffee Kings' such as George Kaltenbach, B.G. Arnold, Hermann Sielcken and Guzman Blanco.[63] The fall in prices came at an inopportune time for the Malayan coffee planters. On the one hand wage-rates were rising; on the other hand the three- to four-year maturation period meant that the large areas planted during the boom came into bearing when prices were at their lowest ebb. Thus, peak production in each of the western Malay States came in the early years of the twentieth century, bringing much lower returns than those anticipated when the coffee was planted (Fig. 33). Moreover, the Malayan planters had concentrated on Liberian coffee. In general this gave lower yields than

[61] *A.R. Land Department, Selangor, 1898,* 3; *A.R. Selangor Planters' Association, 1899,* 1; *A.R.F.M.S., 1899,* 4; *A.R.F.M.S., 1904,* 7.

[62] *A.R.F.M.S., 1906,* 8.

[63] Dafert, 'On the present condition of the culture of coffee in Brazil'.

Arabian coffee and the beans fetched lower prices on the market because they were larger and more variable. Profits were therefore smaller than they might otherwise have been and, with prices at very low levels, the concentration on Liberian coffee itself contributed to the downfall of the Malayan coffee industry.

The problems facing the planters were not simply the product of changed market conditions; the depredations of disease and pests also played a part in the decline of the coffee industry. The fungus *Hemileia vastatrix* had appeared in Selangor by 1894 and although Liberian coffee was more resistant than Arabian coffee the scourge of Ceylon had some effects on local estates. But one of the greatest causes of distress to the planting community was the destruction wrought by the caterpillars of the so-called coffee clear wing hawk moth *Cephonodes hylas*. During 1899 these caused considerable damage on several Selangor estates, particularly the Petaling Estate. Within a matter of months a similar outbreak occurred in Negri Sembilan. Beginning on the Chinese-owned Kong Fong Estate at Sipiau it spread quickly to the Seremban, Senawang, Terentang and Gadut Estates causing considerable damage, so much so that all the bushes on the Kong Fong Estate were compulsorily removed. Afraid of the damage that would result from a widespread outbreak in Klang the Selangor Government imported a batch of crows from Ceylon in 1902 in the hope that they would combat the potential menace. Clearly the rapid expansion of this devastating pest was possible because many estate owners and the majority of smallholders had ceased to maintain their coffee properly now that prices were low.[64]

Some of the disappointment causing the planters to turn away from coffee was of their own making. During the boom interest centred on the planting of large areas and very little attention was given to the processing and marketing sides of the industry. As prices fell it became obvious that more careful processing was necessary to produce coffee that could compete

[64] 'Report on the Caterpillars of Cephonodes Hylas attacking the Coffee in the District of Sungei Ujong, Negri Sembilan', June 1900, *P.G.G.*, Vol. 13, 1900, 730-3; *A.R. Land Department, Seremban, 1900, 3; A.R. United Planters' Association,* 1902, 4.

on the over-loaded world market. In the later 1890's this produced a noticeable increase in the desire to improve curing
techniques to ensure that a less variable product was placed on
the market. Thus, J.M. Lyon invented a new Liberian coffee
pulper which he exhibited on the Selangor Estate near Kuala
Lumpur in October 1896; this was specifically designed to
overcome problems associated with the variation in the size of
berries and was a decided improvement on the pulpers used
previously. Also, by 1898 Shepherd had installed a new coffee-
pulper on his Balgownie Estate in Ulu Langat; this was described as 'a most ingenious contrivance of his own invention,
and one which appears to be finding general favour amongst
coffee planters'.[65]

The activities of planters such as these were justified by the
report of an investigation undertaken in the coffee-growing
districts of Brazil in 1898 in the hope of finding a way to revive
the Malayan industry. This report maintained that everything
depended upon how the coffee was cured. 'It must be patent to
everyone', it said, 'that the coffee-consuming public want an
article on which they can always rely and in which they will
not be disappointed. Those whose duty it is to supply that want
must turn out an evenly sorted sample of coffee, must find the
exact point at which the coffee is palatable, and must attain
that point'.[66] The report was a clear indication that the Malayan
planters were suffering so badly as a result of decreased prices
because they had paid insufficient attention to the details of
processing. Not everyone, however, was prepared to accept this
sort of criticism and one contemporary observer remarked that
'we have heard it asserted that our curing is faulty and that
our sizing is bad; but our planters are surely sufficiently alive
to their own interests to guard against these alleged defects'.[67]
That many had not been 'alive to their own interests' in this
respect helped to expedite the decline of the coffee industry,
for their product was difficult to sell. This situation was exacerbated by their lack of attention to methods of marketing and

[65] S.F.P., 3rd Series, No. 483, 27 October 1896; M.R. Ulu Langat, April
1898, S.G.G., 1898, No. 325, 220.
[66] A.R. Negri Sembilan, 1898, 11.
[67] Selangor Journal, Vol. 5 No. 25, 20 August 1897, 401.

advertising during the flush of the boom. In effect, the Malayan planters produced poor coffee which only brought profits when demand was high and supply was unusually low; under normal market conditions their position was unenviable.

Although the situation was grim in the late 1890's many coffee planters and Government officials in Selangor remained optimistic. The demand for new land had decreased but large extensions of the planted area were made within existing estates, particularly in Klang. Whilst replacement or abandonment were the fate of coffee in all other states, with the opening of the new century optimism continued to run high in Selangor. In 1900 the coffee on all European-owned estates here was carefully tended in anticipation of the improvement in market conditions which was 'confidently foreseen by those whose experience lends weight to their opinion'.[68]

The great determination of the Selangor planters to tide over the crisis appeared to have been justified when prices began to rise in 1904. This improvement in market conditions produced a slight revival of coffee planting in the state, mainly in the vicinity of Klang; during 1907 coffee was again 'being planted up, either separately or in conjunction with rubber'.[69] This new planting, however, was not accompanied by a marked increase in the total crop area for simultaneously older coffee was cut out to make way for maturing rubber. In the long run this was the fate of almost all the coffee in Selangor.

Elsewhere confidence in the future of the industry was shaken immediately prices began to fall and the planters were quick to seize upon other crops to the detriment of coffee. In Perak, for instance, a preference for rubber was apparent by 1897 and within a year the new crop had been planted on several estates, including the Cecily, Selinsing and Yam Seng Estates. Similar developments were occurring in Negri Sembilan and Selangor and apart from rubber, several other crops, notably coconuts, attracted the attention of European planters. This switch to other crops was favoured by the United Planters' Association and, at least initially, was regarded by some planters as a temporary phase whilst they waited for 'better

[68] A.R. Selangor, 1900, 3.
[69] A.R. Selangor, 1907, 5.

times for coffee', in most cases the new crops being interplanted with the coffee. By the beginning of the twentieth century however, virtually all applications for new agricultural land in the western Malay states emanating from Europeans were for the planting of crops other than coffee, the majority being granted for rubber planting. It became the general rule for coffee to be removed as the interplanted rubber matured and within a short while the acreage of rubber greatly exceeded that of coffee. This change was accompanied by the winding up of a number of coffee companies and by the purchase of coffee estates by newly-formed rubber companies.

With the first onset of the depression some estate owners looked to tin mining as a means of overcoming their difficulties. Thus, towards the end of 1898 blocks were cut out of the Kamuning and Heawood Estates in Perak for mining purposes; in the same year several planters in Selangor applied for mining rights over their estates and the Government 'dealt with them in a liberal spirit'. Some planters turned to other activities to tide them over their financial difficulties as did the Glassford brothers who supplied the Selangor Public Works Department with laterite; a few even entered Government service.[70]

Apart from causing a change of interest, the coffee depression also resulted in the abandonment of estates. During 1898 two coffee estates in Sungei Ujong 'went under the hammer' and the White Rose Coffee Estate near Bukit Mas in Batang Padang was abandoned. Further estates were abandoned in the subsequent two years and in 1901 the estates of Leybourne Davidson and the Batu Tiga Planting Syndicate in Klang reverted to the Government. Thereafter, the remaining estates turned to other crops.[71]

The expansion of rubber planting during the first decade or so of the present century ensured the demise of the coffee indus-

[70] *M.R. Kuala Kangsar*, November 1898, *P.G.G.*, Vol. 12, 1899, No. 24, 15; *A.R. Land Department, Selangor, 1898*, 3; L.U. Stafford, 'Planting in Selangor in the Old Days', *British Malaya*, Vol. VIII No. 12, April 1934, 256; Allen and Donnithorne, op. cit. 108.

[71] *A.R. Negri Sembilan, 1898*, 11; *M.R. Batang Padang*, June 1898, *P.G.G.*, Vol. 11, 1898, No. 469, 510; *A.R. Negri Sembilan, 1900*, 2; *A.R. Klang, 1901*, 1.

try. By 1902 the European coffee estates in Malaya had 'to a great extent been planted up with Para, which will eventually dispossess the coffee ... [although] well-opened and well-managed estates on well-situated land yield a small profit even at present low prices'.[72] A year later Liberian coffee had completely lost favour and on most estates was regarded merely as a catch-crop to be used in conjunction with rubber planting. By 1905 even in Selangor, the last stronghold of the industry in Malaya, such coffee as remained only received attention when it did not interfere with the growth of the rubber with which most of the 'fields' had been planted. Here the amount of coffee remaining 'lessens year by year, as it is cut out when the rubber trees attain an age at which they require the full use of the ground'.[73] Thus the area planted with coffee in Kuala Lumpur District declined from about 3,000 acres in 1904 to 1,380 acres in 1906, the area planted to coffee on European estates in Klang declined by nearly 50 per cent. during 1907 alone, and at that date only 180 acres of coffee remained in Kuala Selangor.[74]

By the end of the first decade of the twentieth century cultivation had virtually ceased in Perak and Negri Sembilan; in 1909 coffee was estimated to occupy less than 6,000 acres in the Federated Malay States, almost all of which was planted as a catch-crop for rubber.[75] Most of this lay in Klang and as the industry declined it tended to retreat to what had for long been its major centre of concentration. In this District coffee planting was revived slightly in the period 1910-13 when higher prices and the planting of *Coffea robusta* made it a profitable catch-crop on the many newly-planted rubber estates; indeed, in 1913 a total of about 10,000 acres of coffee, mostly interplanted with rubber and heavily concentrated around Klang, existed in Selangor.[76] But even in Selangor the area planted with coffee declined noticeably after 1913 as the rubber matured. Although there was a further slight resurgence of coffee planting in

[72] *A.R.F.M.S., 1902*, 4.

[73] *A.R. Selangor, 1905*, 5.

[74] *A.R. Registry of Titles, Selangor, 1905*, 4; *A.R. Registry of Titles, Selangor, 1906*, 2; *A.R. Klang, 1907*, 2; *A.R. Kuala Selangor, 1907*, 2.

[75] *A.R.F.M.S., 1909*, 8.

[76] *A.R. Selangor, 1913*, 2.

Selangor when rubber prices fell in the late 1910's henceforth the industry was of minor significance.

The Role of the Coffee Boom in the Agricultural History of Malaya

Coffee served as an important pioneer crop in the western Malay states in the late nineteenth century. The expansion of large-scale coffee planting rarely involved the replacement of other crops on existing plantations; rather it heralded the extension of large-scale agricultural enterprise into new areas and was accompanied by the addition of a new and experienced element to the existing planting community. Virgin land was cleared for the new estates and in consequence, the frontier of settlement and the minor road network were pushed outwards with the existing main communication lines determining, as in nineteenth-century Brazil, the general directions of the advance (Fig. 31). Just as there were advancing frontiers associated with the crops discussed in previous chapters, so the development of the coffee industry in the last quarter of the nineteenth century was accompanied by a frontier advance, particularly in Selangor.

Nevertheless, in terms of area occupied, numbers employed and value of exports coffee was never the most important crop produced by plantation agriculture in Malaya in the pre-rubber era. Only in Selangor was coffee planting the major form of large-scale agricultural enterprise; on average this state produced over three-quarters of the coffee exported from the Federated Malay States in the years subsequent to the boom. The importance of the coffee boom in the agricultural history of Malaya as a whole has been over-emphasized in the past. This has resulted mainly from the limelight accorded to coffee planting in both official and unofficial publications. As a plantation crop coffee was widely cultivated in the western Malay states, but it was overwhelmingly important only in Selangor.

During the 1890's the Governments of these states were preoccupied with the idea that agricultural development could only be effected by the encouragement of European planters, and their reports focussed attention upon the success that they were achieving in this respect during a period in which European planters were concentrating upon coffee cultivation. Yet sugar, tapioca and gambier and pepper remained export crops of supreme importance, albeit largely in Chinese hands, in western Malaya throughout the brief and variable history of the coffee industry.

Coffee was the first crop to be cultivated successfully by European planters in many parts of the peninsula. As a result large areas of agricultural land were granted to Europeans on which they eventually planted rubber. The expansion of coffee cultivation brought with it the first planting capital, management personnel and imported agricultural labour, mainly Tamil and Javanese, to many parts of the Malay states, and the channels by which these came to Malaya were later extended to supply the needs of the rubber industry. It was also accompanied by the formulation of an agricultural policy by which the Governments concerned hoped to establish the large-scale European agricultural enterprise which they regarded as a fundamental requirement for agricultural development. The basic features of this policy were easy land terms, sizable planting loans and measures designed to ease the labour situation; when rubber took the place of coffee a favourable official agricultural policy already existed.

At the same time the influx of European planters and the expansion of coffee cultivation were accompanied by the establishment of Planters' Associations which in turn gave the European planting community much greater cohesion; it acquired a new stature and was in a much stronger position in its negotiations with the Government. Although coffee planting in general was a short-lived and unsuccessful enterprise, it did permit a considerable number of European planters to learn something of local conditions in Malaya; it also taught them caution and restraint when their attention was first diverted to rubber and this aided the successful expansion of the latter crop in the early years of the twentieth century.

Belfield estimated that it required an investment of over $44,000 to open, plant and maintain 100 acres of coffee for the first six years, and that if the price of coffee stood at $25 per pikul then the return from the fourth, fifth and sixth years would total about $27,500.[77] Even with the high prices of the boom it took four or five years to repay the cost of opening a coffee estate; with the low prices of the late 1890's and early 1900's it took considerably longer. This slow and by no means certain return on investment was the main factor limiting Chinese interest in coffee planting. It had another important effect, however, for it stimulated a change from the typical proprietary European estate of the 1880's and early 1890's to local- or foreign-based company ownership, and with it the development of 'agency-houses' through which foreign capital could be acquired to finance planting activities. Later these became the cornerstones of the expanding rubber industry in Malaya.

---

[77] H.C. Belfield, *Handbook of the Federated Malay States*, 2nd edition, London, 1904, 164.

PART III

THE RUBBER PLANTATION INDUSTRY

10

RUBBER PLANTING IN MALAYA, 1877-1908
FAITH REPLACES SCEPTICISM

IN PARTS I AND II IT WAS SEEN THAT with the exception of spices, which ceased to be of importance by the 1860's, it was the rapid expansion of rubber planting in the first decade and a half of the present century that gave the *coup de grâce* to the production of the typical nineteeth-century export crops. For various reasons this expansion confirmed the shift from Chinese to European dominance of commercial agricultural enterprise in Malaya. It also paved the way for plantation agriculture to become increasingly monocultural.

The Experimental Phase

A series of technical developments caused an increasing world demand for rubber products in the late eighteenth and nineteenth centuries; of particular importance were Charles Goodyear's discovery of the vulcanization process in 1839; the growth of the electrical industry; and the expanding use of pneumatic tyres, first for bicycles and later for automobiles, in the 1880's, 1890's and early 1900's. World consumption of raw rubber rose from about 100 tons in 1820 to some 50,000 tons by the end of the century; almost the whole of this was obtained from wild rubber-producing plants in the Amazon basin.[1]

Natural rubber is a polymer of an unsaturated hydro-carbon and occurs in a large number of plants. Most of these plants contain too little rubber for economic extraction or it is difficult to obtain free from contaminants; in some cases extraction of rubber results in the destruction of the plant.[2] During the

---

[1] T.R. McHale, 'Changing Technology and Shifts in the Supply and Demand for Rubber: An Analytical History', *Malayan Economic Review*, Vol. IX No. 2, October 1964, 26-29.

[2] P.R. Wycherley, 'A Botanist's Approach to Natural Rubber Production', *New Scientist*, Vol. 9 No. 225, 9 March 1961, 620.

pioneer phase in the history of the rubber plantation industry attempts were made to grow several of these rubber-producing plants on a plantation basis. Ceara rubber (*Manihot glaziovii*), *Geta rambong* (*Ficus elastica*), *Castilloa elastica*, Para rubber (*Hevea brasiliensis*), and several others attracted attention. Within a short while, however, interest centred almost entirely on *Hevea brasiliensis*. Of all the known rubber-producing plants this one gave 'the highest yield of rubber latex with the highest yield of rubber proportionate to extraneous matter per tree and per unit area over a several-year period'. It thrived on a wide range of soils and was remarkably resistant to both disease and insect pests in South-East Asia, the major scene of the industry's development.[3] Moreover, it is relatively easy to extract rubber from *Hevea* by tapping and to prepare the product in a nearly pure form; the rubber content in latex vessels close to a tapping cut is quickly restored by synthesis and the bark regenerates after tapping, thus giving the *Hevea* tree a long productive life.[4]

The origin of the modern plantation industry dates from the early 1870's when *Hevea* seeds were first sent to Kew Gardens, England. The story of how H.A. Wickham collected 70,000 seeds in the area between the Tapajos and Madeira rivers in the central Amazon in 1876, which he then dispatched to Kew, is sufficiently well-known to require further elaboration. The seeds reached Kew in June 1876, about 4 per cent. germinated, and later in the year a large proportion of the seedlings were sent to Ceylon. A few were also sent to Singapore, but these apparently died. A further consignment of twenty-two seedlings arrived in Singapore in 1877 and towards the end of the year nine of these were planted by the side of the Residency at Kuala Kangsar, Perak.[5]

[3] McHale, op. cit. 32.

[4] Wycherley, op. cit. 620-1.

[5] H.N. Ridley, *The Story of the Rubber Industry*, London, n.d., 7; Burkill, *Dictionary of the Economic Products of the Malay Peninsula*, Vol. 1, 1150; M.J. Kennaway, *Cavalcade of Rubber*, Singapore, 1936, 1-2; P.R. Wycherley, 'The Singapore Botanic Gardens, and Rubber in Malaya', *Gardens' Bulletin, Singapore*, Vol. XVII, pt. 2, December 1959, 176.

The seedlings planted in Singapore and Kuala Kangsar thrived. As early as 1879 Hugh Low at Kuala Kangsar reported that 'The Heveas are 12 to 14 feet high. They take to the country immensely'. Three years later he observed that 'all kinds of India rubber succeed admirably' in the Government Gardens at Kuala Kangsar; seeds and plants of *Hevea brasiliensis* had been sent to Java, Singapore, Ceylon and India, and he stated that 'supplies will be forwarded on application to any person or institution which will take care of these valuable plants'. The first Para rubber tree to flower in the East did so at Kuala Kangsar in March 1880 and this tree bore fruit for the first time the following year, as did the trees in Singapore.[6]

In 1883 specimens of rubber were collected from the six-year-old trees at Kuala Kangsar and sent to England for a report, signifying the first attempt at tapping in Malaya and the first sample of cultivated rubber to be despatched from the peninsula to Europe.[7] Swettenham claims that whilst in Perak in 1884-5 he planted out four hundred seeds from the original Kuala Kangsar trees.[8] Rubber now appeared to offer some hope of promise as a plantation crop, and Heslop Hill was persuaded to plant a few trees on his coffee estates at Linsum in Negri Sembilan in 1883 and at Weld Hill in Selangor in 1885. In 1887 seeds from the Kuala Kangsar trees were planted in the museum grounds at Taiping and in the garden of the District Magistrate at Parit Buntar, and before 1890 Heslop Hill had also planted several hundred trees along the sides of the roads on his newly-acquired Kamuning Estate in Perak.[9]

As Jenkins remarks these first plantings were quite unsystematic and were undertaken 'not as a venture but for the purpose of observation'; moreover, Wycherley suggests that Heslop Hill

[6] 'Para Rubber', *Kew Bulletin*, No. 142, October 1898, 271; *Accounts and Papers*, 1884, Vol. LV, C-4192, Encl. 1 in No. 13, *A.R. Perak, 1882*; P. Schidrowitz and T.R. Dawson, eds., *History of the Rubber Industry*, Cambridge, 1952, 53.

[7] *Accounts and Papers*, 1884, Vol. LV, C-4192, Encl. 1 in No. 21, *A.R. Perak, 1883*.

[8] Swettenham, *British Malaya*, 263.

[9] 'Para Rubber', *Kew Bulletin*, No. 142, October 1898, 272; *Straits Times*, 23 November 1899.

planted these trees merely to provide seed should the crop realize its potentialities. It is believed that 'the rubber was very inferior and that Mr. Hill got no further at this date than growing scattered trees from seed'; the rubber was planted as shade trees on the roadsides of his coffee estates.[10]

During the 1880's, however, even the minor interest that had been generated declined. The rising price of coffee diverted the attention of Government officials away from the unproven and untried crop, and the planters who arrived from Ceylon came to open new coffee estates, not to conduct experiments. At the same time, there was a drop in world rubber prices as large supplies from Africa moved on to the world market and this trend was not reversed until the early 1890's (Fig. 34). Economic discouragement merely enhanced the doubts already in the minds of many in Malaya. Murton, Director of the Botanical Gardens in Singapore, argued that local rubber-producing plants were as suitable as *Hevea,* and he insisted that the cost of cultivating this exotic would hardly be repaid. His successor, Cantley, held similar views and several others believed that the potential production of wild rubber in South America alone might be far in excess of the world's needs.[11] The results of attempts to tap the existing trees served to increase the growing scepticism, and an attempt to tap the Kuala Kangsar trees in 1889 was so disappointing that Swettenham, having decided that there was no future for *Hevea* in Malaya, 'ordered the destruction of several of the original Kuala Kangsar trees and discouraged further interest'.[12]

In November 1888 H.N. Ridley arrived in Singapore to become Director of the Botanical Gardens. Convinced that there was a bright future for rubber as a plantation crop he immediately set to work to care for and augment the stock of *Hevea brasiliensis* in his charge. He insisted on the potential value of

---

[10] R.O. Jenkins, 'Rubber, Introduction and Expansion with Special Reference to Malaya', *British Malaya,* Vol. 26 No. 4, August 1951, 298; Wycherley, 'The Singapore Botanic Gardens and Rubber in Malaya', 179; Kennaway, op. cit. 7-8.

[11] Jenkins, op. cit. 298.

[12] Wycherley, 'The Singapore Botanic Gardens and Rubber in Malaya', 178.

this exotic and began a series of experiments to prove his point. Para rubber was first tapped in the East by Dr. Trimen in Ceylon in October 1882; en route from England to Singapore Ridley called at Ceylon in 1888 to observe Trimen's methods. He began tapping experiments on the trees in Singapore in 1889, and the next year exhibited some of the rubber which he produced at the Singapore Horticultural Show. In 1891 he sent samples of rubber to London for a report, and these were pronounced excellent. Although he had to be relatively careful because of the limited number of trees at his disposal, Ridley quickly improved upon the tapping methods devised by Trimen.

Apart from his work as a scientific investigator, Ridley also did his utmost to persuade planters and others in Malaya that Para rubber was worth their attention as a plantation crop. By 1893 plants and seeds were distributed to Government officers in the Malay states and Ridley was using every method in his power to popularize the crop. Indeed, one writer reports that it was his practice to 'stuff seeds into the pockets of planters and others begging them to make a trial': and among planters he earned the soubriquet of 'mad Ridley' or 'rubber Ridley'.[13] In 1893 Heslop Hill sent a sample of rubber produced from the trees on the Linsum Estate to the Officer-in-Charge of Sungei Ujong and asked that it be valued. In the accompanying letter he said that he had 'hundreds if not thousands of trees' on his estate and would be glad to supply 'any quantity of seed that the Goverment [sic] may wish to buy'.[14]

Nevertheless, Ridley's efforts met with little success in the early 1890's. It is reported, for instance, that Heslop Hill could not be persuaded to accept further plants from Ridley because 'he had plenty of trees and they were of no use'.[15] Rapidly rising coffee prices dominated the minds of the planters; most Government officials were even less interested in rubber. Indeed, Ridley claims that at this time he was reprimanded by the Governor

[13] Song Ong Siang, *One Hundred Years' History of the Chinese in Singapore*, Singapore, 449.

[14] *N.S.S.F., Misc. 2051/93.*

[15] O. Marks, 'The Pioneers of Para Rubber Planting in British Malaya', *British Malaya*, Vol. 1, February 1927, 282.

for growing 'exotics' and was ordered to desist.[16] The doubts
current among planters and officials in Malaya in the early
1890's were in fact well-founded. Rubber had never been grown
on plantations before, it was indigenous to another part of the
world, it took six to seven years to mature, its productive life
on plantations was unknown, new sources of rubber were being
exploited in Africa and the future of the market appeared
uncertain.

Several factors swung things in Ridley's favour. The price
of rubber on the world market improved in the mid-1890's and
within a while coffee prices fell disastrously (Fig. 34). The
Malayan coffee planters were in a mood to accept a new crop
and became more sympathetic to Ridley's ideas. Moreover, the
experiments were now giving much greater reason for
confidence.

By the late 1890's rubber had been planted on an experimental basis in several parts of Perak and it was now clear that
it was a hardy plant tolerant of a wide variety of soils and
topographic conditions. Thus, Wray concluded in 1898 that
'it will thrive in any locality, from the bakau swamps to the
foot-hills, and on any soil from rich alluvium to old mine
heaps'.[17] At the same time tapping experiments were more
widely undertaken and continued to produce very satisfactory
results. Curtis began tapping the trees in the Waterfall Gardens,
Penang in 1896. L. Wray began experiments at Taiping in 1897
and was followed the next year by R. Derry at Kuala Kangsar.
In April 1898 Derry reported that many trees had been tapped
and that samples had been valued in London at 2s 8d and 3s
per pound and considered 'equal to Brazilian produced rubber,
and also worth 1s per pound more than that usually sent home
from the Straits'.[18] Samples were also sent to London from
Penang in 1898 and were very well received; reports on further
samples from Penang and Perak in 1899 were extremely prom-

---

[16] H.N. Ridley, 'How Rubber Started in Malaya', *Young Malayans*, 6
February 1954, 44 quoted by Allen and Donnithorne, op. cit. 110.

[17] L. Wray, 'Rubber Growing in Perak', *Perak Museum Notes*, Vol. 2,
pt. 2, 1898, 94.

[18] 'Para Rubber', *Kew Bulletin*, No. 142, October 1898, 271.

ising.[19] Moreover, these experiments showed that continuous production was possible without damaging the trees. By now planters were sufficiently confident in the new crop to begin planting sizable parts of their estates. But although commercial planting had begun the initial experiments were not complete.

Derry joined Ridley in Singapore in 1904 and together they conducted a series of tapping experiments which established 'a number of principles and carried the technique far towards that currently employed'. With the establishment of a Department of Agriculture in the Federated Malay States in 1905 experimental work also began in Kuala Lumpur. Other developments at this time included the type of knife to be used for tapping, the advantages of morning over afternoon tapping and recommendations on suitable planting distances. Almost all the early estates were planted at densities of well over 200 trees per acre; these experiments showed that stands of about 150 trees per acre, or even less, could make tapping more economical and increase the useful life of the trees.[20]

Most of the early planters were fervent believers in the practice of clean-weeding. As early as January 1903 Ridley cautioned against this.[21] The first Director of Agriculture in the Federated Malay States, J.B. Carruthers, also argued strongly against the practice which he considered costly, and the cause of some soil erosion and loss of moisture in the surface layers of the soil. Almost from its inception his Department had investigated the use of 'a substitute for weeds' as a cover-crop and in 1907 he suggested the use of *Crotolaria striata*, *Mimosa pudica* and *Desmodium triflorum*.[22] By 1908 experiments had solved most of the major cultural problems concerning the new industry.

Pioneer Plantings, 1895-1904

Rubber was first planted on a commercial basis in Malaya in the mid-1890's on estates previously opened for other crops.

[19] Ibid. 273; 'Para Rubber in Penang' and 'Para Rubber in Perak', *Kew Bulletin*, Nos. 145-6, January and February 1899, 21-22.
[20] Wycherley, 'The Singapore Botanic Gardens and Rubber in Malaya', 178-9.
[21] *N.S.S.F.*, N.S. 544/1903.
[22] *A.R. Director of Agriculture, F.M.S.*, 1907, 10-13.

Some confusion exists as to who deserves the credit for the
initial planting but in either 1895 or 1896 the Kindersley
brothers planted a five-acre stand of *Hevea* on their Inch
Kenneth Estate near Kajang in Selangor and Tan Chay Yan
planted forty acres, interplanted with *Ficus elastica,* at Bukit
Lintang to the north-east of Malacca town. The former estate
was opened originally for coffee; Tan was one of the Malacca
tapioca planters.[23]

During this pioneer phase most rubber was interplanted with
existing crops as these became relatively less remunerative or as
their cultivation was discouraged by Government action. It is
broadly true to say that the first wave of planting had its greatest
effects on the coffee estates, which were suffering most from
economic difficulties, but that after the opening of the new
century interplanting of rubber became general on almost all
existing estates and fresh land was alienated for the new crop.

Several factors stimulated the planting of rubber in Malaya
during this pioneer phase, and amongst these economic considerations played a major role. As world demand for rubber
increased during the 1890's prices rose quickly; concurrently
coffee prices fell disastrously and the Malayan planters began
to search for alternative crops. At its meeting in August 1897
the United Planters' Association of the Federated Malay States
discussed the various crops which could be cultivated in place
of coffee and interest was quickly diverted to 'some less expensive and more profitable form of cultivation'.[24]

Some interest was shown at this stage in a variety of crops
including coconuts and ramie, but rubber appeared to offer
the brightest prospects. As a result, rubber-producing plants
were planted either among existing crops or in small pure
stands on several existing estates. At this time *Hevea brasiliensis*
remained an exotic, an untried and unproven crop never before

[23] Burkill, *Dictionary of the Economic Products of the Malay Peninsula*
Vol. 1, 1151; Jenkins, op. cit. 298; Ridley, *Story of the Rubber
Industry*, 8; J.H.M. Robson, *Records and Recollections (1889-1934)*
Kuala Lumpur, 1934, 25; Wycherley, 'The Singapore Botanic Gardens
and Rubber in Malaya', 180.

[24] *Selangor Journal*, Vol. V No. 25, 20 August 1897, 401; *A.R.F.M.S.*
1897, 3; *A.R. Selangor, 1897*, 7.

cultivated on an estate basis, and several planters preferred to try other rubber-producing plants. Ceara rubber was interplanted with coffee on the Batang Kali Estate in Ulu Selangor in the late 1890's and *Geta rambong* had been planted in many areas, including Muar, Malacca, Ulu Langat and Kuala Selangor before the turn of the century. Uncertainty about the potentialities of these different crops led to the planting of mixed stands, usually of Para rubber and *Geta rambong*. This latter crop retained some degree of popularity during the first decade of the twentieth century, especially on coastal estates, but by about 1910 it had almost completely given way to *Hevea* in Malaya.

There was, in fact, considerable scepticism about the future of *Hevea brasiliensis* among both planters and Government officials in Malaya in the late 1890's. Some of these doubts were dispersed by the tapping experiments conducted by Derry on the trees at Kuala Kangsar, and rubber produced from these trees was sold on the London market in 1899. This first consignment of Para rubber from Malaya to reach the markets of Europe realized a price of 3s 10d per pound and did much to consolidate interest in the new crop.[25] In the same year the Federated Malay States Government voted a sum of $4,000 in its estimates for 1900 for the purpose of carrying out experiments with rubber and other products. This may appear an insignificant sum, but in view of the fact that at this date a Government Department of Agriculture did not exist it clearly represents increasing and positive interest in the new crop on the part of the Government.[26]

In the late 1890's, however, the economic motives persuading planters to try rubber were strongly reinforced by the introduction of special land regulations in the Federated Malay States. These regulations, introduced in August 1897, provided that land granted for rubber planting should carry a quit-rent of only ten cents per acre for the first ten years, at the end of which time it would be raised to fifty cents an acre. On concessions of one thousand acres or less, at least one-tenth of the total area

[25] C. Baxendale, 'The Plantation Rubber Industry', *Agricultural Bulletin of the Federated Malay States,* Vol. 1 No. 5, December 1912, 181.
[26] *A.R. Selangor Planters' Association, 1899,* 1.

was to be planted with 'gutta of any description, every year, no other form of cultivation being permitted so long as the land pays a quit rent of ten cents per acre only'; one-twentieth of the total area of concessions of between one and two thousand acres was to be planted each year, and one-thirtieth of the total area of concessions of two to three thousand acres. The produce of these concessions was to be subject to a duty of $2\frac{1}{2}$ per cent. *ad valorem* for fifteen years from the date of commencing work and thereafter subject to whatever duties might be in force, up to a maximum of 5 per cent.[27]

The last three years of the nineteenth century witnessed a noticeable growth of the desire to plant rubber, particularly in Selangor and Perak, although only a relatively small area was actually planted. Planting was restricted almost entirely to areas in which European-owned estates had already been opened; it took the form either of interplanting among existing crops or of new planting on land acquired for the purpose adjoining or closeby the existing estates.

As a result of the special regulations F.A. Stephens applied for a 1,000-acre block of land adjoining his Jebong Estate in Matang in October 1897. He began opening the land almost immediately and during 1898 planted out 16,000 rubber seedlings.[28] By the beginning of 1898 some eighty acres of rubber had also been planted on the Yam Seng Estate and the crop had been planted along the sides of the roads on the Selinsing Estate in this District.[29] A few acres had been planted both on the Cecily Estate and at Sitiawan by 1897, and in the following year a 3,280-acre block was granted to H.A.W. Aylesbury for rubber and coconuts in Lower Perak.[30] Some interest was also shown in the Kuala Kangsar and Kinta Districts at this time. In the case of the former, European planters acquired 2,100 acres under the special regulations during 1897, a year later it

27 *N.S.S.F., R.G.* 2139/97.

28 *M.R. Matang,* October 1897, *P.G.G.,* Vol. 10, 1897, No. 742, 969; *A.R. Matang, 1897, P.G.G.,* Vol. 11, 1898, 160; *A.R. Lands, Mines and Surveys, F.M.S., 1898,* 9.

29 *M.R. Matang,* January 1898, *P.G.G.,* Vol. 11, 1898, No. 136, 127.

30 *A.R. Lower Perak, 1897, P.G.G.,* Vol. 11, 1898, No. 204, 211; *A.R. Lands, Mines and Surveys, F.M.S., 1898,* 15.

was reported that the Sultan was prospecting for suitable land at Senggong to induce the Malay population to take an interest in rubber, and in 1899 Gordon Brown acquired 1,000 acres at Sungei Siput which he named the Sungei Krodah Estate.[31] Rubber planting also attracted some attention from the Chinese in Perak before the turn of the century and in 1899 Chong Ong Sien was in the process of opening a large plantation at Kota Bahru in Kinta.[32] During 1897 about 35,000 rubber seeds were supplied to intending planters by the Government Gardens at Kuala Kangsar. The following year the Government Gardens in Perak sold 32,000 seeds and 59,700 seedlings and the Forest Department established extensive nurseries; the Government Gardens at Taiping supplied 11,000 seeds to the Yam Seng Estate and 3,000 seeds to the Jebong Estate during 1898.[33] *Hevea brasiliensis* had already been planted on estates in several Districts of Perak by 1900, but in this phase the coastal District of Matang was the main centre of operations.

Rubber was interplanted with coffee on many estates in Selangor during the last years of the century, particularly in Klang. In most cases, however, these coffee planters merely planted rubber whilst they waited 'for better times for coffee' for in general they remained unconvinced that the prospects of this new and untried crop were brighter than those of coffee; indeed, rubber planting was still 'considered by sober-minded people as a hopeless gamble'.[34]

The acquisition of land in Selangor specifically for the purpose of rubber planting dates from the introduction of the special regulations in 1897. In that year a 500-acre block near Serendah in Ulu Selangor was granted on special terms to 'some gentlemen desirous of planting gutta', and applications were also received for land in Klang. Early the next year there were applications for a large amount of land for rubber in Kuala Langat, and the cultivation of this new crop was 'very greatly

[31] *A.R. Kuala Kangsar, 1897, P.G.G.*, Vol. 11, 1898, No. 205, 215-16; *A.R. Kuala Kangsar, 1898*, 3; *A.R. Kuala Kangsar, 1899*, 2.

[32] *A.R. Kinta, 1899*, 2.

[33] *A.R. Perak, 1897*, 3; *A.R. Perak, 1898*, 15; L. Wray, 'Rubber Growing in Perak', *Perak Museum Notes*, Vol. 2, 1898, 95.

[34] Swettenham, *British Malaya*, 368.

extended' in Klang District during 1898. By the end of 1897 small stands of *Hevea* had been planted on eight different estates in Selangor and two years later the crop had been planted on estates in every district. At this stage rubber planting was mainly the preserve of the Europeans, but Chinese soon began to follow suit on both large and small holdings. During 1898 Lau Boon Tit planted fifty-four acres with rubber on his Semenyih Estate in Ulu Langat and in June, 1899 there were fifteen applications from Chinese for smallholdings in Kuala Langat on which they intended to plant coffee as a catch-crop for rubber.[35]

The area devoted to *Hevea* in Selangor, as either mixed or pure stands, increased rapidly. During 1898 alone 389,500 trees were planted in the state; the following year 1.6 million imported and locally grown seeds were sown in nurseries and these produced about one million plants almost all of which were planted out before the end of the year.[36] Clearly, it is extremely difficult to arrive at any estimate of the total area occupied by rubber in this early period when pure stands varied from a fraction of an acre to over fifty acres and when large areas were interplanted with one or more crops. It has been estimated however, that Para rubber occupied over 7,000 acres, either as pure stands or as an interplanted crop, in Selangor by 1901.[37]

The only other state in which *Hevea* was of any importance by the turn of the century was Negri Sembilan, and again to a large extent it was European coffee planters who made the first move. By 1900 some rubber had been planted on several of the coffee estates in the Coast and Seremban Districts. On the other hand, however, the acquisition of new land specifically for rubber was of very little importance in Negri Sembilan. One of the few examples of the process here is the Government Rubber Estate established near Seremban in 1898. The idea of establishing this estate was proposed by Heslop Hill in 1898; the proposal was favourably received by the Government and work

[35] *A.R. Ulu Selangor, 1897*, 1; *A.R. Klang, 1897*, 3; *M.R. Kuala Langat* April 1898, S.G.G., 1898, No. 302, 206; *A.R. Klang, 1898*, 3; *A.R. Kuala Langat, 1899*, 3; Wright and Cartwright, op. cit. 393.

[36] *Straits Times*, 17 March 1900; *A.R. Selangor Planters' Association 1899*, 1; *A.R. Selangor, 1899*, 28.

[37] *A.R. Selangor, 1901*, 3.

began immediately. Ownership was divided equally between the Negri Sembilan Government and Heslop Hill and the estate was worked by Hill using prison labour supplied by the Government. After a short while the Government appears to have regretted entering upon this venture and in 1904 offered to sell its half share to Hill for $29,572.[38] In fact, a marked expansion of rubber planting did not occur in Negri Sembilan until the new century was two or three years old.

With the turn of the century confidence in the future of rubber planting in Malaya mounted annually. Trees planted by the pioneers during the preceding decade were now reaching maturity, satisfactory tapping methods had been evolved, and more and more samples were sent to England where they realized high prices. Over 130 pounds of rubber were dispatched to England from the Linsum Estate in Negri Sembilan in 1902 and sold for 3s 10d per pound, despite the fact that the exporter classed this consignment as 'Number two quality'.[39] Some tapping was done on the Matang, Selinsing and Jepong Estates in Perak during 1903, although even a year later the Jebong Estate was the only estate in Perak on which regular tapping was undertaken.[40] No estate was in general bearing in Selangor in 1903, but most had sent samples to England for examination and valuation.[41] In all cases the results obtained by these pioneers were extremely encouraging, and faith in the future of rubber became widespread amongst local planters and Government officials.

It had for long been the general official desire to stimulate agricultural development, and it was widely believed that one of the most effective ways of doing so was to encourage the European 'capitalist or planting industry'.[42] At the same time officialdom held a view of the planting industry which regarded it as long-term land development; rubber, with its long matura-

---

[38] N.S.S.F., Misc., 3090/98, Misc. 1989/99, Misc. 1899/1901, Misc. 3075/ 1903 and R.G. 89/1904.

[39] A.R. Negri Sembilan, 1902, 3.

[40] A.R. Lands, Mines and Surveys, F.M.S., 1903, 4; A.R. Larut and Krian, 1904, 5.

[41] A.R. Selangor, 1903, 3.

[42] Willis, Report upon Agriculture in the Federated Malay States, 90.

tion period and its apparently long productive life, fitted their picture of the type of crop upon which the development of commercial agriculture should be based. It was, in fact, in complete contrast to the crops cultivated hitherto by Chinese in many parts of western Malaya; crops which enabled the Chinese to make quick returns but which offered little hope of permanent land development of the type envisaged by Government.

In order to stimulate the replacement of Chinese shifting cultivation by 'permanent' agriculture the Governments of the western Malay States began to introduce a special clause, stipulating that a 'permanent' crop such as rubber or coconuts must also be planted, into all new grants of land made to Chinese after 1900 for tapioca or gambier and pepper cultivation (see Chapters 3 and 4). Initially the new clause had minimal effects, but the rising price of rubber and relatively strict enforcement soon led to the widespread planting of rubber among catch-crops of tapioca or gambier on Chinese-owned estates.

The process whereby rubber estates replaced former Chinese shifting cultivation was encouraged by further Government legislation in Negri Sembilan. Here, as the old Chinese leases expired the land concerned reverted to Government. In November 1903 the Resident suggested that this land, formerly under tapioca or gambier and pepper but now covered with *lalang* and *belukar*, should be offered to planters for the cultivation of 'permanent products' on extremely favourable terms. The suggestion was approved and appeared as a Government *Notification* offering special 'lalang terms' in January 1904. These terms offered the land at a nominal rent of a dollar per 100 acres for the first seven years and thereafter at a dollar per acre.[43] This greatly stimulated the acquisition of land for rubber in Negri Sembilan, particularly among European planters. The two Government actions noted here did much to alter the former patterns of export-orientated agriculture in the western states.

By 1902 almost every coffee estate in Malaya had been interplanted with rubber and the sugar planters of Province Wellesley and Perak were also beginning to show an interest in the new crop. Confidence in rubber had risen to such an extent that

[43] *N.S.S.F., N.S. 5032/1903; N.S.G.G.,* 4 January 1904, No. 20.

some planters were beginning to cut out the interplanted crops, especially coconuts, and as more rubber approached maturity this practice became general. In some instances almost mature coconuts were removed to make way for newly-planted rubber.[44]

By about 1903 the tempo of applications for new land for rubber planting in the western Malay states began to increase. Twenty-one applications for blocks of over fifty acres were received by the Seremban Land Office during that year, eleven of these, coming from both Europeans and Chinese, were for blocks exceeding 200 acres; at the same time Towkay Chang On Siu of Perak wrote to the Negri Sembilan Government asking for 1,000 acres of land for rubber planting in the state and the Malacca Rubber Company applied for 6,000 acres in mukim Ayer Kuning, Tampin. In fact, applications were received for a total of about 20,000 acres in Negri Sembilan during 1903. Amongst other large blocks granted here that year were the 3,000 acres applied for by V.R. Wickwar on behalf of E.S. Grigson of Colombo and a block of the same size granted to W.J. Coates on behalf of an English syndicate; these grants reveal the practice of local planters acting as acquiring agents for overseas persons which was not uncommon at this time.[45]

The area planted with rubber in western Malaya was noticeably extended in the first years of the twentieth century (Table 16). By 1904 about 15,000 acres held by European planters in Selangor had been planted with Para rubber, either as sole crop or among existing crops; in Negri Sembilan almost 4,900 acres were under rubber in the Seremban District by 1904, with another 1,800 acres (including 280 acres under *Geta rambong*), planted in the Coast District.[46] The crop was gaining in importance in Perak, Province Wellesley and Malacca, and the first commercial plantings had been made in Johore and Kedah. Although rubber had been planted in many parts of the western

---

[44] See for example F.C. Roles, 'Rubber Development in Malaya' in Wright and Cartwright, op. cit. 354.

[45] *A.R. Seremban Land Office, 1903,* 4; *A.R. Tampin, 1903,* 2; *A.R. Negri Sembilan, 1903,* 4; *N.S.S.F., N.S. 2451/1903* and *R.G. 2106/ 1903.*

[46] *A.R. Selangor, 1904,* 3; *A.R. Seremban Land Office, 1904,* 4; *A.R. Coast, 1904,* 1.

TABLE 16

FEDERATED MALAY STATES: RUBBER ACREAGE, 1897-1904

Year	Acres
1897	345
1898	1,761
1899	3,227
1900	4,693
1901	5,965
1902	7,239
1903	11,239
1904	19,239

Source: *A.R. Director of Agriculture, F.M.S., 1907*, 7.

N.B. The figures produced by the Department of Agriculture at this time do not always agree with estimates prepared by state officials.

Malay states by 1904, certain Districts stand out as the 'core areas' of the new industry—the Klang District of Selangor, the Seremban District of Negri Sembilan (and to a much lesser extent the Coast District of the same state), and the coastal District of Matang in Perak. In all cases the earliest phase of the rubber industry in Malaya is connected with accessible west coast areas in which commercial agriculture concerned with other crops, chiefly coffee, had already gained a foothold. By 1904 rubber was quickly supplanting all previous export-orientated crops; the way had been paved for the first rubber boom.

The First Rubber Boom, 1905-8

Rising rubber prices and the increased confidence in the crop induced by the success achieved on the pioneer plantings resulted in a very marked extension of planting activities after 1904.[47] Virtually every existing estate began converting to rubber by interplanting and by planting newly-cleared fields; concurrently there was an increasing rush for new land, particularly in the western Malay States, and by 1908 rubber planting had extended into every state of Malaya.

In Perak applications were received during 1905 for over

[47] By May 1905 the price of cultivated rubber had risen to 6s 10d per pound; it fell to 6s 1¾d by the end of the year, but rose to 6s 3d in March and April 1906. Thereafter, prices began to fall. By August 1907 the price stood at 5s 2d per pound and in December had dropped to 3s 8d. Wright and Cartwright, op. cit. 358.

10,000 acres for rubber in Matang, 12,000 acres in Lower Perak and over 6,000 acres in Batang Padang.[48] The following year witnessed a tremendous rush for land in the state. In Kinta seventeen applications were received for a total of about 9,500 acres, mostly near Ipoh and Batu Gajah; some 13,000 acres were alienated in Lower Perak during 1906 and already 'most of the available road frontage and accessible land [was] now occupied' in Batang Padang.[49] Planting on the newly-alienated land began immediately, large-scale planting of rubber was vigorously undertaken on existing estates, and the sugar estates were 'fast being planted up with rubber'. By 1906 approximately 7,000 acres had been planted with rubber in Krian with sugar acting as a catch-crop over large areas; in Lower Perak a total of 31,000 acres had been alienated for rubber, and 6,500 acres had been planted, of which some 1,300 acres were interplanted with *Geta rambong* or other crops.[50] The rush for new land in Perak diminished in 1907 and 1908, but planting continued apace, and the acreage devoted to Para rubber alone mounted rapidly as catch-crops, including sugar, coffee, tapioca and tea, were removed.

Selangor experienced a similar extension of planting activities in this period. The attention of the former coffee planters was now firmly fixed on rubber; no new land was planted with coffee and the area devoted to the crop declined annually. Although coffee cultivation was now more profitable than formerly, the larger returns to be obtained from rubber prevented the planter, 'except in a very few cases, from considering the planting or tending of coffee as worth his attention'.[51] Other interplanted crops, notably coconuts, were also quickly removed.[52]

[48] *A.R. Larut and Krian, 1905*, 5; *A.R. Lower Perak, 1905*, 2; *A.R. Batang Padang, 1905*, 2.

[49] *A.R. Kinta, 1906*, 2; *A.R. Lower Perak, 1906*, 3; *A.R. Batang Padang, 1906*, 6.

[50] *A.R. Larut and Krian, 1906*, 5; *A.R. Lower Perak, 1906*, 2-3.

[51] *A.R. Director of Agriculture, F.M.S., 1908*, 3.

[52] It is reported that on one estate in Selangor during 1906 130 acres of healthy and well-grown coconuts just coming into bearing and 'worth fully $275 to $300 per acre' were cut down to make room for rubber little over a year old. *A.R. Inspector of Coconut Plantations, F.M.S., 1906*, 3.

The acquisition of land for rubber planting had already progressed far in this state by 1905. In that year the Resident-General observed that almost all the accessible land between the Klang and Selangor rivers had been taken up for the crop.[53] Nearly 25,000 acres were under cultivation on European-owned estates in Klang by 1906; more than 5,000 acres had been planted in Kuala Lumpur District, over 3,000 acres in both Kuala Selangor and Ulu Langat and an area in excess of 2,000 acres in both Ulu Selangor and Kuala Langat.[54]

Here as elsewhere the existing communication network determined the lines upon which rubber planting extended. The Klang valley, with its road and rail links between Kuala Lumpur and Port Swettenham, was the major axis of development in Selangor, and indeed in the whole peninsula, at this time. By the end of 1908, when over 80,000 acres had been planted with rubber in Selangor, almost two-fifths of the planted area lay in Klang District; in fact, at that date more rubber had been planted here than in the whole of Negri Sembilan. Significantly, in commenting upon the decline in applications for land for rubber in Selangor in 1908 Belfield remarked that 'almost the whole of the suitable land within reasonable distance of existing means of communication [had] been already taken up'.[55] Outside the Klang valley planting activities at this time were tied closely to the coastal roads north and south of Klang and to the north-south road and rail connexions along the foothills.

In Negri Sembilan the acreage planted to rubber increased five-fold between 1905 and 1908 (Table 17). This increase was effected by the operation of three different processes; interplanting of rubber among existing crops, opening up and planting of virgin land and re-occupation and planting of abandoned land. The Government actions noted earlier did much to reinforce rising prices as motivations for this expansion. European planters started to take up land abandoned by the Chinese in the Coast District during 1905 under the special 'lalang terms'.

[53] A.R.F.M.S., 1905, 5.
[54] A.R. Klang, 1906, 2; A.R. Kuala Langat, 1906, 1; A.R. Kuala Selangor, 1906, 2; A.R. Ulu Selangor, 1906, 2.
[55] A.R. Selangor, 1908, 4 and xi.

TABLE 17

FEDERATED MALAY STATES : RUBBER ACREAGE, 1905-8

State	1905	1906	1907	1908
Selangor	25,758	44,821	61,552	82,246
Perak	11,934	29,612	46,167	56,706
Negri Sembilan	5,718	10,663	17,656	27,305
Pahang	15	483	860	1,791
Total	43,425	85,579	126,235	168,048

Source: *A.R. Director of Agriculture, F.M.S., 1906, 5; A.R.F.M.S., 1907, 8; A.R.F.M.S., 1908, 9.*

By 1908 over 11,000 acres had been planted with rubber in this District of which 'nearly 2,000 acres [was] planted on land, which five years ago or less was abandoned to lalang', and an increasing number of the older Chinese estates were now passing into European hands.[56]

The introduction of the special cultivation clause into all new grants of land to Chinese tapioca and gambier planters was also beginning to have effects. It was reported in 1906 that there was a growing tendency for Chinese to plant rubber among their tapioca and gambier.[57] There were, in fact, a growing number of reasons for doing so; firstly, many began to plant rubber 'with an eye to the European purchaser', and secondly, when permission was given to plant tapioca or gambier as a catch-crop it was generally stipulated that rubber trees should be planted first.

There was a spate of applications for new land in Negri Sembilan in 1905 and 1906. Most of these, coming from both Europeans and Chinese, concerned land in the Seremban and Coast Districts. The Seremban Land Office, for example, received applications for a total of 30,280 acres during 1905 and for 29,000 acres the following year.[58] Legally planting could begin once an application was approved, but title to the land could not be issued until it had been surveyed and the boundaries

[56] *A.R. Coast, 1908, 2.*
[57] *A.R. Coast, 1906, 2.*
[58] *A.R. Seremban Land Office, 1905, 1; ibid. 1906, 1.*

ascertained. Many planters, and particularly planting companies, were unwilling to commence operations before they obtained a title. This rush for land completely overwhelmed the Land Office staff which was totally inadequate to deal with applications on this scale. The problem was accentuated by the inaccuracy of existing surveys and maps, and the resultant delay in issuing titles caused considerable frustration among planters wishing to begin work quickly.[59] Despite these problems however, planting of rubber on newly-acquired land progressed rapidly.

The figures produced by the Department of Agriculture, Federated Malay States, indicate that over 10,000 acres had been planted with rubber in Negri Sembilan by the end of 1906 (Table 17); this is probably an under-estimate, for elsewhere it has been suggested that the total planted area exceeded 15,000 at this date.[60] Despite a lull in applications in 1907 and 1908 the development of existing estates was actively continued. This expansion and the location of much of the planted area was dramatically described by the Resident of Negri Sembilan in 1907. He wrote 'The area under rubber increases day by day, and day by day new clearings appear in the country. Along the railway line between the Selangor boundary and Malacca there is a nearly continuous extent of rubber planted'.[61] The Seremban and Coast Districts remained the dominant centres of activity. The main foci of development were the Sungei Ujong Railway and the Seremban-Pengkalen Kempas road on the one hand, and the northwest-southeast aligned road and railway passing from Selangor through Seremban to the Malacca frontier on the other.

More than four-fifths of the total area planted with rubber by 1906 lay in the western Malay States of Perak, Selangor and

---

[59] For example, J.J. Craigie applied for a block of land in January 1906. He deposited the required survey fee ($1,150), in the Land Office in February 1907. When nothing had been done by August 1907 he complained that 'we wish to start planting at the New Year and the long delay in issuing title to the land is keeping us from commencing operations'. *N.S.S.F., Misc. 2365/1907.*

[60] *N.S.S.F., R.G. 1663/1907.*

[61] *A.R. Negri Sembilan, 1907, 3.*

Negri Sembilan, and the rush for new land that characterized this first boom had its greatest efforts in these states (Table 18). Malacca was the only other state in which planting was underway on a large scale, and here interplanting with tapioca was the general rule, most of the estates being Chinese-owned. In Province Wellesley most of the existing estates were also turning to the new crop and some planting had been done in neighbouring Kedah. Elsewhere, relative isolation and poor communications discouraged rubber planting.

TABLE 18

MALAYA: ESTATE RUBBER STATISTICS, DECEMBER 1906

State	Number of Estates	Total planted Acreage	Acreage planted during 1906
Selangor	119	44,821	19,063
Perak	87	29,612	17,678
Negri Sembilan	25	10,663	4,945
Pahang	11	483	468
Straits Settlements	5	11,341	4,098
Johore	7	2,310	1,355
Total	254	99,230	47,607

Source: A.R. Director of Agriculture, F.M.S., 1906, 5-6.

The east coast states were almost completely unaffected by the developments in commercial agriculture that had characterized western Malaya during the nineteenth century. They therefore lacked the bases upon which rubber planting expanded so rapidly in the western states; there were no existing estates which could be quickly and cheaply converted to rubber, there was no existing estate labour force, there were no railways and an almost complete deficiency of roads. When new land could still be obtained west of the main range there was little to attract planters eastwards. Nevertheless, the period 1905-8 did see the beginnings of the rubber industry, admittedly on a very small scale, in Pahang and in Kelantan. At the same time development quickened in Johore where the proposal to build a north-south railway from Gemas to Johore Bahru promised to open vast new areas.

Although Chinese gambier and pepper planting was extensive in nineteenth-century Johore and directly or indirectly provided the Government with a considerable revenue, very little attempt had been made to develop suitable communications. Nevertheless, by 1907 rubber planting was underway on several European-owned estates (including the Lanadron, Nordanal and Jementah Estates) in the Muar District and on one or two estates, such as Mount Austin, close to Johore Bahru; significantly such roads as did exist in Johore in 1907 were almost entirely confined to these two Districts[62] (Fig. 35A).

The proposed railway, which was finally completed in 1909, and the ruler's willingness to grant large blocks of land on favourable terms soon stimulated the acquisition of new land in this state. The Malay Peninsula (Johore) Rubber Concessions Limited were granted 50,000 acres, consisting of twenty blocks each of 2,500 acres, by the side of the new railway in the northern part of the state (Fig. 35A). Planting began on this land in 1906, it being the object of the company to partly develop the land and then sell it in blocks to rubber planting companies; the first block was sold in this way before 1908. At the same time The Rubber Estates of Johore Limited, for whom Messrs. Guthrie and Co. Ltd. acted as agents, were granted three blocks of land totalling 25,000 acres, comprising two blocks of 10,000 acres and one of 5,000 acres. All three blocks fronted the new railway (Fig. 35A). Planting began on the 10,000-acre block near Gemas in 1906 and some 2,000 acres were planted with rubber within the first two years. Work did not begin on the 10,000-acre block at Labis or the 5,000-acre block at Layang-Layang until after 1908.[63]

Kelantan, still outside the British sphere of influence in the peninsula and far-distant from the Straits Settlements, evoked little interest until the time of the first boom. The development of the rubber industry here really dates from 1905 and owes much to the existence of the Duff Development Company Limited. Robert W. Duff accompanied Hugh Clifford's expedition to Trengganu and Kelantan in 1895 as a police official. In February 1900, when District Officer of Ulu Selangor, he was

[62] Swettenham, *British Malaya*, 307.
[63] Wright and Cartwright, op. cit. 360-3.

invalided out of the service and returned to England. Here he succeeded in interesting several businessmen in a project to trade in Kelantan. Later the same year he obtained a title, or 'a partnership agreement with the Sultan', for a huge area in interior Kelantan; this title placed the administration of the area in his hands and conferred on him powers of legislation and taxation and sole commercial rights of every description. Together with several European assistants, Duff moved to Kelantan early in 1901 and established his headquarters at Kuala Lebir[64] (Fig. 35B). The rising price of rubber persuaded the Duff Development Company to advertise its concession for planting purposes in 1906. At the same time the Kelantan Government publicized the conditions upon which it was prepared to grant land for planting. Graham reports that these efforts 'resulted in the receipt of numerous inquiries, in many cases followed by actual selection of land'.[65] By 1907 over 16,000 acres had been granted to companies for rubber planting; although work had started on some of this, probably only a very small area had been planted. More than half of the alienated acreage was in the hands of subsidiaries of the Duff Development Company.[66] Fundamentally, it was the existence of this unusual company that brought the inaccessible and relatively unknown state of Kelantan within the orbit of the first rubber boom.

The first rubber boom caused an unprecedented expansion of plantation agriculture in Malaya; an expansion which, unlike those associated with the export crops grown during the nineteenth century, affected all parts of the peninsula. From the 'core areas', related as they were to existing patterns of commercial agriculture, estate rubber cultivation was extended into many virgin areas. With very few exceptions, of which Kelantan is clearly one, this extension of the planting frontier followed closely the lines determined by the developing communication network. Soils and topography played little part in fostering or hindering this extension for rubber will grow on a very wide

[64] A. Wright and T.H. Reid, *The Malay Peninsula: A Record of British Progress in the Middle East*, London, 1912, 152-60.
[65] W.A. Graham, *Kelantan*, Glasgow, 1908, 82.
[66] Ibid. 137-8.

variety of soils and under diverse topographic conditions. Accessibility and official encouragement were the controlling factors.

By 1908 rubber was the main interest of the planting industry in Malaya; it was no longer an unknown and unproven exotic and was rapidly replacing all previous export-orientated crops. The total area planted with rubber in Malaya increased almost five-fold between 1905 and 1908 and in the latter year exceeded 240,000 acres, a larger area than had been occupied hitherto by any single agricultural product. Exports were still small, for most of the rubber was immature but plantation agriculture was quickly becoming monocultural. It was also becoming increasingly European-dominated.

Official Promotion of the Planting Industry

The development of commercial agriculture in nineteenth-century Malaya resulted mainly from Chinese and European private enterprise. Government assistance was minimal, there was no official agricultural policy, and the pioneer planters provided virtually all the essentials of development. Towards the end of the century, however, the Government, both in the Malay States and the Straits Settlements, started to take an increasing interest in agriculture as the idea spread that the promotion of cultivation was the soundest way to ensure the opening up and settlement of the country. Commercial agriculture was particularly welcomed as the speediest way of achieving this end, not least because it also provided a potential source of revenue. Existing Chinese systems of commercial agriculture were frowned upon for they appeared to offer little hope of permanent land development. In the Government mind the development of commercial agriculture became synonymous with the European planting industry; European planters came to be regarded as 'the backbone of the country ... deserving of the utmost encouragement which Government can give them'.[67]

A definite bias towards the European planting industry became apparent in the 1890's; during the subsequent decade it

[67] *A.R. Lower Perak, 1906*, 6.

became increasingly obvious. To facilitate the growth of commercial agriculture in Malaya three fundamentals were
essential: capital, labour and accessible land on easy terms. All
three were in relatively short supply during the nineteenth
century, and it was the ability of the Chinese to overcome this
shortage in their own particular ways that enabled them to
achieve considerable success in the production of export crops
at an early date. By the end of the century, however, Government had accepted the principle that if the desired expansion
of European planting activities was to occur then some official
effort to provide these essentials of development was necessary.

The rise of the coffee industry in the western Malay States
was accompanied by the first efforts in this direction. Land
regulations were introduced that offered large blocks of land
on favourable terms designed to discourage speculation; loans,
in some cases up to a total of $40,000 were made to coffee planters
and others to permit them to develop their properties; and
legislation was passed in an attempt to promote an inflow of
immigrant Indian labour to provide a work-force for the new
European estates.

The rapid expansion of rubber planting after 1900 is related
closely to an intensification of Government encouragement.
Special land regulations were introduced in the Federated
Malay States to encourage rubber planting as early as 1897. By
1900 no new land was granted to Chinese gambier or tapioca
planters unless they agreed also to plant some 'permanent
product'; in 1904 special 'lalang terms' were offered to planters
willing to take up the large stretches of land already abandoned
by the Chinese shifting cultivators in Negri Sembilan. Moreover, under the existing general land regulations virgin land
could be acquired on attractive terms; indeed, one of their basic
purposes was to promote the opening of estates.

That favourable land terms were not alone sufficient to cause
an expansion of planting activities is shown by the marked
reluctance of planters to open estates in Pahang. Accessibility
governed the choice of site for new estates, both before and after
the coming of rubber, and to the Europeans this meant land
adjoining a road or railway.

The initial road and rail network in Malaya appeared in the

late nineteenth century to serve the needs of the tin miners; the chief mining areas were strung along the western foothills of the main range and communications linked these to each other and to points of export at the coast. This pattern determined the lines of expansion followed by the coffee planters and the early rubber planters. Government was constantly involved in extending the road and rail network, for it was recognized that by such extensions plantation agriculture could be pushed into new areas. Since the existing network formed the base-line for these extensions the orientation towards the west coast remained. This orientation and its effects on the distribution of rubber are particularly clearly evident in the case of the railways. By 1900 short, unconnected lines had appeared to link the mining areas of Larut, Kinta, interior Selangor and Seremban with the coast at Port Weld, Teluk Anson, Klang and Port Dickson respectively, togther with a short line from Bukit Mertajam to Prai in Province Wellesley. Work began to unite these various lines by joining them along the foothill zone and by July 1903 through rail connexion between Prai and Seremban had been achieved. Simultaneously, a plan to achieve a continuous rail link between Johore Bahru and Prai emerged. After lengthy negotiations with the Sultan, work on the Johore railway started in March 1904 and was completed five years later. By this time a total of $46 million had been spent on railway development in Malaya; this development was restricted to the western side of the peninsula, and the alignment of the railway exerted a very strong pull on planters opening new land for rubber[68] (Fig. 35A).

Away from the railway European planters sought land fronting an existing or proposed road. During the coffee boom such land had been granted to all who applied, whether European planters or Malay smallholders. As a result, particularly in Selangor, there was very little unalienated land fronting existing roads at the time of the first rubber boom. In many cases at the time of the first rubber boom European planters bought up existing Malay smallholdings in order to acquire road frontage for their estates; in Klang for instance, estate owners

[68] Chai Hon-Chan, *The Development of British Malaya, 1896-1909,* Kuala Lumpur, 1964, 189-94.

and managers paid out a total of $15,412 to buy up 400 acres of smallholdings for this purpose during 1906.[69] At the same time, the growing bias in favour of European planters is revealed by the action taken by the Selangor Government to 'abate this nuisance'. Wherever possible roadside smallholdings that could be classed as 'abandoned' were resumed by the Government. Moreover, in 1905 Belfield issued an order to all District Officers to the effect that no land abutting on a Government road was 'to be alienated to a native without the previous sanction of the Resident'. 'Meanwhile', he wrote, 'I am attempting to concentrate native gardeners in specified areas, and to discourage the occupation by them of land which may be usefully reserved for scientific planting.'[70] Henceforth land with rail or road frontage was to be reserved for estates in Selangor, and to a very large extent these were European-owned.

A precedent for the granting of loans from public funds to aid planters and others develop their properties was established in the Malay States as early as 1890. This became a feature of Government agricultural policy in the Federated Malay States when the High Commissioner gave his approval to a special 'Loans to Planters' scheme in July 1904. Under this scheme the Government could advance loans to *bona fide* planters 'in order to encourage agriculture'. The loans were to be made over a period not exceeding seven years; they were subject to interest at a rate of 6 per cent. and the Government had first charge on the estates affected.[71] Sizable loans were taken up by both individual planters and companies in each of the three western Malay States. The vast majority of these went to Europeans; amongst the few exceptions are loans made to Japanese planters in Negri Sembilan and to Chinese in Perak.

The scheme was liberally used and within a short while the Federated Malay States Government had advanced a total of one and a half million dollars to planters.[72] In May 1908 the Resident-General called a special meeting of the Residents in Kuala Lumpur to discuss the scheme, and in August that year

[69] *A.R. Klang, 1906,* 2.
[70] *A.R. Selangor, 1905,* 3-4.
[71] *A.R. Negri Sembilan, 1904,* 19.
[72] Chai Hon-Chan, op. cit. 161.

he informed the acting Resident of Negri Sembilan that the fund was exhausted.[73] Loans made to planters in the later months of 1907 appear to have been special ones from state funds, such as that granted to T.H. Tedlie to develop his Bukit Kubu Estate in Negri Sembilan.[74] The introduction of this 'Loans to Planters' scheme is a clear indication of the desire of the Federated Malay States Government to make every effort to encourage the development and extension of the planting industry, if needs be by providing it with financial backing. In the long run however, Government funds were totally insufficient to meet the capital needs of the new industry the expansion of which, even in the period up to 1908, was based on the flow of capital from outside Malaya.

The development and expansion of the rubber plantation industry in Malaya depended upon immigrant labour mainly from southern India. The nucleus of an Indian estate labour force in Malaya had already been created by the sugar planters of Province Wellesley and Perak and by the coffee planters of the western states before the spread of rubber planting; in the former case it comprised mainly indentured labour, in the latter case unindentured or 'free' labour. Rubber planting is in fact relatively less labour-intensive than either sugar or coffee planting, particularly during its five- to seven-year maturation period. Nevertheless, the firm belief in clean-weeding held by most of the earlier rubber planters necessitated comparatively large work-forces on the estates established prior to 1908, and as more rubber came into tapping there was an increased demand for labour.

Various types of legislation had been introduced in the late nineteenth century in an attempt to stimulate the flow of Indian labour migrants to Malaya, but in general the numbers available were always insufficient. After the turn of the century, however, the Malayan authorities began to assume a larger role in supervising Indian immigration; 'ideas were forthcoming from planters and officials which suggested that the government

[73] N.S.S.F., R.G. 1349/1908 and N.S. 1120/1908.
[74] N.S.S.F., N.S. 1120/1908.

might be able to act effectively to increase the numbers of Indian immigrant laborers' entering the country.[75] The rubber planters, many of whom had recently turned from coffee, tended to prefer the 'free' Indian labour imported under the *kangany* system to the indentured labour common on the sugar estates. *Kangany*-recruited labour was considered cheaper and physically superior, and as 'free' labour it was initially less subject to official control and inspection. The number of labourers recruited under this system for work on estates in the Federated Malay States rose from 2,064 in 1903 to 7,543 in 1905.[76] Nevertheless, it was still insufficient to satisfy the demands of the growing plantation industry. Indeed, although the total labour force employed on estates in the Federated Malay States increased markedly in 1906-7, a year later it showed signs of declining (Table 19).

TABLE 19

FEDERATED MALAY STATES : ESTATE LABOUR FORCE, 1906-8

Race	1906	1907	1908
Tamils	29,358	43,824	43,515
Javanese	4,070	6,029	4,999
Chinese	3,533	5,348	6,595
Malays	1,499	2,872	1,961
Total	38,360	58,073	57,080

Sourse: *A.R.F.M.S., 1906*, 7; ibid. 1907, 9; ibid. 1908, 10.

At a joint meeting in 1906 the United Planters' Association, the Johore Planters' Association and the Malay Peninsula Agricultural Association expressed the desire that Government should establish a 'central labour bureau' to help alleviate the problem. In an effort to arrive at a solution the Resident-General of the Federated Malay States visited India in 1906, and on his return made several recommendations, the most important of

[75] J.N. Parmer, *Colonial Labor Policy and Administration*: *A History of Labor in the Rubber Plantation Industry in Malaya, 1910-1941*. Monographs of the Association for Asian Studies, No. IX, New York, 1960, 38.

[76] *A.R.F.M.S., 1905*, 14.

which was the formation of a quasi-official Immigration Committee. This Committee was appointed in March 1907, its chief duty being to advise the Government on Indian immigration. At its first meeting however, it was decided that its immediate task was to devise a scheme to import labour on a large scale. It recommended, in fact, the establishment of a special fund to help finance the importation of labour; the recommendation was accepted and legislation enacted in late 1907 and early 1908 in the Federated Malay States, Straits Settlements and Johore for the establishment of a 'Tamil Immigration Fund'. This fund was to provide free passages to Malaya for all Tamil immigrants. It was expected to stimulate an increased flow of labour by preventing deductions from wages on account of recruiting expenses; it was also expected to prevent malpractices by recruiters and *kanganies* in India. Moreover, it was designed to make all employers of Tamil labour, whether planters or otherwise, bear their fair share of the cost of importation by making them pay an assessment according to the number of days worked by the Tamil labour in their employment.[77] This scheme, arising out of joint concern on the part of the planters and the Government, paved the way for the importation of Indian labour on a large scale in the boom years after 1908.

As a result of growing Government interest in agricultural development, in 1904 J.C. Willis, Director of the Botanical Gardens, Ceylon, was asked to prepare a report on agriculture and make recommendations as to its future in the Federated Malay States. His major criticism was the 'lack of concentration of effort and of a definite policy on the part of the Government ... [for] there is no one whose special business it is to attend to agricultural matters of policy'. Willis was strongly in favour of encouraging European planters. He urged that a definite agricultural policy for the Federated Malay States should be based on three aims: in the first place, the country must be made attractive to capitalists, peasants and labourers to promote the inflow of capital, settlers and labour; further, agriculture should be made as attractive as other forms of enterprise; finally, a special department should be established

[77] Parmer, op. cit. 38-39; R.N. Jackson, op. cit. 115.

to improve the technical side of agriculture.[78] These recommendations were readily accepted in the Federated Malay States. A Department of Agriculture was instituted immediately, and J.B. Carruthers, the first Director of Agriculture, assumed duty on 1 February 1905. The basic aims of the new Department were to conduct experiments and to give advice and information on agricultural matters; to this end suitably qualified staff were appointed and the Department began immediately to compile agricultural statistics. In a relatively short while the main centre of agricultural research in Malaya shifted from Singapore to Kuala Lumpur.

Willis also suggested that the Government should publicize the Federated Malay States abroad to intending planters and capitalists; in fact, two years earlier a *Handbook of the Federated Malay States* had been compiled by H.C. Belfield, and several similar publications appeared before the end of the decade.

The Growth of Corporate Ownership

Estimates of the cost of opening and maintaining a rubber estate until the trees came into bearing tend to vary. Clearly, it was much cheaper to convert an existing estate to rubber by interplanting than it was to open virgin land, for part of the land was already cleared, many of the basic facilities already existed, and the interplanted crop helped to provide an income during the maturation period of the rubber. As a general rule during this early period it cost between £20 and £25 per acre to establish and maintain an estate on new land until the trees matured. In such cases, no income was forthcoming until at least five years after the trees were planted. Thus, the rate of investment was high, the returns delayed. Within seven years of planting, however, an average annual output of 250 lbs. per acre was not unusual, and after ten years a yield of as much as 375 lbs. per acre could be expected, At the prices current in the first decade of the twentieth century rubber planting had emerged as a very profitable field of investment.[79]

[78] Willis, *Report upon Agriculture in the Federated Malay States*, 86-88.
[79] Belfield, op. cit. 167-8; Wright and Cartwright, op. cit. 350; Allen and Donnithorne, op. cit. 111.

Individual planters were rarely in a position to provide the capital necessary to convert an existing estate or to open and maintain new land. The coffee planters in particular had suffered considerable losses as a result of the depression; moreover, their unfortunate experience with coffee tended to make them wary of risking everything again as individuals on the new crop. Baxendale, himself one of the pioneer rubber planters in Malaya, clearly indicates the restricting effects of this capital deficiency in the early stages of the industry. He says:

To attribute this slow development to lack of enterprise would be unjust. If any explanation is required it must be attributed to lack of money. At the time of which I am speaking, we were all coffee or sugar planters, struggling for a bare, very bare, existence. Some of us may have had the privilege of being on terms of a nodding acquaintance with men of means but not many of these could recollect that rubber was useful for any practical purpose except for the erasure of pencil marks.[80]

Lack of capital tended to restrict planting operations in the early years of the century; the introduction of the 'Loans to Planters' scheme in 1904 did something to alleviate this problem but the Government was in no position to provide financial backing for the tremendous expansion of planting activities caused by rising prices in 1905 and 1906. To a large extent this spurt of planting activities depended upon capital from outside Malaya, acquired by the formation of limited companies.

The establishment of companies to run estates was not new to Malaya, and the conversion of the typical proprietary estate of the nineteenth century to corporate ownership became marked in the later years of the coffee industry. A similar process was not unusual in the early stages of the rubber plantation industry. There are many examples of individuals, or groups of individuals, acquiring land which they planted with rubber and then either sold to an existing company or floated as a new company. Malcolm Duncan, for instance, opened the Chenderiang Estate in Batang Padang in 1905-6 and floated it as a company in London in 1907, and Lau Boon Tit

[80] Baxendale, op. cit. 181-2.

who began planting rubber on his Semenyih Estate in Ulu
Langat in 1898, sold out to the Asiatic Rubber and Produce
Company Limited in January 1906.[81] In such cases it was not
uncommon for the original planter to accept shares in the
company as part of the purchase price or to remain on the
property in a managerial capacity. The first company to be
formed specifically for the purpose of rubber planting in
Malaya was the Yam Seng Rubber Company, established in
1895. This was followed by the Selangor Rubber Company
Limited, formed under the auspices of Harrisons and Crosfield
Limited to work the Sungei Rengam Estate in April 1899.[82]
But this process of company formation did not really become
active until 1903-4.

Before 1905 it was not an easy matter to raise capital for any
company floated for the purpose of rubber planting; confidence in the new crop was growing steadily among the planting community and among Government officials in Malaya,
but the investing public abroad still had to be convinced that
rubber planting there was a sound investment. It is probably
for this reason that in the early years of the century Ceylon
was an important source of investment for the developing
Malayan industry. In 1903, for example, the estates belonging
to the Seremban Syndicate were sold to the Seremban Estate
Rubber Company Limited, a company capitalized in Ceylon,
for a total of £31,666, the vendors retaining half the sum in
shares in the new company. Growing public confidence in the
Malayan industry is indicated by the fact that Rs100 shares in
this new company were quoted at Rs285 a year after its
foundation.[83]

It was the planting boom of 1905-6 that stimulated the
formation of rubber planting companies and the emergence
of London as the focus of investment activities. As Kennaway
observes, 'it was not till 1905 and after that year that the
stockbrokers and others really began to have confidence in
rubber'.[84] By early 1906 speculation in companies new and old

[81] Wright and Cartwright, op. cit. 381 and 393.
[82] Kennaway, op. cit. 4.
[83] A.R. Negri Sembilan, 1903, 4; A.R. Negri Sembilan, 1904, 5.
[84] Kennaway, op. cit. 14.

had aroused interest in England 'which extended considerably outside the circle of those having direct connection with the East'.[85] The tying of the dollar to sterling at a fixed rate in 1906 provided new encouragement to investors. A rash of new companies appeared, some to develop new land, others to acquire existing estates. In his report on the Federated Malay States for 1905 the Resident-General observed that most of the large estates had been converted into, or sold to, limited liability companies.[86] During 1906 in Klang alone forty-one titles were transferred to companies or syndicates.[87] By 1908 virtually all the existing estates in the western Malay states were in the hands of companies, mostly registered in London. Significantly, of the companies formed to plant rubber in Malaya before the end of 1908 as many as three-fifths were concerned with estates in Selangor and some four-fifths with estates in the three western Malay States.[68]

The period up to 1908 was characterized by the formation of a multiplicity of small rubber planting companies. The vast majority of these were concerned with a single estate, and usually took the name of the estate as the basis for the name of the new company. Very few companies at this time were concerned with land in more than one state, a notable exception being the London Asiatic Rubber and Produce Company Limited with estates in Malacca, Selangor and Perak. In part, of course, this situation resulted from the floating of proprietary estates as separate companies. Bauer offers an additional explanation. He maintains that the pioneers were unable or unwilling to develop very large estates 'as the future of the industry and the techniques of cultivation were entirely conjectural'. The investor, he suggests, 'preferred to spread his risk by investing in a number of companies. Once established the system could not be easily unscrambled, with neighbouring properties

---

[85] Wright and Cartwright, op. cit. 352.

[86] A.R.F.M.S., 1905, 5.

[87] A.R. Selangor, 1906, 3.

[68] Based on information in M.S. Parry and E.M. Muraour, The A.B.C. to Rubber Planting Companies in Malaya, 1st edition, London, 1910.

in different ownership and interspersed with native or Chinese holdings'.[89]

The floating of these small companies in London was to a very large extent undertaken by the large merchant-houses of Singapore, of which the most important were Harrisons and Crosfield Limited and Guthrie and Company Limited. Individual planters and groups of planters generally lacked the experience or contacts necessary to float their estates as companies. Moreover, rubber planting was a new and relatively unproven enterprise so far as the London brokers and investors were concerned: Malaya was a strange and distant land, and cases of speculation in the floating of companies were not unknown.

The merchant- or agency-houses assumed a dominant role in this process because they had well-known and respected names which gave to this new and highly speculative enterprise a degree of integrity and stability attractive to investors. They became the link between the plantations in Malaya and the sources of capital in Europe. They played a fundamental role in the expansion of the new industry which occurred in western Malaya during this early period. But perhaps most important of all is the fact that by paving the way for the investment of huge sums of share-capital from the West, they facilitated the European domination of plantation agriculture in Malaya which accompanied the development of the rubber industry. Undoubtedly this basic change, which occurred between about 1904 and 1908, resulted from the long-term investment of large sums of money required for the cultivation of a crop such as rubber on a plantation basis.

By 1908 plantation agriculture in Malaya had begun to move from a speculative pioneer stage to dependence upon a single crop produced on a modern industrial basis under corporate ownership. A revolution had occurred, and a new organizational framework had emerged. The new order was confirmed by the developments of the succeeding decade.

[89] P.T. Bauer, *The Rubber Industry: A Study in Competition and Monopoly*, London, 1948, 10-11.

11

EPILOGUE
BOOM AND RESTRICTION

THE BASIC FEATURES OF THE ESTATE RUBBER INDUSTRY had already emerged by 1908; channels for the importation of capital, chiefly from Europe and agricultural labour, mainly from south India, had been established; plans were afoot to extend the communication network of the western foothills and coastal plains thus opening new areas for agricultural development; and attractive land regulations had been evolved. Indeed, in little more than a decade the rubber plantation industry had been established. Rubber quickly swept aside all previous plantation crops to become the basis of export-orientated agriculture in Malaya and one of the two pillars of the Malayan economy. Subsequent developments occurred on the basis of patterns established before the end of the first decade of the twentieth century. This chapter presents a brief résumé of these developments to carry the story to 1921, the eve of enforced restriction of rubber production.

The Boom Years, 1909-12

The half decade after 1908 witnessed an unprecedented expansion of interest in the new industry. World demand for rubber increased rapidly as the automobile industry, in particular, was developed. Supplies of wild rubber from Brazil and elsewhere proved insufficient to meet this demand and little of the rubber on the new plantations was yet in bearing. By November 1909 the price of rubber had risen to 9s 8d a pound, a price which gave a phenomenal profit for at this date costs of production on Malayan plantations averaged about 1s to 1s 3d per pound.[1] For a short while in April 1910 prices reached a peak of over 12s per pound; thereafter, they began to fall,

[1] A.R.F.M.S., 1909, 9.

and by October of the same year stood at 4s 9d per pound[2] (Fig. 36).

This fantastic rise in prices had a dual effect on the Malayan rubber industry; it produced a 'Stock Exchange boom' in shares in Malayan plantations, old and new, in London, and a 'planting boom' in Malaya itself. Baxendale observes that during 1909 the income from the older companies attracted the attention of the investing and speculating public in Europe in general—and Britain in particular—'as being unusually large for an agricultural industry'.[3] The few companies with estates with large areas of rubber already in bearing paid phenomenal dividends during this boom period (Table 20).

TABLE 20

DIVIDENDS PAID BY SELECTED RUBBER COMPANIES, 1908-11

Company	Paid up Capital (£)	Area (Acres)	Dividends (Percentages)			
			1908	1909	1910	1911
Petaling Rubber Estate Syndicate Ltd.	22,500	2,205	45	125	325	250
Selangor Rubber Co. Ltd.	30,000	2,466	75	287.5	375	275
Linggi Plantations Ltd.	110,000	9,599	60	165	237.5	131.25*
Kuala Lumpur Rubber Co. Ltd.	180,000	4,000	20	75	57.5	30*
Labu (F.M.S.) Rubber Co. Ltd.	100,000	5,374	7	25	50	45

Source: A.R.F.M.S., 1911, 27.   * interim

The imagination of the British investing public was quickly captured. Dozens of new companies were floated, many to take over existing tapioca or sugar estates on which rubber had been interplanted; other companies, often of more doubtful character, were formed to finance new plantations. During the height

[2] A.R.F.M.S., 1910, 10.
[3] Baxendale, op. cit. 182.

of the boom some companies took up land which was unsuited to rubber cultivation and when prices fell soon afterwards they surrendered the land to the Government. During 1912 Pantai Limited surrendered a grant for 222 acres in Seremban District, 'obviously taken up for purposes of flotation only'.[4] More rubber companies were formed to work land in Malaya in the years 1909 and 1910 than had existed in 1908. Speculation was rife. During 1910 thirty-three estates changed hands in Negri Sembilan alone. In Kedah in the same year there was great activity in dealing in rubber estates and in applications for land for rubber plantations; more than half the estates in the state changed hands.[5]

Most of the companies formed in 1909 and 1910 were over-capitalized in relation to the necessary cost per acre for opening new estates. As the boom waned in the following two years, however, a series of new estates were opened by companies and individuals on a more conservative basis and under careful and experienced management. In these cases the usual rate of investment averaged £25 to £30 per acre until the trees matured. By 1912 sixty rubber planting companies were operating in the Federated Malay States, and in that year they paid dividends varying from 20 per cent. to 275½ per cent., the average being 68 per cent.[6] Although prices were at a peak only for a few months in late 1909 and early 1910, very considerable profits were still made in 1912. At the same time much of the rubber planted during the first boom was beginning to yield and production increased markedly, especially in the western Malay States (Fig. 37).

During this boom period European companies were particularly anxious to acquire land already planted with rubber for this reduced the initial investment and ensured quicker returns; it also helped to attract investors in Britain. There was therefore an increasing tendency for the old Chinese plantations whether of sugar, gambier or tapioca, to pass into the hands of European

[4] *A.R. Seremban Land Office, 1912,* 3.

[5] *A.R. Negri Sembilan, 1910,* 3; *A.R. Kedah, 1328 A.H.,* 13 January 1910-11, January 1911, 12.

[6] C.E. Akers, *Report on the Rubber Industry of the Orient,* London, 1912, 25-26.

companies which offered large sums for interplanted land. Many Chinese and also Malay smallholders began to plant rubber on their land with this end in view. Thus Teo Peng Kim, a resident of Kuala Lumpur, planted a block of land at Temiang in Negri Sembilan which she sold in November 1910 to the United Temiang Syndicate for $30,000. Before the end of the year, in conjunction with Lim Ju Keng, she applied for and was granted 1,000 acres of *lalang* land at Batang Malaka for rubber planting, presumably hoping to repeat her earlier success.[7] Simultaneously Malay smallholders responded to the new method of acquiring wealth, stimulated by the early successes of a few of their kind. In 1909 for instance, a Malay in Matang District, Perak, sold twelve acres of rubber for $8,000; the appetite of the smallholders was 'whetted to plant more for the demented foreigner to buy'.[8]

The prospects of large returns also produced a tremendous increase in planting activities on estates old and new. Between 1909 and 1912 the acreage planted with rubber on estates in Malaya increased by 110 per cent., the number of estates in existence almost doubled and the total area alienated for rubber planting on estates rose by 642,000 acres. The year of greatest activity for the estates was 1911, when 332 new estates were opened, 343,000 acres were alienated for rubber and 180,000 acres were newly planted (Table 21).

TABLE 21

RUBBER ESTATES IN MALAYA, 1908-13
(*as at 31 December*).

Year	Number of Estates	Total Alienated Acreage	Acreage Planted with Rubber
1908	417	762,408	241,138
1909	534	855,992	292,035
1910	632	1,014,414	362,853
1911	964	1,357,698	542,877
1912	1,055	1,498,282	621,621
1913	1,151	1,622,231	708,545

Source: *A.R. Director of Agriculture, F.M.S.* for relevant years.

[7] *N.S.S.F., Tampin 3052/1910.*
[8] *A.R. Perak, 1909, 11.*

This boom had noticeable effects in all parts of Malaya with the exception of Trengganu, but it found its greatest expression in the western states of Perak and Selangor. In each of these states over 70,000 acres were newly planted with rubber on an estate basis between 1909 and 1912. In the case of Selangor 101 new estates appeared and an additional 100,000 acres were alienated for estate rubber; in Perak 149 new estates were opened and an additional 127,000 acres alienated. The alienation of large areas for estate rubber cultivation was also very active in Johore during this period, but a much smaller area was newly planted here during the boom than was the case in Perak and Selangor.

This planting boom took several different forms. There was, in the first place, a very marked extension of planting activities on existing rubber estates and conversion by interplanting was undertaken on all the old estates that had retained their original crops. At the same time, there was a tremendous rush for new land, for both estates and smallholdings, in the areas in which rubber planting was already well established, the areas previously designated 'core areas'. In both cases activity concentrated heavily in western Malaya and was closely tied to existing communication patterns. By 1910 'almost all the available land within reach of existing roads [had] been alienated' in Kinta, and the following year the Resident of Perak observed that the whole face of the country, as seen from the main roads, had been transformed 'from virgin forest to the monotony of miles of rubber trees, and a patch of jungle along our cart-roads will soon be the exception rather than the rule of less than ten years ago'.[9]

To a large extent, therefore, the planting boom merely emphasized distributional patterns that had already emerged by 1908. In discussing the situation in 1912, Akers remarked that rubber cultivation was almost continuous along either side of the railway line from Tampin to Penang, being broken only at intervals by Forest Reserves and mining operations; cultivation was more scattered along the line from Tampin to Singapore, but planting was being actively undertaken.[10] Neverthe-

---

[9] *A.R. Perak, 1910*, 6; *A.R. Perak, 1911*, 11.
[10] Akers, op. cit. 19.

less, the frontier of rubber planting did extend outwards from the earlier centres into completely new areas during this boom period, although frequently the directions in which extensions were made were determined by the construction or planning of new roads and railways, and these almost invariably were linked directly to the existing west coast network. An excellent example of this form of frontier advance is the tremendous interest shown in the acquisition of land for rubber, by both Europeans and Chinese, along the Gemas-Bahau railway in the Kuala Pilah District of Negri Sembilan during 1910.[11] Similarly in Johore there was a 'feverish desire' to plant rubber during the boom years, and the alignment of the recently-completed railway retained an almost magnetic attraction for the planters.[12]

Planting began on an estate basis in Trengganu in 1911, but in general this state, in which virtually nothing was done to evolve suitable land regulations until after 1920, was totally unaffected by the boom. In Kelantan the area planted with rubber on estates doubled during 1911, and planting activities were restricted mainly to the Ulu Kelantan District which contained the Duff Development Company's concession. It was estimated that 11,000 acres had been planted with rubber on estates in this state by the end of 1911, representing about one-quarter of the area that had been planted in the single District of Klang at the same date.[13] Development was equally restricted in Pahang. Planting began on a commercial scale here in 1905 but only 7,700 acres had been planted on estates by the end of 1911.[14] Clearly, lack of communication facilities in the isolated and undeveloped east coast states was the major hindrance to the expansion of estate rubber cultivation, not least because it increased total operative costs. The contrast between Pahang, under British control since 1889, and Kedah, under Malay administration until 1909, is alone sufficient to negate most other explanations of this lack of development to the east of

---

[11] N.S.S.F., K.P. 1308-1310/1910; K.P. 1646/1910; N.S. 1783/1910 and N.S. 2623/1910.
[12] A.R. Johore, 1913, 7.
[13] A.R. Kelantan, 1911, 3.
[14] A.R. Director of Agriculture, F.M.S., 1911, 19.

the main range. Indeed, in 1912 one observer stated that rubber planting in Pahang 'will not prove a golden road to fortune. The labour and transport handicap is no mere bagatelle'.[15]

This expansion of planting activities occurred on the basis of channels of capital and labour supply already established before the boom began. The agency-houses played an increasing role in the development of the industry as a flood of new companies were formed; apart from Guthries, and Harrisons and Crosfield, Sime Darby took a major part in this process. But the 'Loans to Planters' scheme did not cease in 1908. The fund, administered by a Committee of Federal Officers, was still available to provide aid to planters and during 1909 a total of $187,476 was given out in loans.[16] Moreover the introduction of the Immigration Fund in 1908 did much to solve earlier labour problems. The number of south Indian labourers entering Selangor increased from 13,700 in 1908 to 43,500 in 1913, and marked increases were also registered in Perak and Negri Sembilan during the same period.[17] In Negri Sembilan, however, as in several other states, including Kelantan and Johore, a large proportion of the estate labour force consisted of Chinese; indeed, Tamil labour was predominant only on the estates of Perak and Selangor. The estates in Kelantan relied heavily on Chinese *sinkheh* labour recruited on an indentured system. The temporary prohibition of the indentured system here tended to restrict expansion in the later years of the boom, but it was subsequently removed.[18] Elsewhere, rubber planting was expanding in areas in which a Chinese agricultural labour force already existed. Adequate supplies of labour permitted the rapid expansion of planting activities that characterized the boom period.

Encouraging land regulations were already in force in the Federated Malay States by the early years of the twentieth century. After the remaining Malay States came under British influence in 1909 similar regulations were evolved. In Johore the Land Enactment introduced in September 1910 provided for

---

[15] *Greniers' Rubber News*, Vol. 3 No. 19, 22 June 1912, 1.
[16] *A.R.F.M.S., 1909*, 15.
[17] R.N. Jackson, op. cit. 121.
[18] *A.R. Kelantan, 1912*, 2.

the issue of grants in perpetuity on conditions very similar to those in force in the Federated Malay States and produced 'an immediate demand for titles'.[19] With the introduction of the new régime in Kedah, 'the Government adopted a more liberal policy in regard to land for cultivation in order to encourage capitalists to invest money in rubber'.[20] A system of tenure by registration was developed slowly in Kelantan after 1910.[21] Clearly, the planting boom was made possible by the development of extremely favourable conditions in Malaya before rubber prices began to soar.

Another feature of this boom period worthy of comment is the interest it aroused in rubber planting in Malaya among people who had previously had little connexion with local agricultural development. Japanese, for instance, began planting rubber in Johore in 1909 and opened a considerable number of estates, varying in size from less than one hundred to several thousand acres, during 1910 and 1911, particularly in the southern part of the state and in the Batu Pahat District. At the same time, they also began to open rubber estates in Negri Sembilan. Some of the Chinese miners also turned to rubber planting during this period. In 1910 for example, Towkay Chu Shu Ming of the firm of Kong San was granted 500 acres for rubber in mukim Setul, Negri Sembilan, and before the end of the year had acquired several blocks in other parts of the state.[22] There are also several instances of Chinese converting mining titles to agricultural titles to allow rubber planting on the land. This move to plant rubber was not restricted to the miners. Chinese in various other occupations were also planting the crop, often on a relatively small scale; Chong Chee Tin, the proprietor of a coffee-shop in Kuala Pilah town for instance, acquired fifteen acres for rubber at Sungei Petei in Kuala Pilah

[19] F.W.N. Bridges, *Surveys for Title in the Federated Malay States with notes on the Revenue Surveys of the Unfederated Malay States*, Kuala Lumpur, 1930, 47.

[20] Thamsook Ratanapun, *The Development of the North-Western States of Malaya, 1909-1941*. Unpublished M.A. Thesis, University of Hong Kong, March 1961, 147-8.

[21] Bridges, op. cit. 52.

[22] *N.S.S.F., N.S. 419/1900* and *Jelebu 1770/1910*.

in 1910.[23] Moreover, wealthy Chinese in the Straits Settlements also began to acquire large blocks of land for rubber planting in the Malay states. In conjunction with the activities of existing Chinese planters and the spread of rubber planting among Malay smallholders, these developments resulted in a marked increase in the Asian-owned rubber acreage in the early 1910's.

Temporary Set-Backs, 1913-14

The price of rubber fell sharply in 1913, and by September stood at 1s 11½d per pound. Lewton-Brain suggested that an immediate cause of this price-fall was probably the strike, followed by floods, that occurred at Akron, the chief manufacturing centre in the United States, during 1913.[24]

The effects of this drastic reduction in prices were apparent immediately, particularly on the European-owned estates. A smaller area was planted with rubber in the Federated Malay States during 1913 than in any year since 1909. Some estate managers applied for licences to prospect for tin, and permission was given to several Chinese in Negri Sembilan to take one crop of tapioca from land already granted to them for rubber planting.[25] The Collector of Land Revenue, Seremban, reported that 'the sudden and unexpected fall in the price of rubber was followed by a diminution of enthusiasm, and led to a number of small applications being withdrawn'.[26] Johore experienced similar effects. The planting of new land by Europeans in this state almost ceased during 1913 and 1914, although the activities of the Japanese planters continued unchecked.[27] In contrast, in many parts of western Malaya the Chinese continued to acquire and to plant new land, and in Kedah during 1913 the Chinese towkays had in no way 'lost their confidence in the future of plantation rubber; and the Chinese planters, of the "market-gardener" class, who own and cultivate their separate small holdings of ten or fifteen acres, [were] clearing and planting with undiminished vigour'.[28]

[23] N.S.S.F., K.P. 1645/1910.
[24] A.R. Director of Agriculture, F.M.S., 1913, 2.
[25] N.S.S.F., K.P. 34/1913; Tampin 698/1913 and Tampin 2236/1913.
[26] A.R. Seremban Land Office, 1913, 4-5.
[27] A.R. Johore, 1913, 9 and A.R.Johore, 1914, 13.
[28] A.R. Kedah, 1331 A.H., 11 December 1912-30 November 1913, 21.

The outbreak of the first World War in 1914 temporarily augmented the effects of the reduction in prices. The Director of Agriculture, Federated Malay States, reported that it dislocated the market for a time, but the recovery in the case of rubber was very rapid, and after the first week or two prices were remarkably steady 'largely due to the extraordinary demand for certain rubber articles for the use of the Allied Forces'.[29] The outbreak of hostilities in Europe produced other difficulties, particularly with regard to the financing of the newer estates, some of which had a certain amount of trouble for a time in obtaining remittances. Moreover, many European estate managers and assistants volunteered for service. Their departure seriously reduced efficiency at a time when huge areas were coming into bearing. In consequence, new planting was restricted during 1914 and tapping was done on a more conservative basis than in the boom years. Nevertheless, exports continued to rise (Fig. 37).

In many cases the financial problems created by these setbacks were reduced by the assistance obtainable from the Planters' Loan Fund. During 1913 the capital of this Fund was increased by $1 million, although this was available only to private owners and syndicates and to local companies.[30] In 1914 a Planters' Loan Board replaced the earlier organization and immediately suggested that the capital of the Fund should be raised from $4 to $5 million. The outbreak of war, however, prevented the implementation of this suggestion. It was now the general policy of the Board to discourage the speculative opening of land and for this reason it laid down a general rule 'not to recommend any loan on plantings of less than two years'. The Board also decided that henceforth no dividend or bonus was to be taken by the owners of an estate on which a loan had been granted until the loan had been repaid, and that all profits derived from the estate should be devoted to the repayment.[31] Clearly, the years 1913 and 1914 witnessed the beginning of the end of unlimited agricultural expansion under strong Government encouragement.

[29] *A.R. Director of Agriculture, F.M.S., 1914*, 2.
[30] *A.R. Director of Agriculture, F.M.S., 1913*, 3.
[31] *N.S.S.F., N.S. 2385/1915.*

These temporary set-backs were not without their beneficial effects so far as the long-term development of the rubber plantation industry was concerned. They marked the end of the period of intense speculation which typified the boom years, they focussed attention on the need to improve processing and marketing techniques and to increase the general level of efficiency.

In 1913 the price of 'plantation' rubber was considerably lower than the price of 'wild' rubber. Mr. Arthur du Cros, Managing Director of the Dunlop Rubber Company Limited, suggested that the basic reasons for this difference could be traced to the lack of uniformity in the processing of 'plantation' rubber and to the fact that it was 'indifferently graded'.[32] During the boom years the efforts of planters and companies were directed to the planting of large areas of rubber; few had given much consideration to processing and marketing at a time when prices were extremely high. By 1913, however, when prices had fallen drastically, large areas were approaching maturity and it became increasingly necessary to ensure that manufacturers received a product which satisfied their needs.[33] Before 1911 very few estates possessed factories designed or equipped for the processing of rubber and in most cases either old coffee stores or temporary buildings were used. The period 1911-14 witnessed a complete change as greater attention was paid to processing and marketing. Special factories were constructed on most estates and engine-driven machinery was widely installed. The temporary set-backs of 1913 and 1914 had induced a considerable improvement in the all-round efficiency of the industry.

Enthusiasm Renewed, 1915-17

Rubber prices reached a more encouraging level in 1915, chiefly because of the large demand for rubber for war purposes and the enormously increased purchases of the United States. The following year the Director of Agriculture, Federated Malay States, noted that the price of rubber had ruled consistently high throughout the year, 'and in spite of high freight

---

[32] *Financial Times*, 4 November 1913.

[33] L. Wray, 'The Packing of Plantation Rubber', *Agricultural Bulletin of the Federated Malay States*, Vol. 1 No. 8, March 1913, 301-4.

rates and higher cost of materials on this side the profits continue to be very considerable'.[34] Although production was rising rapidly as the rubber planted in the boom years matured, the prospects of profits at the level now reaped by those who had planted half a decade or more before stimulated a new wave of land acquisition and planting in the period 1915-17. Planting activities were renewed on existing estates, new land was taken up in the as yet unoccupied parts of the 'core areas' and large-scale expansion occurred in several less developed districts. The European estate acreage was enlarged by all three processes, but to a very large extent this was an era of rapid planting on the part of smallholders, both Malay and Chinese, particularly in the western Malay States.[35]

The Kuala Pilah District of Negri Sembilan provides an excellent example of the way in which this sudden spurt of activity affected previously less developed areas. The District Officer reported that in 1916

The demand for rubber land throughout the year was extraordinary, far exceeding that in the 'boom' year. All nationalities joined in the rush and at the end of the year practically the whole of the road and railway frontage in the district had been applied for. The demand for land was a genuine one and there was practically no speculation in jungle land.

In fact, the total number of applications for land grants in this District in 1916 exceeded the total received in the years 1905 to 1915 added together.[36] The rush for land was equally spectacular in other west coast areas. In Johore, applications were received for about 315,000 acres during 1916, at the same time there was a marked increase in the demand for land in southern Kedah, and there was an 'overwhelming demand for land for rubber planting' in Perak.[37] By the end of 1917 over 610,000 acres had been planted with rubber on estates in the Federated Malay States, and over one million acres had been

[34] A.R. Director of Agriculture, F.M.S., 1916, 1.

[35] A.R. Planters' Association of Malaya, 1915, 4 and A.R. Negri Sembilan, 1915, 7.

[36] A.R. Kuala Pilah, 1916, 2-3.

[37] A.R. Johore, 1916, 9; A.R. Kedah, 1334 A.H., 9 November 1915-27 October 1916, 2; A.R. Perak, 1916, 3.

so planted in the whole of Malaya. Statistics relating to the smallholding acreage at this date do not exist. Clearly, however, there was a very marked increase in the smallholding rubber acreage in the middle years of the second decade of the twentieth century, and in some Districts of western Malaya as much as half the total rubber acreage lay on smallholdings in 1917.[38] It may be that as much as 625,000 acres had been planted with rubber on smallholdings in Malaya by this date.[39]

By 1917, however, the unfettered expansion of plantation agriculture was coming to an end. The rush for land which characterized 1915 and 1916 placed an unbearable strain on the Land Office Staff in many Districts and resulted in the closure of the application books. In December 1916 the Land Office books were closed until further notice in the Rembau and Kuala Pilah Districts of Negri Sembilan, although in the latter case applications were still considered for land to the east of the railway from Gemas to Pahang. The books were also closed in Tampin District in February 1917 and in Kedah and Pahang in the same year. The result was a marked decline in the rate of alienation of land for rubber planting. To some extent, the passing of the Malay Reservations Enactment in 1913 had begun to have similar restricting effects, for technically it made it impossible for estate owners to buy up land already planted by Malay smallholders and also tended to limit the areas in which new land was available for estate expansion. Nevertheless, planting continued on land already alienated to estates.

Falling Prices and Restriction of Output, 1918-21

The improvement in market conditions during 1915 and 1916 was merely a temporary result of enhanced war-time demand. Conditions worsened in 1917 and prices on the Singapore market fell from 77 cents a pound at the beginning of 1918 to

[38] E.g. by 1917 28,200 acres had been planted with rubber on estates in Kuala Kangsar District and an estimated 29,000 acres on smallholdings; for Larut District the figures were 30,735 acres and 27,000 acres respectively. *A.R. Perak, 1917*, 3-4.

[39] Estimate based on Tables 129-131 in D.M. Figart, *The Plantation Rubber Industry in the Middle East*, Washington, 1925, 274-5.

37 cents a pound in August, a price at which few estates could continue to produce at a profit.[40] 1918 was, in fact, a year of crisis for the Malayan rubber industry.

The severe reduction in prices was coupled with other basic problems. In the first place, the export of rubber from British colonies to places other than the United Kingdom was restricted. Yet the Imperial Government had also imposed restrictions on facilities for shipping rubber from Malaya to the United Kingdom, and in 1918 the space available in British ships for such exports amounted to a mere 2,000 tons per month. Moreover, in May 1918 the United States Government decided to restrict imports of rubber and established a quota at the rate of 100,000 tons per annum, a marked reduction on her 1917 imports of 177,000 tons. This was a major blow to the Malayan industry, for at this time Malaya produced some 63 per cent. of the world output of plantation rubber, and the United States imported about 70 per cent. of total world production.[41]

As a result of these problems exports of Malayan rubber declined and the industry suffered severely (Fig. 37). Indeed, the Malayan rubber industry weathered the 1913 slump very much more easily than the problems it faced five years later. By 1918 over 691,000 acres were in bearing on estates in Malaya, representing three times the acreage in bearing in 1913, and comprising about three-fifths of the total planted estate acreage in 1918 (Table 22).

The estates were, in fact, faced with drastically reduced rubber prices at a time when costs of production and freight charges were rising. In consequence, there was a very substantial fall in profits in 1918. The majority of companies either greatly reduced or completely passed over dividends and in some cases they recorded a loss on the year's working.[42] Demand for new land was minimal. Few estates undertook new planting;

---

[40] *A.R. Negri Sembilan, 1918*, 7.

[41] *Report of the Commission Appointed by His Excellency the High Commissioner for the Malay States to enquire whether any action should be taken by the Government to give protection or assistance to the Rubber Industry*, Singapore, 1918, 1-7, hereafter cited as *Report of the Protection Commission, 1918*.

[42] *A.R. Planters' Association of Malaya, 1918*, 6.

TABLE 22

MALAYA: ESTATE RUBBER STATISTICS, 1918

	Federated Malay States	Straits Settle-ments	Johore	Kedah Kelantan and Trengganu	Total
Number of Estates	1,126	248	148	192	1,714
Total Alienated Area (Acres)	1,094,217	266,743	363,688	253,442	1,978,090
Planted with rubber at 31 December	672,106	167,789	166,116	118,232	1,124,243
Planted with rubber alone	660,020	163,514	164,280	109,237	1,097,051
Rubber interplanted with other crops	12,086	4,275	1,836	8,995	27,192
Acreage in bearing	447,175	107,539	89,945	46,776	691,435
Planted during the year	50,484	14,600	3,741	9,598	78,423

Source: A.R. Planters' Association of Malaya, 1921, Appendix E.

indeed, the practice of interplanting immature rubber with tapioca spread markedly in Negri Sembilan and in some areas newly cleared land was planted with hill padi.[43] Some estates obtained mining leases over parts of their lands, and interest was awakened in the possibility of diversifying plantation agriculture. Thus, in November 1918 the Advisory Committee of the Federated Malay States Department of Agriculture suggested that the Director should request the Resident of Negri Sembilan to reserve a block of at least 2,000 acres for the establishment of a large-scale experimental plantation. The stated object of the proposal was 'to encourage the development of new agricultural industries in this country'.[44] It was at this time that interest was first shown in oil palm as a plantation crop in Malaya.

Early in 1918 there was considerable pressure from the Rub-

[43] A.R. Negri Sembilan, 1918, 4.
[44] N.S.S.F., Fed. 3444/1918.

ber Growers' Association for the restriction of rubber output, and in July 1918 the Planters' Association of Malaya asked the Government to intervene to assist the industry. At the time the Government felt that there was insufficient cause to warrant intervention. In the same month, however, the Colonial Office wrote to the Malayan authorities suggesting a scheme of controlled output and fixed prices.[45] A Committee comprising planters and Government officials was appointed on 16 August 1918 to advise the Government whether any action was necessary to protect or assist the rubber industry; on 2 September the Committee became a Commission. The Committee immediately recommended that as a temporary measure the Government should cease to collect the export duty on rubber, and was strongly in favour of restricted output and guaranteed prices. In its full report the Commission recommended that the assistance and protection to be given to the rubber industry 'should take the form of an arrangement between the British and Dutch Governments for restriction by law of their output of plantation rubber'. It suggested that estates of fifty acres or more should be licensed for an output of a fixed number of pounds per acre over a specified period and that a 'coupon system' should be applied to holdings of less than fifty acres. This scheme for the restriction of output was to be accompanied by price control, and a minimum price of one dollar per pound was to be guaranteed.[46] But immediate action was not taken on these recommendations and with the armistice in November 1918 the idea of restriction was shelved temporarily.[47]

The situation improved somewhat during 1919. Prices rose a little and exports increased noticeably (Figs. 36 and 37). But this post-armistice improvement was short-lived and the industry was caught in the general depression of 1920. Rubber prices fell steadily during 1920 from $1.12 per pound in January to 32 cents per pound in December. By 1921 the outlook was dismal. Vast areas were reaching maturity at a time when profits were negligible; most of the European companies had long been

---

[45] *A.R. Planters' Association of Malaya, 1918,* 6.

[46] *Report of the Protection Commission, 1918,* 7-9 and 13; *A.R. Planters' Association of Malaya, 1918,* 8.

[47] *A.R.F.M.S., 1918,* 8.

accustomed to operate on a rising market but they now found 'that they were unable to recover their costs which had been inflated during the years of prosperity by extravagance in administration and by the reckless planting of unsuitable land'.[48]

In September 1920 the Rubber Growers' Association sent a telegram to its local committee in Kuala Lumpur pointing out the grave situation regarding the anticipated world surplus of rubber in 1920 and 1921; it recommended immediate restriction of output by Malayan producers. Representatives of the local committee of the Rubber Growers' Association, the Planters' Association of Malaya and the Rubber Producers' Association of Malaya held a joint meeting in Kuala Lumpur on receipt of this telegram. They supported the idea of restriction and recommended that part of the tapping area on existing estates should be rested and that a scheme on the lines of the Report of the 1918 Commission should be introduced.

The Government expressed its willingness to legislate to provide for compulsory curtailment of output 'if rubber growers and the rubber producers [were] unanimously in favour of legislation'. There was in fact little doubt about the wishes of those connected with the estates. The Rubber Producers' Association of Malaya decided upon a scheme for restricting the output of its members as from 1 September 1920. At the same time the directors of local rubber companies held a meeting in Kuala Lumpur and passed a resolution in favour of legislation, and the Planters' Association of Malaya called on the Government to begin immediate restriction to reduce output to 75 per cent. of 'normal'.[49] This latter suggestion was instituted by voluntary agreement among the British and Dutch companies, which between them controlled most of the estate acreage in Malaya and the Netherlands East Indies, in November 1920. This voluntary restriction continued until December 1921, but proved ineffective because outsiders increased their production. The companies therefore demanded Government

[48] Allen and Donnithorne, op. cit. 121.
[49] 'Minutes of Ordinary Meeting of the Planters' Association of Malaya, 27 September 1920', *Agricultural Bulletin of the Federated Malay States*, Vol. 8 No. 3, July, August and September 1920, 221-4.

intervention to impose compulsory restriction on all producers, and in October 1921 the Stevenson Committee was appointed by the British Government. The restriction scheme proposed by this Committee was approved by the British Government and came into effect in November 1922.[50] The introduction of this scheme marks the close of what might be termed the foundation period in the history of the Malayan rubber industry. Thereafter, for long periods production and new planting were officially restricted in a way which contrasts markedly with the encouragements previously offered to planters by Government.

The End of an Era

By 1921 rubber reigned supreme in the agricultural economy of Malaya. More than three-fifths of the total cultivated area was devoted to this crop and plantation agriculture had become virtually monocultural, dependent upon a product typified by price instability. This was by no means a new situation in Malaya. Throughout the nineteenth and early twentieth centuries commercial agriculture in Malaya was always a highly speculative venture, whether undertaken by Chinese or Europeans. Rising prices brought a rapid expansion of the area planted to specific crops, declining prices saw an immediate restriction of planting activities and frequently a change of emphasis from one crop to another. The history of commercial agriculture in nineteenth-century Malaya is the story of a series of booms, each associated with a different crop, each accompanied by an extension of the frontier of agricultural activity, and each subsiding rapidly as the relative profitability of the crops concerned declined.

As a form of speculative commercial agriculture the rubber plantation industry in early twentieth-century Malaya differed in two important respects from these earlier waves of activity. The nineteenth century was characterized by a marked regional concentration of different forms of plantation agriculture; rubber, on the other hand, was planted to a greater or lesser degree in all parts of the peninsula. Moreover, when prices fell drastically in the late 1910's rubber was not swept aside as was the case with the earlier crops. The economy of the country had now passed the pioneer phase, the social and economic welfare of the population depended to a considerable extent upon the rubber plantation industry, an industry largely backed by the share-capital of British investors. Neither the companies nor the Government were prepared to let the rubber industry suffer the fate of its predecessors.

Although rubber had became the dominant plantation crop in all parts of Malaya the industry was heavily concentrated in west coast areas. The major zone of concentration comprised Johore, the western Malay states of Perak, Selangor and Negri Sembilan, and to a lesser extent Malacca and Kedah; the east coast states of Pahang, Trengganu and Kelantan together contained less than 6 per cent. of the total area planted with rubber in Malaya in 1921 (Table 23). This imbalance in the agricultural development of the areas to the west and east of the main range pre-dates the advent of rubber; the expansion of rubber planting in the early twentieth century merely confirmed the the historical and economic factors that had favoured west coast areas for more than a century.

Any form of plantation agriculture exists to export its products. It can therefore only survive in areas where this is possible. The states of western Malaya lay relatively close to the Straits Settlements, each with its port facilities and its contacts with the major world markets for tropical agricultural produce. Moreover, the 'tin rush' which the western Malay States experienced during the second half of the nineteenth century served to open up vast areas for potential development by stimulating a rapid expansion of transport facilities. Development, as a general rule, begets more development. Communication facilities were extended on the basis of existing networks, planters looking for new land for rubber in the first decade and a half of the present century preferred locations close to roads and railways and therefore rarely turned their attention to the east of the main range. Greater accessibility gave western Malaya a head start on the lands to the east; the imbalance persists today.

Rubber planting began as an estate venture in Malaya. Expansion during the pioneer phase was largely estate-sponsor-

RUBBER IN MALAYA, 1921

Geographical Region	ESTATES			SMALLHOLDINGS			TOTAL ACREAGE PLANTED WITH RUBBER
	Planted Acreage (a)	Acreage in bearing (b)	Percentage (b) over (a)	Planted Acreage (a)	Acreage in bearing (b)	Percentage (b) over (a)	
Perak	235,493	164,305	69.7	233,677	151,816	64.9	469,170
Selangor	282,586	207,125	73.3	116,898	71,882	61.5	399,484
Negri Sembilan	210,743	116,895	55.5	68,677	42,907	62.5	279,420
Western Malay States	728,822	488,325	67.0	419,252	266,605	63.6	1,148,074
Singapore	33,654	19,605	58.2	21,273	9,611	45.2	54,927
Penang	48,492	34,540	71.2	45,688	13,908	30.4	94,180
Malacca	117,730	88,135	74.9	57,230	36,700	64.1	174,960
Straits Settlements	199,876	142,280	71.2	124,191	60,219	48.5	324,067
Johore	224,096	130,187	58.1	214,890	94,423	43.9	438,986
Kedah	108,700	44,992	41.4	75,751	28,493	37.6	184,451
Perlis	n.a.	n.a.	—	n.a.	n.a.	—	2,000
Other West Coast States	332,796*	175,179*	52.6	290,641*	122,916*	42.3	625,437
Pahang	36,178	14,421	39.9	50,799	21,369	42.1	86,977
Trengganu	5,602	1,592	28.4	1,500†	n.a.	—	7,102
Kelantan	n.a.	n.a.	—	n.a.	n.a.	—	33,395
East Coast States	41,780‡	16,013‡	38.3	52,299‡	21,369+	—	127,474
Total Malaya	1,303,274=	821,797=	63.1	886,383=	471,109§	—	2,225,052

† estimate   * excluding Perlis   ‡ excluding Kelantan   + Johore only

n.a. not available   § excluding Kelantan, Perlis and Trengganu   = excluding Kelantan and Perlis

Source: Figart, op. cit. Tables 129, 130 and 131, 274-5.

ed and rubber only rose to prominence as a smallholders' crop during the 1910's. Despite the tremendous rate of new planting on smallholdings between 1910 and 1921 almost three-fifths of the total planted area lay on estates in the latter year (Table 23) and estates produced more than two-thirds of the total Malayan output. The industry remained estate-dominated, and to a very large extent the estates were European-owned. Indeed, in each of the three western Malay States over three-quarters of the total estate acreage was in European hands. Approximately a fifth of the total estate acreage in Malaya was Chinese-owned in 1921, Chinese ownership being most important in Johore, Malacca and Kedah. Japanese ownership remained a notable feature in Johore.

This study has been concerned with the attempts of Chinese and European pioneers to establish plantation agriculture in Malaya and with the varying factors influencing those attempts. It has sought to show that throughout much of the nineteenth century the Chinese achieved considerably greater success in these attempts than did their European counterparts and it has been suggested that the basic reason for this difference lies in the greater suitability of the Chinese cultivation system and methods of organization to the frontier conditions that typified nineteenth century Malaya. With the turn of the century however, the situation changed.

With the notable exception of spices which had ceased to be of significance by the 1860's, maximum production of all the early plantation crops in Malaya was achieved in the first years of the twentieth century; thereafter, these crops disappeared rapidly. British control, in various forms, had extended over a large part of the peninsula by the late 1880's, and by 1919 included the whole of present-day Malaya. As the new administration took root, a policy emerged which clearly favoured the European planter at the expense of the Chinese. Government began to provide the bases of agricultural development—communication facilities, land on easy terms, loans and imported labour—in forms designed to serve the European interest in plantation agriculture in Malaya. It was the foundation of the rubber industry on these bases that sounded the death-knell for the various nineteenth-century export crops and confirmed the growing dominance of Europeans in the commercial agriculture of Malaya. Based on corporate ownership and financed by an overseas share-holding public the development of this industry outdated Chinese methods more suited to the earlier phase. By 1921 plantation agriculture in Malaya was organized on the lines of a western capitalist enterprise.

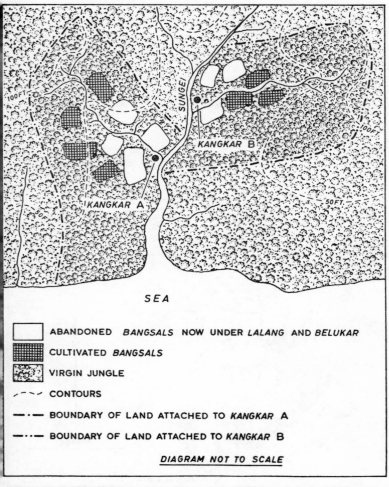

Fɪɢ. 2. SCHEMATIC PLAN OF *KANGKARS* AND *BANGSALS*

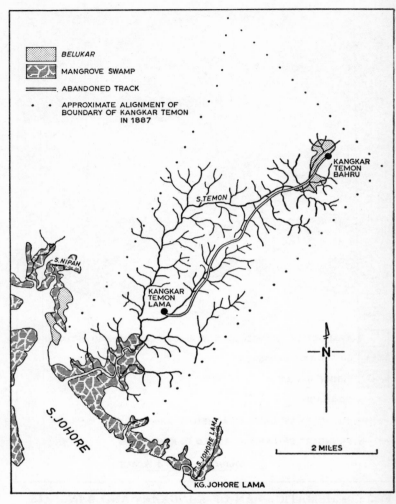

FIG. 3. KANGKAR TEMON LAMA AND KANGKAR TEMON
      BAHRU

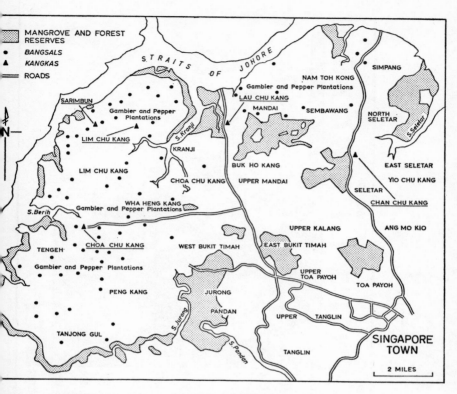

FIG. 4. *KANGKARS* AND *BANGSALS* IN SINGAPORE, 1885
Based on *Map of the Island of Singapore and Its Dependencies, 1885*
(P.R.O., London, Straits Settlements No. 18).

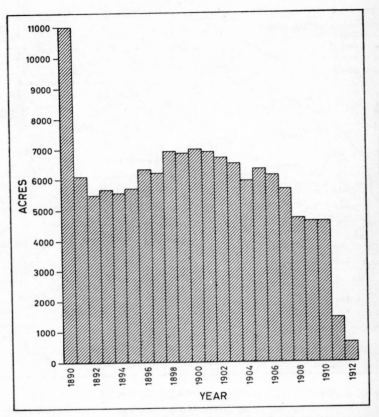

FIG. 5. ACREAGE OF GAMBIER AND PEPPER IN SINGAPORE,
1890–1912

Source: Straits Settlements Blue Books for relevant years.

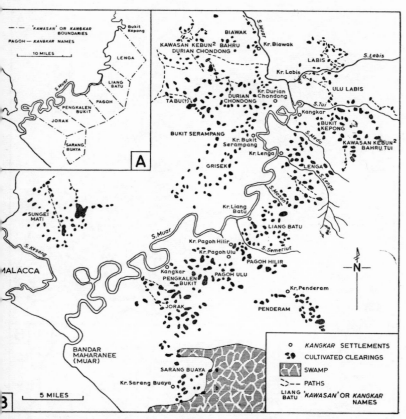

FIG. 6. GAMBIER AND PEPPER PLANTATIONS IN THE MUAR
VALLEY, JOHORE, A. 1887 AND B. 1904

Based on *Map of the Territory and Dependencies of Johore, 1887*
(R.G.S. Map Collection) and *Map of Muar and Batu Pahat, 1904*
(Photostat in Historical Map Collection, Department of Geography,
University of Malaya).

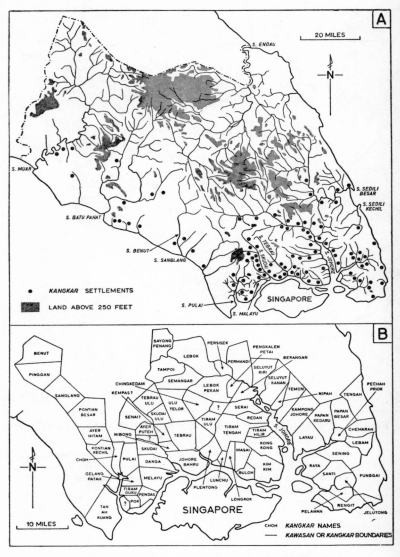

FIG. 7. A. *KANGKAR* SETTLEMENTS IN JOHORE, 1887
B. *KANGKAR* OR *KAWASAN* BOUNDARIES IN
SOUTHERN JOHORE, 1887
Based on *The Singapore and Straits Directory for 1887*, Singapore,
1887, 249-50, and *Map of the Territory and Dependencies of Johore,
1887* (R.G.S. Map Collection).

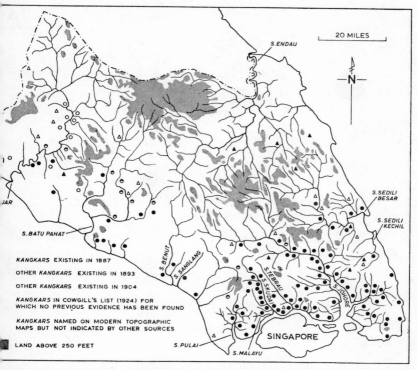

FIG. 8. ALL KNOWN *KANGKAR* SETTLEMENTS IN JOHORE

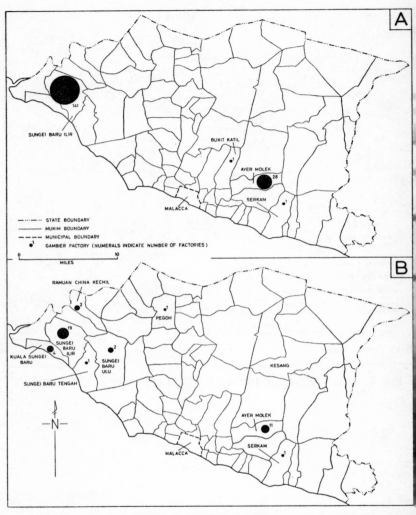

FIG. 9. GAMBIER FACTORIES IN MALACCA, A. 1882 AND B. 1887
Source: Straits Settlements Blue Book, 1882 and 1887.

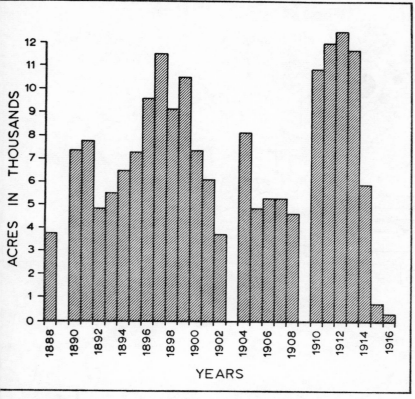

FIG. 10. ACREAGE OF GAMBIER AND PEPPER IN MALACCA, 1888–1916

Source: Straits Settlements Blue Books for relevant years.
N.B.   Figures for 1889, 1903 and 1909 are unavailable.

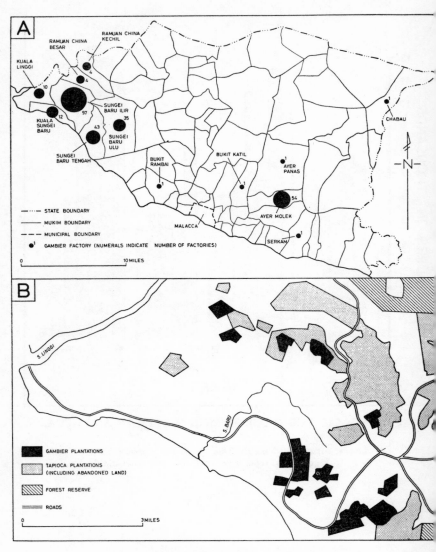

FIG. 11. A. GAMBIER FACTORIES IN MALACCA, 1895 B. LAND
USE IN WESTERN MALACCA, 1894

Based on *Straits Settlements Blue Book, 1895* and *Tracing of the
Malacca Territory, 1894* (National Archives of Malaysia, Petaling
Jaya).

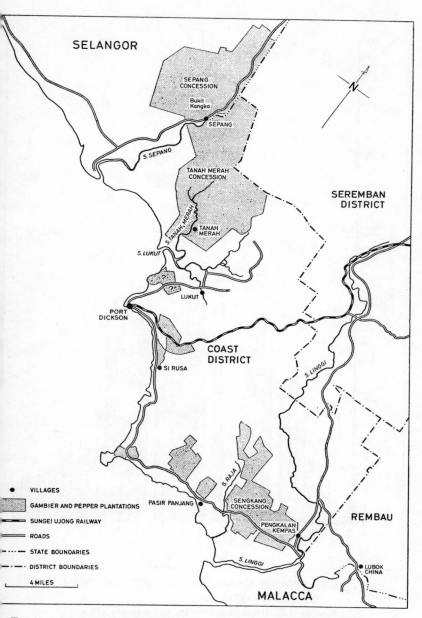

SELANGOR

SEPANG
CONCESSION

Bukit
Kangka

• SEPANG

S. SEPANG

TANAH MERAH
CONCESSION

S. TANAH MERAH

• TANAH
MERAH

SEREMBAN
DISTRICT

S. LUKUT

LUKUT

PORT
DICKSON

COAST
DISTRICT

• SI RUSA

S. LINGGI

• VILLAGES

GAMBIER AND PEPPER PLANTATIONS

SUNGEI UJONG RAILWAY

ROADS

STATE BOUNDARIES

DISTRICT BOUNDARIES

4 MILES

PASIR PANJANG •

S. RAJA

SENGKANG
CONCESSION

PENGKALAN
KEMPAS

REMBAU

S. LINGGI

• LUBOK
CHINA

MALACCA

Fig. 12. GAMBIER AND PEPPER PLANTATIONS IN NEGRI
SEMBILAN AND SELANGOR, 1901

Based on information contained in official reports and on *Map of
the Negri Sembilan, 1903* (P.R.O., London, Straits Settlements,
No. 40).

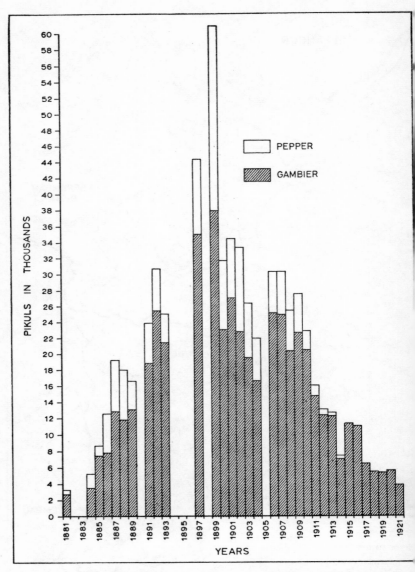

FIG. 13. EXPORTS OF GAMBIER AND PEPPER FROM NEGRI
SEMBILAN 1881–1921

Source: A.R. Negri Sembilan for the relevant years.

N.B.   Figures for 1882-3, 1890, 1894-6, 1898 and 1905 are unavailable.

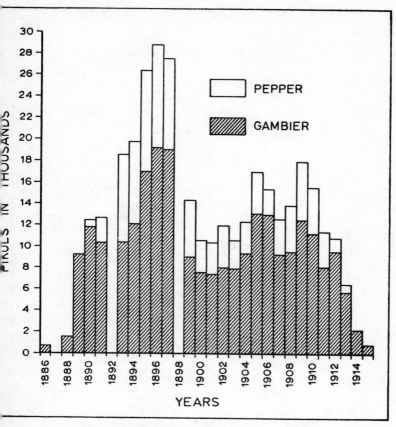

FIG. 14. EXPORTS OF GAMBIER AND PEPPER FROM
SELANGOR, 1886–1915

Source: *A.R. Selangor* for the relevant years.
N.B.   Figures for 1887, 1892 and 1898 are unavailable.

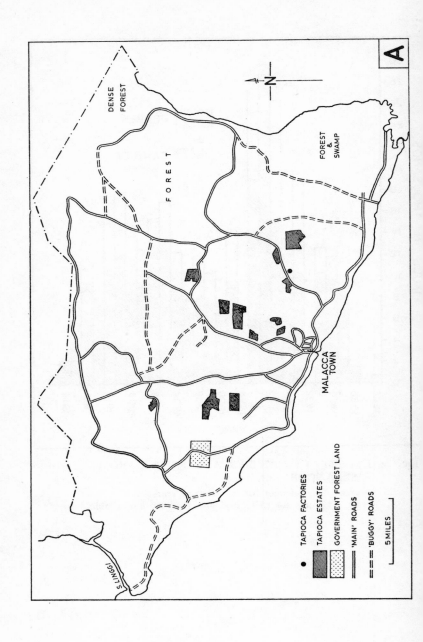

DENSE FOREST

FOREST

FOREST & SWAMP

MALACCA TOWN

S. LINGGI

N

A

TAPIOCA FACTORIES
TAPIOCA ESTATES
GOVERNMENT FOREST LAND
'MAIN' ROADS
'BUGGY' ROADS

5 MILES

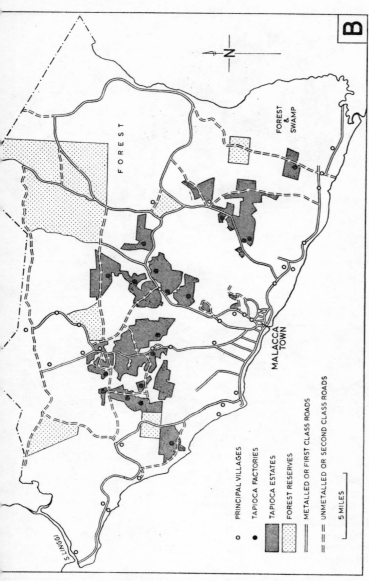

FIG. 15. TAPIOCA PLANTATIONS IN MALACCA, A. 1867 AND
B. 1878

Based on *Map of the Malacca Territory, 1867* (Historical Map
Collection, Department of Geography, University of Malaya) and
Map of the Malacca Territory, 1878 (P.R.O., London, Straits
Settlements, No. 15).

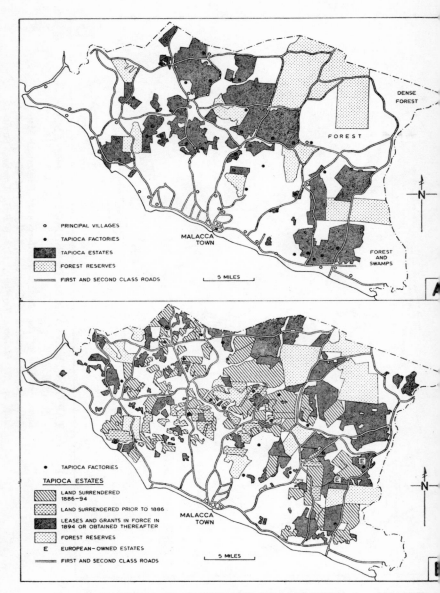

FIG. 16. TAPIOCA PLANTATIONS IN MALACCA. A. 1886 AND
B. 1894
Based on *Map of the Malacca Territory, 1886* and *Tracing of the
Malacca Territory, 1894* (National Archives of Malaysia, Petaling
Jaya).

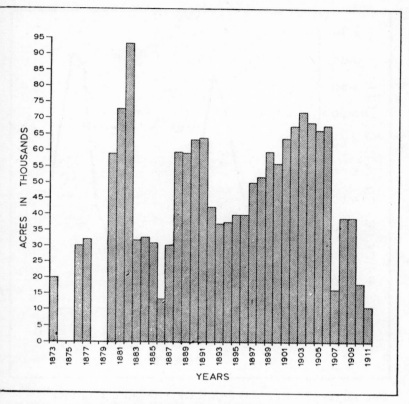

FIG. 17. ACREAGE OF TAPIOCA IN MALACCA, 1873–1911

Source: Straits Settlements Blue Book for the relevant years.

N.B.   Figures for 1874-5. 1878-9 are unavailable.

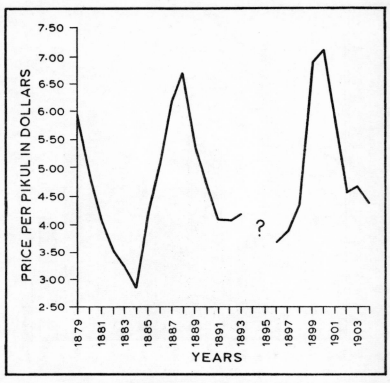

FIG. 18. AVERAGE SALE PRICE OF TAPIOCA, 1879–1904

Sources: N.S.S.F., Sel. 507/94; A.R. Malacca, 1901, 21; N.S.S.F., Tampin 2962/1902 and Tampin 3762/1902; A.R. Lands and Mines Dept., Coast District, 1904, 4 (N.S.S.F., P.D. 839/1905).

(The prices quoted in these various sources do not conform to a standard pattern, some referring only to small flake, and some to medium and small flake *and* pearl; others appear to be average prices for all tapioca exports. For the purpose of this graph, which is intended merely to give an indication of general price movements, these figures have been generalized.)

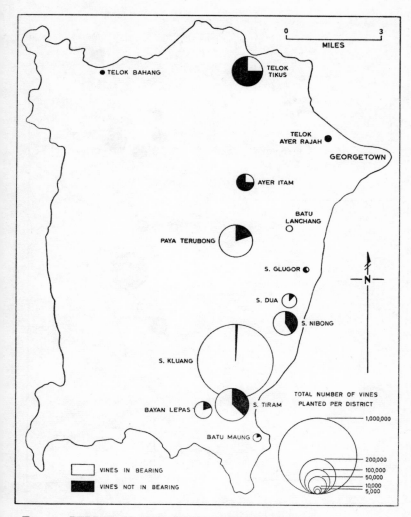

FIG. 19. PEPPER PLANTATIONS IN PENANG, 1818

Source: Enclosure in Report of Finance Committee, Penang
Consultations, 7 October 1818, *SSR* (IOL), Vol. LXVII, 287,
quoted by Stubbs Brown, op, cit. as Appendix VIB.

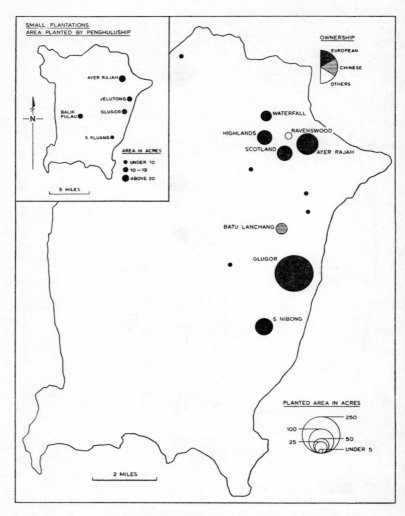

FIG. 20. CLOVE PLANTATIONS IN PENANG, 1843
Source: Penang Gazette, Vol. 2 No. 44, 11 May 1844.

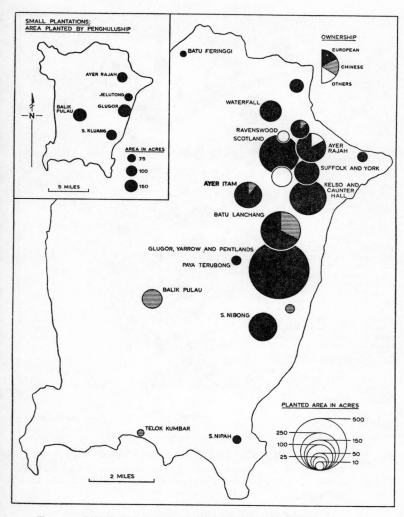

SMALL PLANTATIONS:
AREA PLANTED BY PENGHULUSHIP

BATU FERINGGI

AYER RAJAH

JELUTONG

GLUGOR

BALIK
PULAU

S. KLUANG

AREA IN ACRES
75
100
150

5 MILES

OWNERSHIP
EUROPEAN
CHINESE
OTHERS

WATERFALL

RAVENSWOOD
SCOTLAND

AYER
RAJAH

SUFFOLK AND YORK

AYER ITAM

KELSO AND
CAUNTER
HALL

BATU LANCHANG

GLUGOR, YARROW AND PENTLANDS

PAYA TERUBONG

BALIK PULAU

S. NIBONG

PLANTED AREA IN ACRES
500
250
150
100
50
25
10

TELOK KUMBAR

S. NIPAH

2 MILES

FIG. 21. NUTMEG PLANTATIONS IN PENANG, 1843
Source: *Penang Gazette*, Vol. 2 No. 44, 11 May 1844.

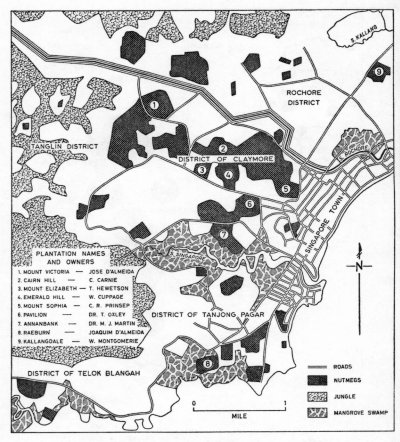

PLANTATION NAMES
AND OWNERS

1. MOUNT VICTORIA — JOSE D'ALMEIDA
2. CAIRN HILL — C. CARNIE
3. MOUNT ELIZABETH — T. HEWETSON
4. EMERALD HILL — W. CUPPAGE
5. MOUNT SOPHIA — C. R. PRINSEP
6. PAVILION — DR. T. OXLEY
7. ANNANBANK — DR. M. J. MARTIN
8. RAEBURN — JOAQUIM D'ALMEIDA
9. KALLANGDALE — W. MONTGOMERIE

ROADS
NUTMEGS
JUNGLE
MANGROVE SWAMP

Fig. 22. NUTMEG PLANTATIONS IN SINGAPORE, 1846

Based on *Plan of Singapore Town and Adjoining Districts from actual Survey by John Turnbull Thomson*, 1846 (R.G.S. Map Collection).

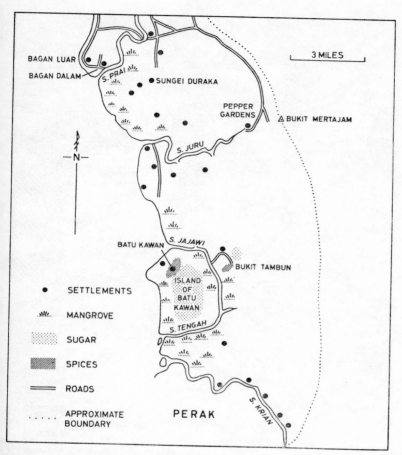

FIG. 23 SOUTHERN PROVINCE WELLESLEY, 1839

Based on *Plan of Prince of Wales Island and Province Wellesley by J.T. Thomson, 20 November 1839* and *Plan of Province Wellesley and part of Prince of Wales Island. Drafted by J.A. Marsh ... from an Original Drawing by J.T. Thomson ... 2 December 1840* (Survey Office, Penang).

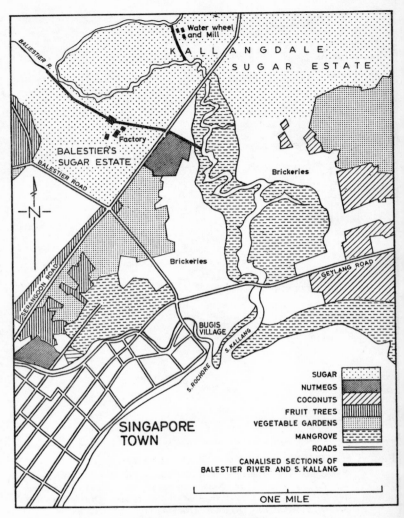

FIG. 24. SUGAR ESTATES IN SINGAPORE, 1846

Based on *Plan of Singapore Town and Adjoining Districts from actual Survey by John Turnbull Thomson, 1846* (R.G.S. Map Collection).

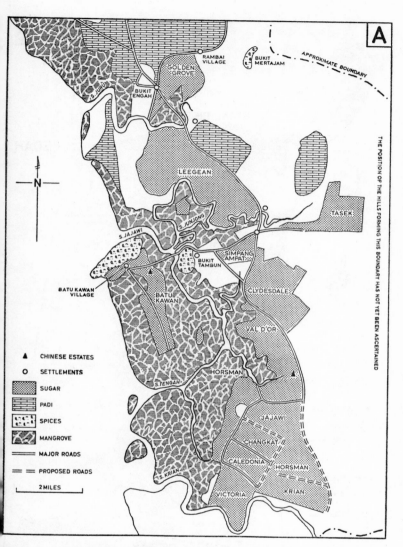

FIG. 25. SUGAR ESTATES IN PROVINCE WELLESLEY, A. 1853
and B. 1897

Based on *Map of Prince of Wales' Island or Pulo Penang and
Province Wellesley ... made in 1853 by J. Moniot* (P.R.O., London,
Straits Settlements, No. 6) and *Map of Pinang Island, 1897* (Survey
Office, Penang).

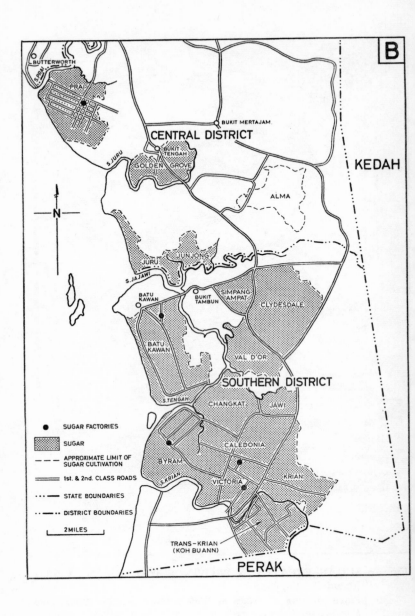

B

BUTTERWORTH
S.PRAI
PRAI
BUKIT MERTAJAM
CENTRAL DISTRICT
S.JURU
BUKIT TENGAH
GOLDEN GROVE
ALMA
KEDAH
JUNJONG
JURU
S.JAJAWI
BATU KAWAN
BUKIT TAMBUN
SIMPANG AMPAT
CLYDESDALE
BATU KAWAN
VAL D'OR
SOUTHERN DISTRICT
S.TENGAH
CHANGKAT
JAWI

● SUGAR FACTORIES

▨ SUGAR

– – APPROXIMATE LIMIT OF SUGAR CULTIVATION

═══ 1st. & 2nd. CLASS ROADS

····· STATE BOUNDARIES

··─·· DISTRICT BOUNDARIES

├── 2 MILES

CALEDONIA
BYRAM
S.KRIAN
VICTORIA
KRIAN

TRANS–KRIAN
(KOH BUANN)

PERAK

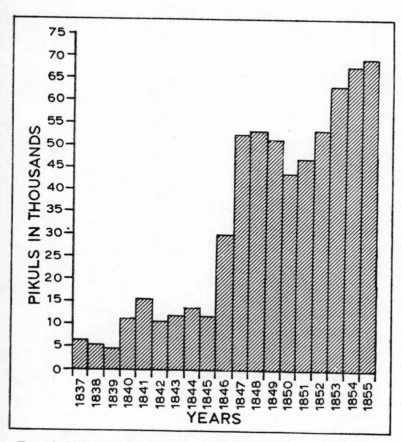

FIG. 26. EXPORTS OF SUGAR FROM PENANG, 1837–55
Source: Penang Gazette, Vol. XIV No. 10, 8 March 1856.

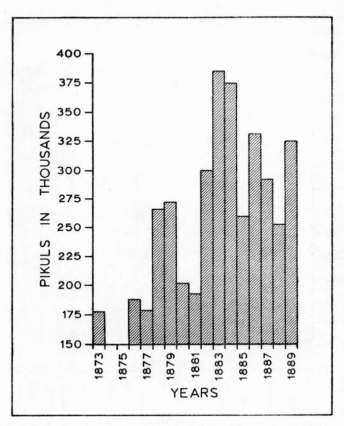

FIG. 27. EXPORTS OF SUGAR FROM PENANG, 1873–89
Source: Straits Settlements Blue Books for relevant years.
N.B.   Figues for 1874-5 are unavailable.

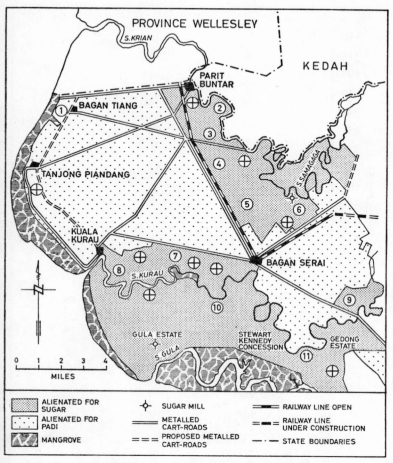

FIG. 28. SUGAR ESTATES IN KRIAN DISTRICT, 1901

Based on information contained in official reports.

Key numbers: 1. Sin Tai Li Estate
2. Guan Seng Estate
3. Eow Seng Estate
4. Tali Ayer Estate
5. Sungei Bogak Estate
6. Samagaga Estate
7. Jin Seng Estate
8. Siang Aik Estate
9. Kwah Bak Heng Estate
10. Eng Joo Estate
11. Ong Ban Seng Estate

Crosses indicate other Chinese-owned sugar estates.

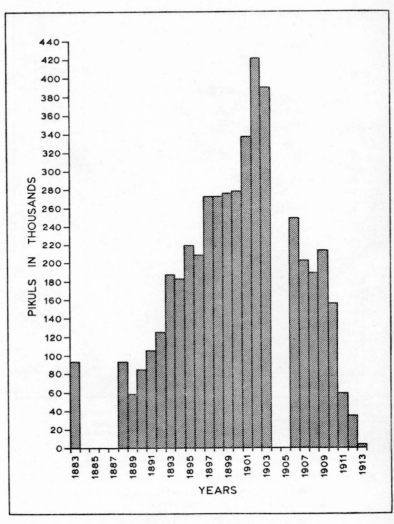

FIG. 29. EXPORTS OF SUGAR FROM PERAK, 1883–1913
Source: A.R. Perak for relevant years.
N.B.   Figures for 1884-7, 1904-5 are unavailable.

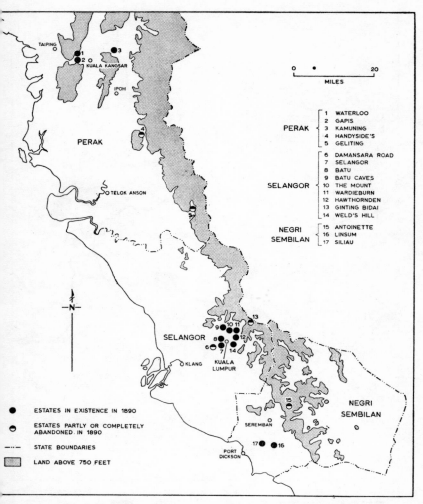

FIG. 30. PIONEER COFFEE ESTATES IN THE WESTERN MALAY
STATES, 1877–90
Based on information contained in official reports.

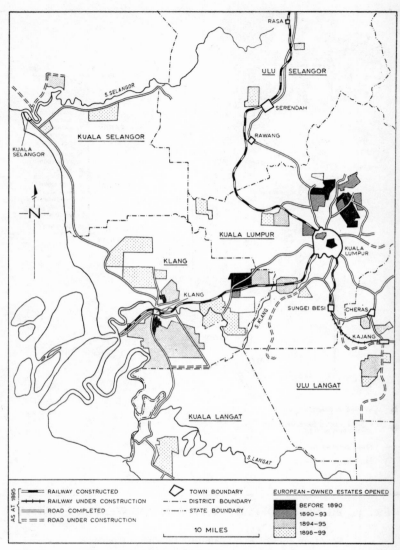

FIG. 31. EXTENSION OF EUROPEAN ESTATE OWNERSHIP IN
SELANGOR, 1890–1899
Based on information contained in official reports.

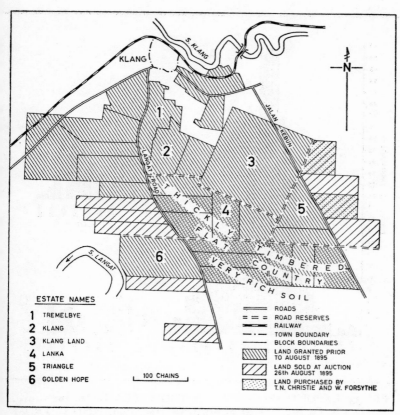

FIG. 32. LAND INVOLVED IN THE KLANG FLASCO, 1895

Based on sketch plan in 'Sale of State Agricultural Land in the Klang and Kuala Langat Districts of the State of Selangor', *Selangor Government Gazette*, Vol. VI, 1895, No. 340, 403.

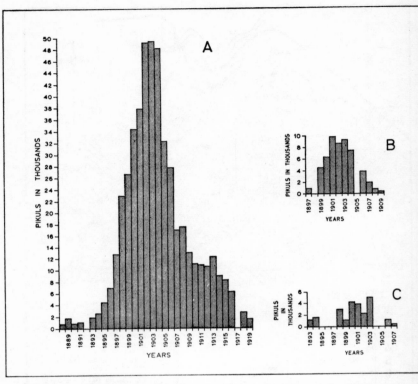

FIG. 33. EXPORTS OF COFFEE, A. FROM SELANGOR, 1888–1919,
B. FROM NEGRI SEMBILAN, 1897–1907 AND C. FROM
PERAK, 1893–1907

Source: A.R. Selangor, A.R. Negri Sembilan and A.R. Perak for
the relevant years.

N.B.   Figures for Selangor for 1892 and 1917, for Negri Sembilan
for 1898 and 1905 and for Perak for 1895-7, 1904-5 are
unavailable.

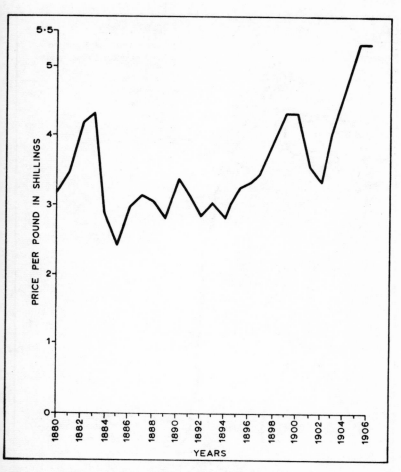

FIG. 34. PRICE OF FINE PARA RUBBER, 1880–1906 (I.e. Price of 'Wild or Uncultivated' Rubber)

Source: 'Para Rubber: The Rise and Fall in Prices of the Forest Product for the last 30 years and of the Cultivated Form for the past 4 years', *Kew Bulletin*, No. 7, New Series, 1906, 241-2.

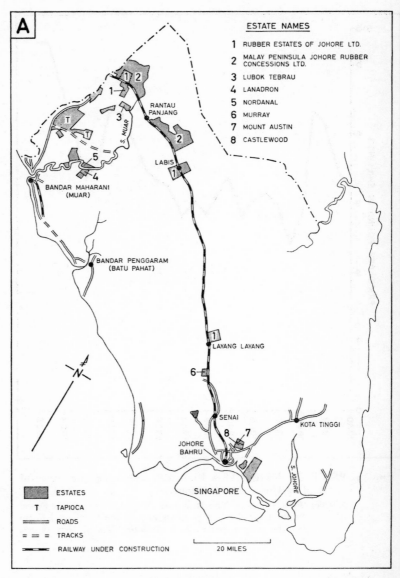

ESTATE NAMES

1 RUBBER ESTATES OF JOHORE LTD.
2 MALAY PENINSULA JOHORE RUBBER CONCESSIONS LTD.
3 LUBOK TEBRAU
4 LANADRON
5 NORDANAL
6 MURRAY
7 MOUNT AUSTIN
8 CASTLEWOOD

RANTAU PANJANG

LABIS

BANDAR MAHARANI (MUAR)

BANDAR PENGGARAM (BATU PAHAT)

LAYANG LAYANG

SENAI

KOTA TINGGI

JOHORE BAHRU

SINGAPORE

S. MUAR

S. JOHORE

N

ESTATES
T TAPIOCA
ROADS
= = = TRACKS
RAILWAY UNDER CONSTRUCTION

20 MILES

FIG. 35. A. ESTATES IN JOHORE, 1907 AND B. ESTATES IN KELANTAN 1907

Based on *Map of Johore by Dato Bintara Luar, 1907* (Photostat, Historical Map Collection, Department of Geography, University of Malaya) and *Map of Kelantan* in W.A. Graham, *Kelantan*. Glasgow, 1908, opposite page 138.

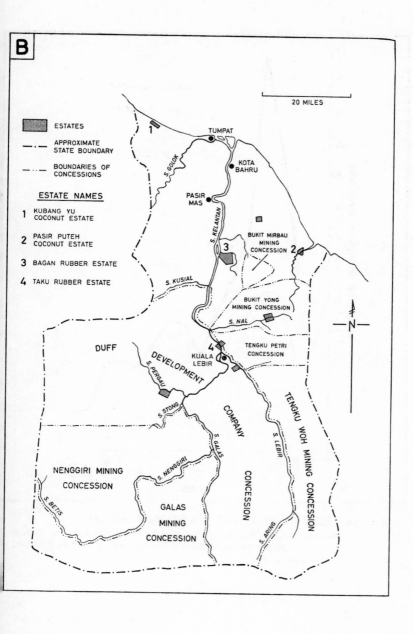

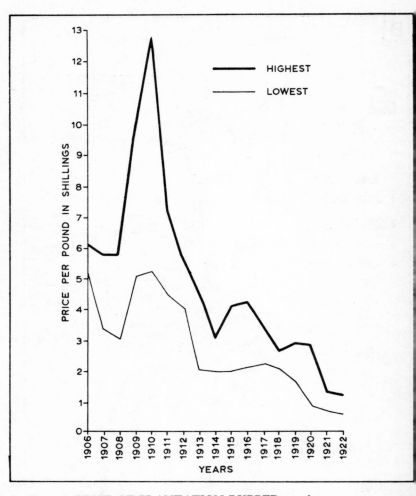

FIG. 36. PRICE OF PLANTATION RUBBER, 1906-22

Source: A.R.F.M.S., 1906-9; Labour Research Department, *British Imperialism in Malaya* (Colonial Series No. 2), London, 1926, 40.

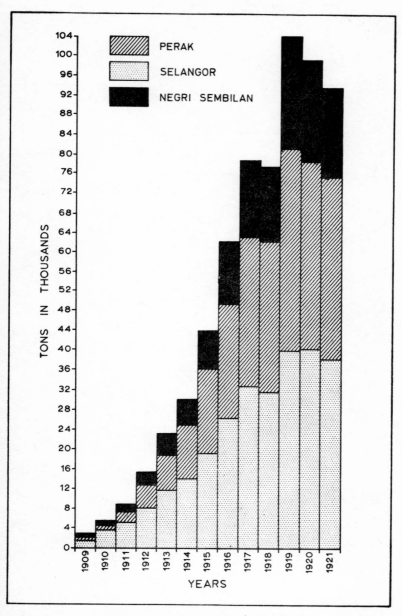

FIG. 37. EXPORTS OF RUBBER FROM THE WESTERN MALAY
STATES, 1909–21
Source: Annual Reports of Perak, Selangor and Negri Sembilan
for the relevant years.

BIBLIOGRAPHY

Abbreviations used in footnotes

A.R.	*Annual Report.*
A.R.F.M.S.	*Annual Report, Federated Malay States.*
A.R.S.S.	*Annual Report, Straits Settlements.*
F.M.S.	Federated Malay States.
J.I.A.	*Journal of the Indian Archipelago and Eastern Asia* (Singapore).
JMBRAS	*Journal of the Malayan Branch, Royal Asiatic Society* (Singapore); as from Vol. XXXVII, pt. 1, 1964, *Journal of the Malaysian Branch, Royal Asiatic Society.*
JSBRAS	*Journal of the Straits Branch, Royal Asiatic Society* (Singapore), succeeded by *Journal of the Malayan Branch, Royal Asiatic Society* in 1923.
J.S.S.S.	*Journal of the South Seas Society* (Singapore).
(M.) J.T.G.	*(Malayan) Journal of Tropical Geography* (Singapore and Kuala Lumpur).
M.A.J.	*Malayan Agricultural Journal* (Kuala Lumpur).
M.R.	District Officer's *Monthly Report.*
N.S.G.G.	*Negri Sembilan Government Gazette.*
N.S.S.F.	*Negri Sembilan Secretariat Files* (followed by file number).
P.G.G.	*Perak Government Gazette.*
P.R.O.	Public Records Office, London.
R.G.S.	Royal Geographical Society, London.
S.F.P.	*Singapore Free Press* (Singapore).
S.G.G.	*Selangor Government Gazette.*
S.S.B.B.	*Straits Settlements Blue Book.*
S.S.G.G.	*Straits Settlements Government Gazette.*
S.S.R. (IOL)	*Straits Settlements Records* (India Office Library).

1. Government Documents, Reports and Publications

Unless stated otherwise these were consulted in the National Archives of Malaysia, Petaling Jaya.

Annual Reports (Titles vary).

Straits Settlements, 1855-66 (C.O. 275/1 and 2, Public Records Office, London).

Malacca, 1887, 1888, 1890, 1891 and 1893.

Federated Malay States, 1896-1921.

Director of Agriculture, Federated Malay States, 1905-21.

Negri Sembilan, 1895-1921.

Perak, 1895-1921.

Selangor, 1889-1921.

Johore, 1913-21.

Kedah, September 1905-August 1906; September 1906-February 1908; 1909-21.

Kelantan, August 1903-August 1904; August 1904-May 1905; 1911-21.

Government Gazettes

Straits Settlements, 1875, 1884-90.

Negri Sembilan, 1894, 1896, 1898, 1900-9.

Perak, 1888-1910.

Selangor, 1891, 1898-1909.

Malacca Diary, *Straits Settlements Records* (India Office Library), August 1826-May 1828, Vols. 165-8 (microfilm, University of Malaya Library).

Negri Sembilan Secretariat Files, 1887-1921.

Parliamentary Papers

The annual bound volumes were consulted in the State Papers Room, British Museum. In footnotes these are referred to as *Accounts and Papers*; year of presentation, volume of year, Command Paper number, enclosure reference and title of individual report follow in that order.

Report of the Commission appointed by His Excellency the High Commissioner for the Malay States to enquire whether any action should be taken by the Government to give protection or assistance to the Rubber Industry, Singapore, 1918.

Selangor State Council Minutes, 1877-1921 (microfilm, University of Malaya Library).

Straits Settlements Blue Books (Singapore), 1870-1921 (State Papers Room, British Museum).

2. *Miscellaneous*

Kew Bulletin (i.e. Bulletin of Miscellaneous Information, Royal Gardens, Kew, London), 1888-1910.

Perak Museum Notes, Perak Government Printing Office, Taiping, Vol. 1 No. 1—Vol. 2, pt. 2, 1893-8 (microfilm, University of Malaya Library).

Planters' Association of Malaya, *Annual Report*, 1915, 1916, 1918-21.

Selangor Planters' Association, *Annual Report*, 1899.

3. Newspapers

Unless stated otherwise these were consulted in the National Library, Singapore.

Grenier's Rubber News (Kuala Lumpur), 2 October 1909-21 September 1918; 11 January 1919-30 June 1920. Various issues. British Museum—Colindale.

Malacca Observer and Chinese Chronicle (Malacca), Nos. 50-65, 27 January-24 August 1829. British Museum—Colindale.

Malacca Weekly Chronicle and Mercantile Advertiser, Nos. 1-104, 7 January 1888-28 December 1889. British Museum—Colindale.

Malay Mail (Kuala Lumpur), 1896 onwards. Various issues.

Penang Gazette (Penang), April 1838-March 1839, 1844, 1847, 1849-50, 1852, 1856, 1863.

Selangor Journal (Kuala Lumpur), Vol. 1, 23 September 1892-Vol. 5, 3 September 1897. National Archives of Malaysia.

Singapore Chronicle (Singapore), 1827-30 (microfilm, University of Malaya Library); 1833-4 and 1836-7.

Singapore Free Press (Singapore), 1837-96. Various issues.

Straits Times (Singapore), 1845 onwards. Various issues.

4. Unpublished Theses

CANT, R.G. *An Historical Geography of Pahang, 1888-1939.* Ph.D. Thesis, University of Malaya (Kuala Lumpur), October 1965.

JACKSON, J.C. *Chinese and European Agricultural Enterprise in Malaya, 1786-1921: A Geographical Study of Expansion and Change.* Ph.D. Thesis, University of Malaya (Kuala Lumpur), April 1965.

LIM LEONG BEE. *The Introduction of Rubber in Perak, 1895-1910.* B.A. Hons. academic exercise, Department of History, University of Malaya (Singapore), 1953.

LOOI SIK CHEONG. *The Sugar Industry in the Straits Settlements with special reference to Province Wellesley, 1840-1913.* B.A. Hons. academic exercise, Department of History, University of Malaya (Singapore), 1961.

NAVARATNARAJAH, P. *The Introduction of Rubber to the State of Negri Sembilan, 1895-1910.* B.A. Hons. academic exercise, Department of History, University of Malaya (Singapore), 1957.

NGUI, DAWN. *The Early Rubber Industry in Selangor, 1895-1910.* B.A. Hons. academic exercise, Department of History, University of Malaya (Singapore), 1954.

SADKA, EMILY. *The Residential System in the Protected Malay States, 1874-1895*. Ph.D. Thesis, Australian National University, December 1960.

STUBBS BROWN, M. *A History of Penang, 1805-1819*. M.A. Thesis, University of Malaya (Kuala Lumpur), April 1963.

THAMSOOK RATANAPUN. *The Development of the North-Western States of Malaya, 1909-1941*. M.A. Thesis, University of Hong Kong, March 1961.

WAN KING CHEONG. *Coffee Planting in Selangor, 1880-1900*. B.A. Hons. academic exercise, Department of History, University of Malaya (Singapore), 1954.

ZAHARAH HAJI MAHMUD. *Change in a Malay Sultanate: An Historical Geography of Kedah up to 1939*. M.A. Thesis, University of Malaya (Kuala Lumpur), April 1966.

5. Books and Articles

AINSWORTH, L. *The Confessions of a Planter in Malaya: A Chronicle of Life and Adventure in the Jungle*, London, 1933.

AKERS, C.E. *Report on the Rubber Industry of the Orient, including Ceylon, the Malay Peninsula, Java and Sumatra*, London, 1912.

ALLEN, G.C. and DONNITHORNE, A.G. *Western Enterprise in Indonesia and Malaya: A Study in Economic Development*, London, 1957.

D'ALMEIDA, W.B. 'Geography of Perak and Selangor, and a brief sketch of some of the adjacent Malay States', *Journal of the Royal Geographical Society*, Vol. XLVI, 1876, 357-80.

'Annual Remittances by Chinese Immigrants to their Families in China', *J.I.A.*, Vol. 1, 1847, 35-37.

ASIMONT, W.F.C. *Hevea brasiliensis or para rubber in the Malay Peninsula*, London, 1908.

BALESTIER, J. 'View of the State of Agriculture in the British Possessions in the Straits of Malacca', *J.I.A.*, Vol. 11, 1848, 139-50.

BARTLEY, W. 'Population of Singapore in 1819', *JMBRAS*, Vol. XI, pt. 2, 1933, 177.

BASTIN, JOHN. *The Changing Balance of the Early Southeast Asian Pepper Trade*, Papers on South-East Asian Subjects, Department of History, University of Malaya, Kuala Lumpur, No. 1, 1960.

—— *Essays on Indonesian and Malayan History*, Eastern Universities Press, Singapore, 1961. Monographs on South-East Asian Subjects, No. 2.

BAUER, P.T. *The Rubber Industry: A Study in Competition and Monopoly*, London, 1948.

BAUMGARTEN, F.L. 'Agriculture in Malacca', *J.I.A.*, Vol. III, 1849, 707-23.

BAXENDALE, C. 'The Plantation Rubber Industry', *Agricultural Bulletin of the Federated Malay States*, Vol. 1, No. 5, December 1912, 180-91.

BEGBIE, P.J. *The Malayan Peninsula, embracing its history, manners and customs of the inhabitants, politics, natural history, etc. from its earliest records*, Madras, 1834.

BELFIELD, H.C. Compiler. *Handbook of the Federated Malay States*. 2nd edition, London, 1904.

BIRD, ISABELLA L. (Mrs. Bishop). *The Golden Chersonese and the Way Thither*, London, 1883.

BLYTHE, W.L. 'Historical Sketch of Chinese Labour in Malaya', *JMBRAS*, Vol. XX, pt. 1, 1947, 64-114.

BRADDELL, T. 'Notices of Singapore', *J.I.A.*, Vol. VII, 1853, 325-57; Vol. VIII, 1854, 97-111, 329-48, 403-19; Vol. IX, 1855, 53-65, 442-82.

—— 'Notes on the Chinese in the Straits', *J.I.A.*, Vol. IX, 1855, 109-24.

—— *Singapore and the Straits Settlements Described; and the Arrangements of the future Government of these possessions considered as distinct from the General Question of the Government of India under the East India Company*, Penang, 1858.

—— *Statistics of the British Possessions in the Straits of Malacca; with explanatory notes*, Penang, 1861.

BRIDGES, W.F.N. *Surveys for Title in the Federated Malay States with Notes on the Revenue Surveys of the Unfederated Malay States*, Kuala Lumpur, 1930 reprinted, 1951.

BUCKLEY, C.B. *An Anecdotal History of Old Times in Singapore. From the foundation of the Settlement on 6th February, 1819, to the transfer to the Colonial Office as part of colonial possessions of Crown on 1st April, 1867*, Singapore, 1902, 2 Vols.

BURKILL, I.H. *A Dictionary of the Economic Products of the Malay Peninsula*, London, 1935, 2 Vols.

—— 'Pepper, Nutmegs and Rubber', *British Malaya*, October 1953, 587-9; Part 2, *British Malaya*, November 1953, 647-50.

CAMERON, J. *Our Tropical Possessions in Malayan India: being a descriptive account of Singapore, Penang, Province Wellesley, and Malacca; their peoples, products, commerce, and government*, London, 1865.

CANT, R.G. 'Pahang in 1888: The Eve of British Administration', *J.T.G.*, Vol. 19, 1964, 4-19.

—— 'Historical Reasons for the Retarded Development of Pahang State, Eastern Malaya', *New Zealand Geographer*, Vol. 21 No. 1, 1965, 26-37.

CAVENAGH, MAJOR GEN. SIR ORFEUR. *Reminiscences of an Indian Official*, London, 1884.

CHAI HON-CHAN. *The Development of British Malaya, 1896-1909*, Kuala Lumpur, 1964.

CLODD, H.P. *Malaya's First British Pioneer: The Life of Francis Light*, London, 1948.

COLLINGWOOD, C. 'On Nutmeg and other Cultivation in Singapore', *Journal of the Linnean Society, (Botany)*, Vol. X No. 41, 1867, 45-54.

COOPE, A.E. 'The Kangchu System in Johore', *JMBRAS*, Vol. XIV, pt. 3, 1936, 247-63.

COWAN, C.D. 'Early Penang and the Rise of Singapore, 1805-32', *JMBRAS*, Vol. XXIII, pt. 2, 1950, 1-210.

—— *Nineteenth-Century Malaya: The Origins of British Political Control*, London, 1961.

COWGILL, J.V. 'Chinese Place Names in Johore', *JMBRAS*, Vol. 11, pt. 3, 1924, 221-51.

CRAWFURD, J. 'Agriculture of Singapore', *J.I.A.*, Vol. 111, 1849, 508-11.

DALE, W.L. 'The Rainfall of Malaya, Part 1', *J.T.G.*, Vol. 13, 1959, 23-37.

DALY, D.D. 'Surveys and Explorations in the Native States of the Malayan Peninsula, 1875-82', *Proceedings of the Royal Geographical Society and Monthly Record of Geography*, No. VII, July 1882, 393-412.

DAVIDSON, G.F. *Trade and Travel in the Far East; or recollections of twenty-one years passed in Java, Singapore, Australia and China*, London, 1846.

DAVIES AND CO. *Local Rubber Companies: A Guide to Investors*, Singapore, 1914.

DAVIS, DONALD 'The Browns of Glugor', *Straits Times Annual, 1961*, Singapore, 25-27.

DICKINSON, A.H. 'The History of the Creation of the Malacca Police', *JMBRAS*, Vol. XIX, pt. 2, 1941, 251-83.

DUNMAN, W. *Tales of Malaya*, Singapore, 1931.

EARL, G.W. *The Eastern Seas, or voyages and adventures in the Indian Archipelago, in 1832-33-34, comprising a tour of the island of Java, visits to Borneo, the Malay Peninsula, etc., also an account of the present state of Singapore,* London, 1837.

EARL, G.W. *Topography and Itinerary of Province Wellesley,* Penang, 1861.

EMERSON, R. *Malaysia: A Study in Direct and Indirect Rule,* New York, 1937.

F.A.O. *The World Sugar Economy in Figures, 1880-1959,* Commodity Reference Series, No. 1, Rome, n.d.

FIGART, D.M. *The Plantation Rubber Industry in the Middle East,* Washington, 1925.

'Formation of the Establishment on Poolo Peenang', *Miscellaneous Papers Relating to Indo-China,* Vol. 1, 1886, 26-37.

FORREST, THOMAS. *A Voyage to New Guinea and the Moluccas etc. performed in the Tartar Galley belonging to the Honourable East India Company during the years 1774, 1757, and 1776,* London, 1780.

GARNIER, REV. K. 'Early Days in Penang', *JMBRAS,* Vol. 1, pt. 1, 1923, 5-12.

GOSLING, L.A.P. 'Migration and Assimilation of Rural Chinese in Trengganu' in Bastin, J. and Roolvink, R. eds., *Malayan and Indonesian Studies,* Oxford, 1964, 203-21.

GRAHAM, W.A. *Kelantan. A State of the Malay Peninsula,* Glasgow, 1908.

GREENSTREET, V.R. and LAMBOURNE, J. *Tapioca in Malaya,* Department of Agriculture, Straits Settlements and Federated Malay States, General Series, No. 13, Kuala Lumpur, 1933.

GRIST, D.H. Compiler. *An Outline of Malayan Agriculture,* Department of Agriculture, Straits Settlements and Federated Malay States, Malayan Planting Manual No. 2, Kuala Lumpur, 1936.

GULLICK, J.M. 'Kuala Lumpur, 1880-1895', *JMBRAS,* Vol. XXXIII, pt. 4, 1955, 1-172.

—— *A History of Selangor, 1742-1957,* Singapore, 1960.

HAMILTON, ALEXANDER. *A New Account of the East Indies.* Edited by Sir William Foster. London, 1930, 2 Vols.

HARE, G.T. *Federated Malay States: Census of Population, 1901,* Kuala Lumpur, 1902.

HERVEY, D.F.A. 'A Trip to Gunong Blumut', *JSBRAS,* No. 3, 1879, 85-115.

—— 'The Endau and Its Tributaries', *JSBRAS,* No. 8, 1881, 93-132.

HILL, THOMAS HESLOP. *Reports on Johore,* Singapore, 1879.

HUNTER, W. 'Remarks on the Species of Pepper, which are found on Prince of Wales's Island', *Asiatick Researches,* Vol. 9, 1807, 383-93.

HUNTER, W. 'Plants of Prince of Wales Island', *JSBRAS*, No. 53, 1909, 50-127.

Intelligence Division, War Office, *Précis of Information Concerning the Straits Settlements and the Native States of the Malay Peninsula*, London, 1891-2.

JACKSON, JAMES C. 'Population Changes in Selangor State, 1850-1891', *J.T.G.*, Vol. 19, 1964, 42-57.

—— 'Chinese Agricultural Pioneering in Singapore and Johore, 1800-1917', *JMBRAS*, Vol. XXXVIII, pt. 1, 1965, 77-105.

—— 'Batang Padang Ninety Years Ago', *Malaya in History*, Vol. 10 No. 1, April 1965, 31-38.

—— 'Nutmeg "Mania" in Singapore in the 1840's', *Kajian Ekonomi Malaysia*, Vol. II No. 2, 1965, 24-30.

—— 'Tapioca: a Plantation Crop which Preceded Rubber in Malaya', *Malaysia in History*, Vol. 10 No. 2, 1967, 13-24.

JACKSON, R.N. *Immigrant Labour and the Development of Malaya, 1786-1920*, Kuala Lumpur, 1961.

—— *Pickering: Protector of Chinese*, Kuala Lumpur, 1965.

JENKINS, R.O. 'Rubber. Introduction and Expansion with Special Reference to Malaya', *British Malaya*, Vol. 26 No. 4, August 1951, 196-9.

KENNAWAY, M.J. *Cavalcade of Rubber*, Singapore, 1936.

KIRBY, S.W. 'Johore in 1926', *Geographical Journal*, Vol. LXXI, 1928, 240-60.

KNOWLES, L.C.A. *The Economic Development of the British Overseas Empire*, London, 1924.

Labour Research Department. *British Imperialism in Malaya*, Colonial Series No. 2, London, 1926.

LAKE, H. 'Johore', *Geographical Journal*, Vol. 111, 1894, 281-302.

LEECH, H.W.C. 'About Kinta', *JSBRAS*, No. 4, 1879, 21-33.

—— 'About Slim and Bernam', *JSBRAS*, No. 4, 1879, 34-45.

LEES, F. 'Chinese Settlement in the Kulai Sub-District of Johore, Malaysia' in Steel, R.W. and Prothero, R.M. eds. *Geographers and the Tropics: Liverpool Essays*, London, 1964, 277-96.

LEITH, SIR GEORGE. *A Short Account of the Settlement, Produce, and Commerce, of Prince of Wales Island in the Straits of Malacca*, London, 1804.

LITTLE, R. 'Diseases of the Nutmeg Tree', *J.I.A.*, Vol. 111, 1849, 678-81.

LOGAN, J.R. 'The Probable Effects on the Climate of Pinang of the Continued Destruction of its Hill Jungle', *J.I.A.*, Vol. 11, 1848, 534-6.

Logan, J.R. 'Journal of an Excursion from Singapur to Malacca and Pinang', *Miscellaneous Papers Relating to Indo-China and the Indian Archipelago*, 2nd Series, Vol. 1, 1887, 1-20.

Low, Capt. (later Lt.-Col.) James. *A dissertation on the soil and agriculture of the British settlement of Penang or Prince of Wales Island in the Straits of Malacca, including Province Wellesley on the Malayan Peninsula; with brief references to the Settlements of Singapore and Malacca, and accompanied by incidental observations on various subjects of local interest in these Straits*, Singapore, 1836.

—— 'An Account of the Origins and Progress of the British Colonies in the Straits of Malacca', *J.I.A.*, Vol. III, 1849, 599-617; Vol. IV, 1850, 11-26, 106-18 and 360-79.

—— 'Notes on the Progress of the Nutmeg Cultivation and Trade from the early part of the 17th century to the present day', *J.I.A.*, Vol. V, 1851, 470-87.

Lumsdaine, J. 'Cultivation of Nutmegs and Cloves in Bencoolen', *J.I.A.*, Vol. V, 1851, 78-84.

Macalister, N. *Historical Memoir Relative to Prince of Wales Island, in the Straits of Malacca: and Its Importance Political and Commercial*, London, 1803.

McHale, T.R. 'Changing Technology and Shifts in the Supply and Demand for Rubber: An Analytical History', *Malayan Economic Review*, Vol. IX No. 2, October 1964, 24-48.

McNair, Major J.F.A. *Perak and the Malays: Sarong and Keris*, London, 1878.

Makepeace, W., Brooke, G.E. and Braddell, R. St. J. *One Hundred Years of Singapore. Being some account of the capital of the Straits Settlements from its foundation by Sir Stamford Raffles on 6th February, 1819 to 6th February, 1919*, London, 1921, 2 Vols.

Marks, O. 'The Pioneers of Para Rubber Planting in British Malaya', *British Malaya*, Vol. 2 No. 10, 1927, 281-92.

—— 'The Malay States before Federation: Selangor Forty Years Ago', *British Malaya*, Vol. 8 No. 9, January 1934, 189-92.

Mason, F.R. 'The Clove and Nutmeg Industry in Penang and Province Wellesley', *Malayan Agricultural Journal*, Vol. 19 No. 1, 1931, 4-8.

Mills, L.A. 'British Malaya, 1824-67', ed. by C.M. Turnbull, *JMBRAS*, Vol. XXXIII, pt. 3, 1960, 1-424.

Milsum, J.N. 'Pepper in Malaya', *Malayan Agricultural Journal*, Vol. 18 No. 6, 1930, 274-80.

MOOR, J.H. *Notices of the Indian Archipelago, and adjacent countries; being a collection of papers relating to Borneo, Celebes, Bali, Java, Sumatra, Nias, the Philippine islands, Sulus, Siam, Cochin China, Malayan Peninsula, etc.,* Singapore, 1837.

DE MORGAN, J. *Explorations dans la Presqu'ile Malaise (Royaumes de Pérak et de Patani,* Paris, 1886.

(The) New Atlas and Commercial Gazetteer of the Straits Settlements and Federated Malay States, Shanghai, 1917. Compiled and edited by the Staff of the Far Eastern Geographical Establishment.

NEWBOLD, T.J. *Political and Statistical Account of the British Settlements in the Straits of Malacca,* London, 1839, 2 Vols.

NEWELL, W.H. *Treacherous River: A Study of Rural Chinese in North Malaya,* Kuala Lumpur, 1962.

NIMBALKER, D.P. *Chinese in British Malaya,* Penang, 1935.

Noctes Orientales—being a selection of essays read before the Straits Philosophical Society between the years 1893 and 1910, Singapore, 1913.

OXLEY, T. 'Some Account of the Nutmeg and its Cultivation', *J.I.A.,* Vol. 11, 1848, 641-60.

PARKINSON, C. NORTHCOTE. *British Intervention in Malaya, 1867-1877,* Kuala Lumpur, 1964.

PARMER, J. NORMAN. *Colonial Labor Policy and Administration: A History of Labor in the Rubber Plantation Industry in Malaya, c.1910-1941,* New York, 1960. Monographs of the Association for Asian Studies, No. IX.

PARRY, M.S. and MURAOUR, E.M. *The A.B.C. to rubber planting companies in Malaya,* London, 1910.

PICKERING, W.A. 'The Chinese in the Straits of Malacca', *Fraser's Magazine,* October 1876, (2), 438-45.

PRINSEN GEERLIGS, H.C. *The World's Cane Sugar Industry, Past and Present,* Altrincham, 1912.

PURCELL, V. *The Chinese in Malaya,* London, 1948.

—— *The Chinese in South East Asia,* London, 1951, issued under the joint auspices of the Royal Institute of International Affairs and the Institute of Pacific Relations. Revised edition, 1965.

—— *The Chinese in Modern Malaya,* Singapore, 1960, 2nd revised edition, *Background to Malaya Series,* No. 9.

PUTHUCHEARY, J.J. *Ownership and Control in the Malayan Economy,* Singapore, 1960.

QUINTUS, R.A. *The Cultivation of Sugar Cane in Java,* London, 1923.

RATHBORNE, A.B. *Camping and Tramping in Malaya: Fifteen Years' Pioneering in the Native States of the Malay Peninsula*, London, 1898.

VAN REETH, C.F. *Singapore et la Péninsule Malaise: Intérêts Economiques Belges*, Brussels, 1904.

RIDLEY, H.N. 'Gambir', *Agricultural Bulletin of the Malay Peninsula*, No. 2, February 1892, 20-41.

—— 'Spices', *Agricultural Bulletin of the Malay Peninsula*, No. 6, April 1897, 98-128.

—— *Spices*, London, 1912.

—— *The Story of the Rubber Industry*, London, 1912.

S., A.W. (i.e. A.W. Still). *Dollar Share Values. Malayan Rubber Company Prospects Critically Analyzed*, Singapore, 1911.

SADKA, E. (ed.) 'The Journal of Sir Hugh Low, Perak, 1877', *JMBRAS*, Vol. XXVII, pt. 4, 1954, 1-108.

SANDHU, KERNIAL SINGH. 'Chinese Colonization of Malacca: A Study in Population Change, 1500 to 1957 A.D.', *J.T.G.*, Vol. 15, 1961, 1-26.

—— 'Some Preliminary Observations of the Origins and Characteristics of Indian Migration to Malaya, 1786-1957', in K.G. Tregonning, ed. *Papers on Malayan History*, Singapore, 1962, 40-72.

SCHIDROWITZ, P. and DAWSON, T.R. eds. *History of the Rubber Industry*, Cambridge, 1952. Compiled under the auspices of the Institution of the Rubber Industry.

SHEPPARD, A.M. *A Short History of Negri Sembilan*, Singapore, 1965.

SIAH U CHIN. 'The Chinese in Singapore. General Sketch of the Numbers, Tribes, and Avocations of the Chinese in Singapore', *J.I.A.*, Vol. 11, 1848, 283-90.

(*The*) *Singapore and Straits Directory for 1887*, Singapore, 1887.

SKINNER, A.M. *A Geography of the Malay Peninsula and Surrounding Countries*, Singapore, 1884, Part 1.

SKINNER, G.W. *Chinese Society in Thailand: An Analytical History*, New York, 1957.

SONG ONG SIANG *One Hundred Years' History of the Chinese in Singapore. From the foundation of Singapore on 6th February, 1819 to its centenary on 6th February, 1919*, London, 1923.

STAFFORD, L.U. 'Planting in Selangor in the Old Days', *British Malaya*, Vol. 8 No. 12, April 1934, 255-8.

STEVENS, F.G. 'A Contribution to the early history of Prince of Wales' Island', *JMBRAS*, Vol. VII, pt. 3, 1929, 377-414.

SWETTENHAM (later Sir), FRANK. *About Perak*, Singapore, 1893.

SWETTENHAM (late Sir), FRANK. *British Malaya: An Account of the Origin and Progress of British Influence in Malaya*, London, 1948, revised edition, first published 1906.

TAN TEK SOON. 'Chinese Local Trade', *The Straits Chinese Magazine*, Vol. VI No. 23, September 1902, 89-97.

THOMSON, J. *The Straits of Malacca, Indo-China and China: or Ten years' travels, adventures and residence abroad*, London, 1875.

THOMSON, J.T. 'General report on the residency of Singapore, drawn up principally with a view of illustrating its agricultural statistics', *J.I.A.*, Vol. III, 1849, 618-28, 744-55; Vol. IV, 1850, 27-41, 102-6, 134-43 and 206-19.

THORNTON, T. ed. *Milburn's Oriental Commerce, or the East Indian Traders' Complete Guide*, London, 1825.

Tropical Investors' Guide: Register of Rubber and Tea Companies in Ceylon, Malaya, and Elsewhere, Colombo, 1912.

TUNKU SHAMSUL BAHRIN, 'Indonesian Labour in Malaya', *Kajian Ekonomi Malaysia*, Vol. 2 No. 1, June 1965, 53-70.

TURNBULL, C.M. 'The Johore Gambier and Pepper Trade in the mid-19th Century', *Journal of the South Seas Society*, Vol. XV, pt. 1, 1959, 43-55.

TURNER, G.E. 'A Perak Coffee Planter's Report on the Tamil Labourer in Malaya in 1902', *Malayan Historical Journal*, Vol. 2 No. 1, July, 1955, 20-28.

WALLACE, A.R. *The Malay Archipelago: The Land of the Orang Hutan and the Bird of Paradise. A Narrative of Travel with Studies of Man and Nature*, London, 1869.

WANG GUNGWU. *A Short History of the Nanyang Chinese*, Singapore, 1959, *Background to Malaya Series*, No. 13.

WARD, BARBARA E. 'A Hakka Kongsi in Borneo', *Journal of Oriental Studies*, Vol. 1, 1954, 358-70.

WHEATLEY, PAUL. 'Land Use in the Vicinity of Singapore in the Eighteen-Thirties', *M.J.T.G.*, Vol. 2, 1954, 63-66.

WILLIAMS, L.E. 'Chinese Leadership in Early British Singapore', *Asian Studies*, Vol. 2 No. 2, August 1964, 170-9.

WILLIS, J.C. *A Report upon Agriculture in the Federated Malay States*, Kuala Lumpur, 1905.

—— *Agriculture in the Tropics: An Elementary Treatise*, 2nd edition. Cambridge, 1914.

WINSTEDT, R.O. 'A History of Johore (1365-1895 A.D.)', *JMBRAS*, Vol. X, pt. 3, 1932, 1-170.

WONG, C.S. *A Gallery of Chinese Kapitans*, Singapore, 1963.

WONG LIN KEN. 'The Trade of Singapore, 1819-69', *JMBRAS*, Vol. XXXIII, pt. 4, 1960, 1-315.

WRAY, L. *The Practical Sugar Planter; a complete account of the Cultivation and manufacture of the sugar cane, according to the latest and most improved processes. Describing and comparing the different systems pursued in the East and West Indies and the Straits of Malacca, and the relative expenses and advantages attendant upon each; being the result of 16 years' experience as a sugar planter in those countries*, London, 1848.

WRIGHT, A. and CARTWRIGHT, H.A. *Twentieth Century Impressions of British Malaya*, London, 1908.

—— and REID, T.H. *The Malay Peninsula, a record of British progress in the Middle East*, London, 1912.

WRIGHT, H.R.C. 'The Moluccan Spice Monopoly, 1770-1824', *JMBRAS*, Vol. XXXI, pt. 4, 1958, 1-127.

WYCHERLEY, P.R. 'The Singapore Botanic Gardens and Rubber in Malaya', *Gardens' Bulletin, Singapore*, Vol. XVII, pt. 2, December 1959, 175-86.

—— 'A Botanist's Approach to Natural Rubber Production', *New Scientist*, Vol. 9 No. 225, 9 March 1961, 620-2.

INDEX

251, 264-5; labour in, 252; land grants in, 253.

Kelantan, Sultan of, 233.

Kennaway, M.J. (cited), 212, 214, 243.

Kennedy, Mr., 158, 164.

Kernial Singh Sandhu (cited), 32, 55, 74, 150, 154.

Keru mukim, Tampin, 66, 67, 83.

Kesang, Malacca, 55.

Kew Gardens, rubber seedlings from, 212.

Khoo Sow Chin, 178.

Kimberley, Mr., 62, 179.

Kindersley brothers, 218.

Kinta district, Perak, 161; pigs exported from Malacca to, 55; coffee in, 177, 190-1; rubber in, 220-1, 227, 250; railway in, 236.

Kirby, S.W. (cited), 10.

Klang district, Selangor, pepper in, 181; coffee in, 191-3, 195-7, 200, 202, 203, 204; rubber in, 221-2, 226, 228, 236, 244, 251.

'Klang Fiasco', 196-7.

Klang Railway, 194, 228, 236.

Klang River, 228.

Knowles, L.C.A. (cited), 1.

Koh Bu Ann, 153, 157, 158, 167.

Koh Chap Siam, 40.

Koh Seck Chuan, 60.

Koh Su Toh, 155.

Koh Tiew, 40.

Kong Fong Estate, Negri Sembilan, 200.

Kong San firm, 253.

Kongsis, 3-4, 21, 43, 47, 74, 77, 147: *kongsi*-houses, 160.

Kota Bahru, Kinta, 221.

Kota Stia, Perak, 161.

Kota Tinggi, Johore, 29.

Krian district, Perak, 71, 139, 152, 154-5, 156-8, 159-61, 165, 166-7, 169-71, 172, 173, 227.

Krian Irrigation Scheme, 172.

Krian River, 144.

Kuala Geliting, Perak, 179.

Kuala Kangsar district, Perak, 161, 179, 183, 191, 212-13, 214, 219, 220, 258.

Kuala Langat district, Selangor, 36, 42, 192, 221, 222, 228.

Kuala Lebir, Kelantan, 233.

Kuala Lumpur district, Selangor, gambier and pepper in, 36; tapioca in, 69-70; coffee in, 191-2, 204; rubber in, 228.

Kuala Lumpur Rubber Co. Ltd., 247.

Kuala Lumpur (town), 249; coffee estates near, 180-1, 183-4, 192, 201; auctions of land for coffee within five miles of, 195; rubber experiments at, 217; rubber grown near railway to, 228; meeting of Residents at, 237; agricultural research in, 241; rubber planters' meetings at, 262.

Kuala Muda district, Kedah, 71.

Kuala Panting, Negri Sembilan, 194.

Kuala Pilah district, Negri Sembilan, formed from part of old Negri Sembilan states, 53; tapioca in, 80, 82; coffee in, 194; land bought for rubber estates in, 251, 253, 257, 258.

Kuala Pilah (town), 63, 68, 253.

Kuala Selangor, Selangor, 192, 195, 204, 219, 228.

and coffee, 191, 194, 236; and rubber, 221, 245, 249, 254, 257, 258; sell land to rubber estates, 249.

Malaysia: A Study in Direct and Indirect Rule, xii.

Malay States, non-interference by British in, xiii; British give protection to, xiii, 1, 90, 189; Chinese in, 1, 2; tin-mining in, 89-90; European planters in, 90.

Mangrove forests, 28, 129,140-1, 143, 155, 162, 169.

Manila, 134 136.

Manure, 9, 119, 121, 126, 131, 139, 144, 169.

Marketing, of coffee, 200-2; of rubber, 256.

Marks, O. (cited), 215.

Mason, F.R. (cited), 127.

Matang district, Perak, tapioca in, 71; sugar in, 158-9, 162, 163-5, 167, 169, 170, 171, 172, 173; coffee in, 190-1; rubber in, 220, 221, 226-7, 249.

Matang Estate, Perak, 223.

Mauritius, sugar-planters from, 91, 137, 139, 143, 144, 145; clove plants from, 101; sugar-canes from, 136, 144, 149; 'Mauritius' cane, 144, 149; sugar-processing techniques originating in, 145.

Maxwell, W.E., 39, 192, 194.

Meikle, C., 183.

Meikle, R.S., 183.

Mexican dollars used in Malaya, xi.

Milburn, W. (cited), 111.

Mills, L.A. (cited), 114, 116.

Mitchell, Innis, 178.

Moluccas, 101, 103.

Moniot, Mr., 131.

Montgomerie, Dr. William, 134-5.

Moor, J.H. (cited), 115.

Morrison, A.G., 161.

Mount Austin Estate, Johore Bahru, 232.

Muar district, Johore, 60, 219, 232.

Muar kingdom, Johore, 24.

Muar River, 25, 28.

Muhlinghaus, Mr., 194.

Murray, Mr., 62.

Murton, Mr., 214.

Nairne, Lawrence, 149.

Naning, Malacca, 115; Naning War (1831-2), 115.

Napoleon I, Emperor, 96, 97.

Negapatam, 154, 189.

Negri Sembilan State: British protection (1889) for, xii, 2; gambier and pepper in, 15, 31, 34-51, 64; and pig trade, 55; tapioca in, 56, 61-4, 68, 73, 75, 80, 82-3, 254; population of, 76; abandoned land in, 81; pepper in, 93; coffee in, 176, 183, 193-4, 200, 204, 222; rubber ousts coffee in, 202; rubber in, 213, 215, 222-3, 224-6, 228-31, 235, 237, 248, 249, 251; Japanese planters in, 237, 253; labour in, 252.

Netherlands East Indies, rubber estates in, 262.

Newbold, T.J. (cited), 7.

Newell, W.H. (cited), 3.

New South Wales, 29.

'New Villages', 27.

Nordanal Estate, Johore, 232.

Notices of the Indian Archipelago, 115.

planters sow, 174; interplanted with rubber, 260.

Ridley, H.N., 214-16; (cited), 9,
10, 42, 102, 104, 110, 113, 126,
212, 216-17, 218.

Rioting on plantations, 23.

Rivers: commonest form of
communications in early
days, xiii, 15, 16, 26, 28, 29,
35; settlements in valleys of,
14, 15, 25; early plantations
usually near, 14-15, 19, 21,
24, 28, 76; depots near, 15, 20,
42, 76; settlements near, 26.

Roads: shortage of 15-16;
Johore and, 15, 182, 232;
paths on estates, 16, 21, 73,
181; in Selangor, 39, 184, 228;
planters seek land near, 54,
68, 70, 113, 235-7, 251, 264;
from Malacca to Old Negri
Sembilan, 56, 62, 64, 68, 72,
73, 80; Government en-
courages economic development by building, 91; in
Singapore, 111; in Krian, 156;
planters as contractors for,
181, 184; coffee and, 205; in
East Coast States, 231; tin-
mining and, 235-6.

Robertson, C.J. (cited), xvi.

Robson, J.M.H. (cited), 218.

Rodger, Mr., 44-5, 159, 165.

Roles, F.C. (cited), xviii, 225.

Roslin Estate, Selangor, 183.

Rubana Estate, Matang, 165,
173.

Rubber: expansion of, xvi, 26,
211; European planters dom-
inate on introduction of,
xvi, 211; ousts (a) all other
crops, xvii, 211, 226, 234, 246,
266, (b) gambier and pepper,

18, 26, 30, 43, 48-50, (c) tapioca,
61, 81, 82-3, (d) sugar, 91, 168,
169, 172-4, 227, (e) coffee, 199,
202, 203-4, 206-7, 227; tapioca,
gambier and pepper the most
successful crops before, 6; in
Johore, 25, 225, 231-2, 250, 251,
254, 257, 265-6; interplanted
with (a) gambier and pepper,
26, 41, (b) tapioca, 81, (c)
coffee, 199, 202-3, 204; Chinese
turn to, 43, 48, 49-51; to be
grown with gambier and
pepper, 48; in Selangor, 70,
218, 219, 220-2, 223, 225-6,
227-9, 230-1, 244, 250; in Perak,
71, 168, 202, 216, 220, 221,
224-7, 229, 230-1, 237, 250, 257,
265; in Province Wellesley,
71, 173, 224, 225, 231; in
Kedah, 71-2, 225, 254, 257,
258, 265-6; planted on
abandoned land, 78, 82, 224,
248-9; in Negri Sembilan, 81,
82, 222-6, 228-31, 235, 237, 249,
250,251,254, 257, 258,265;para
(Hevea brasiliensis), 82, 204,
212-13, 215, 219; becomes important, 211; wild, 211, 214,
240, 256; natural, 211; ceara
(Manihot glaziovii), 212, 219;
introduced to Malaya, 212-13;
experiments in tapping rubber trees, 212, 213, 214-15,
216-17, 219, 223; early experiments in growing, 213-14,
216; first commercially planted in 1890, 217-18; in Malacca,
218, 219, 225, 231, 244, 265-6;
in Muar, 219; in Ulu Langat,
219; prices of samples of, 219;
first boom (1905-8) in, 226-34;
in Pahang, 229, 231, 258, 265;

in Straits Settlements, 231; in Kelantan, 231, 232-3, 265; cost of running an estate planted with, 241; restrictions enforced (1922), 246, 258-63; second boom in, 246-54, 257; dividends paid on, 247, 248; backbone of Malayan economy, 264; its output in 1921, 265; in Singapore, 265; in Penang, 265; in Perlis, 265; in Trengganu, 265 (see Geta rambong).

Rubber Growers' Association, 260-1, 262.

Rubber Producers' Association of Malaya, 262.

Rum, 129, 134, 140, 142, 163, 170.

Rumah kechil system of labour, 147, 160-1, 163, 164, 166, 175.

Rupee legal tender in Straits Settlements, xi.

Russell and Co., 136.

Sao Paulo, Brazil, 29.

Schidrowitz, P. and Dawson, T.R. (cited), 213.

Schultze, Captain, 179.

Scott Jones, Mr., 102.

Secret societies, 3, 4, 22, 23.

Sedili districts, Johore, 24.

See Koh Lye, 39.

Segamat district, Johore, 60.

'Selangor cane', 130, 136, 144, 149.

Selangor Estate, Kuala Lumpur, 184, 201.

Selangor river, 228.

Selangor Rubber Co. Ltd., 243, 247.

Selangor State: British protection (1874) for, xiii, 2, 151; gambier and pepper in, 31, 34, 35-6, 38-6, 38-51, 93; pigs imported, 55; tapioca in, 69-70; tin in, 69, 193; coffee in, 176-7, 179-81, 183-4, 187, 188, 191-205 227; pepper in, 184, 191, 193; European coffee-planters attracted to, 189; labour in, 189-90, 252; railways in, 194, 236; rubber ousts coffee in, 202; rubber in, 213, 218, 220-2, 223, 225-6, 227-9, 230, 244, 250, 265-5; land available in, 236-7; grants of land in, 237; rubber companies in, 244.

Selangor, Sultan of, 35, 221.

Selinsing Estate, Perak, 202, 220, 223.

Selinsing mukim, Matang, 158-9, 164.

Semenyih Estate, Ulu Langat, 222, 243.

Sempang Estate, Klang, 196.

Senawang, Negri Sembilan, 193; Estate at, 200.

Sengkang, Negri Sembilan, 35, 36, 39-40, 42, 45, 50.

Sepang, Selangor, 36, 37, 39, 41, 42, 45, 47, 49-50.

Seremban district, Negri Sembilan, tapioca in, 62; coffee in, 180, 193, 222; rubber in, 222, 225-6, 229, 230, 248, 254; railways in, 236.

Seremban Estate, Negri Sembilan, 200.

Seremban Estate Rubber Co. Ltd., 243.

Seremban Land Office, 225, 229-30.

Seremban Syndicate, 243.

Serendah, Ulu Selangor, 221.

Serkam mukim, Malacca, 32.

buy Malay-owned, 159; of
coffee, 191, 194, 236; of rubber,
222, 249, 250, 254, 257, 258,
265-6.

Smith, Christopher, 101, 102.

Smith, Percy Lionel, 178-9.

Smith, Sir Cecil, 183.

Soil: types unimportant in 19th-
century Malaya, xviii; exhausted by (a) gambier and
pepper, 11, 14, 15, 33, 47, (b)
tapioca, 53, 54-6, 61, 67, 70,
77-80; fertile in forests, 87-8;
for spices in Singapore, 111;
for nutmegs, 111, 112, 116,
117; for sugar, 133, 136-7, 139,
143; for coffee, 178, 182, 185,
192, 196; for rubber, 212, 216,
233-4.

Song Gee Gwan, Baba, 63.

Song Ong Siang (cited), 215.

South China, *kongsis* in, 3;
immigrants from, 75; bubonic plague in, 152.

South China Sea, 24.

Southern District, Province
Wellesley, 153.

Spanish dollars used in Malaya,
xi, 13, 98, 130, 135.

Speculation, in land, 194-8, 235,
249; in rubber, 245, 247, 248,
256.

Spices: in Straits Settlements,
87-127; official policy for, 90,
102-4; Penang land regulations for, 90; Dutch monopoly in, 101, 111, 121, 124; in
Province Wellesley, 110; a
long-term crop, 116; in Singapore, 116-17, 128; decline of,
211, 266 (*see* Cloves: Mace:
Nutmegs).

Spices, 102, 104, 126.

Spirit 'farms', 17, 18, 59.

Squatters, Chinese, 10, 23, 89,
106, 109-10, 125, 174.

Sri Menanti state, 53.

Stafford, L.U. (cited), 203.

Statistics, 110, 134, 142.

Steam-powered (a) tapioca factories, 52, 54, 67, (b) sugar
mills, 133, 135, 156, 157, 158,
160, 166, 170 (*see* Machinery).

Steel, R.W. and Prothero, R.M.
(cited), 15.

Stephens, F.A., 164, 190, 220.

Sterling and dollars, xi-xii, 244.

Stevens, F.G. (cited), 95, 104.

Stevenson Committee (1921),
263.

Stewart, Mr., 158, 164.

Straits dollar, xi.

Straits Settlements: rupee
legal tender in, xi; founded,
xiii; Chinese in, 1-3, 4; population of, 5; Chinese financiers
in, 21, 38; European planters
in, 87-91; spices grown in,
87-127; crops grown there to
help pay for administration,
90, 93, 101; labour in, 117, 119,
131; British import duties on
sugar and, 134, 137, 139, 141;
sugar in, 137; transferred
from Government of India
to Colonial Office, 141, 150;
coffee in, 176; rubber in, 231,
265; Government's attitude
to plantation agriculture in,
234; Chinese rubber planters
in, 254; accessible from Western Malay States, 264.

Straits Settlements Bertam
Rubber Co., 174.

Straits Sugar Estate Co., 164-5,
166, 167, 169.